FINANCIAL INTELLIGENCE FOR SUPPLY CHAIN MANAGERS

FINANCIAL INTELLIGENCE FOR SUPPLY CHAIN MANAGERS

Understand the Link between Operations and Corporate Financial Performance

STEVEN M. LEON

Publisher: Paul Boger
Editor-in-Chief: Amy Neidlinger
Executive Editor: Jeanne Glasser Levine
Development Editor: Natasha Wolmers
Editorial Assistant: Kristen Watterson
Cover Designer: Chuti Prasertsith
Managing Editor: Kristy Hart
Project Manager: Namita Gahtori, Cenveo® Publisher Services
Copy Editor: Cenveo Publisher Services
Proofreader: Cenveo Publisher Services
Indexer: Cenveo Publisher Services
Compositor: Cenveo Publisher Services
Manufacturing Buyer: Dan Uhrig

©2016 by Steven M. Leon
Published by Pearson Education, Inc.
Old Tappan, New Jersey 07675

For information about buying this title in bulk quantities, or for special sales opportunities (which may include electronic versions; custom cover designs; and content particular to your business, training goals, marketing focus, or branding interests), please contact our corporate sales department at corpsales@pearsoned.com or (800) 382-3419.

For government sales inquiries, please contact governmentsales@pearsoned.com.

For questions about sales outside the U.S., please contact international@pearsoned.com.

Company and product names mentioned herein are the trademarks or registered trademarks of their respective owners.

Printed in the United States of America

First Printing November 2015

ISBN-10: 0-13-383831-5
ISBN-13: 978-0-13-383831-2

Pearson Education Ltd.
Pearson Education Australia PTY, Limited
Pearson Education Singapore, Pte. Ltd.
Pearson Education Asia, Ltd.
Pearson Education Canada, Ltd.
Pearson Educación de Mexico, S.A. de C.V.
Pearson Education—Japan
Pearson Education Malaysia, Pte. Ltd.
Library of Congress Control Number: 2015950135

Contents

Acknowledgments

Taking on this endeavor took a small dedicated army. I could not have pulled this project off without the support of my family and colleagues. A special thank you goes to my wife and daughter, Tammy and Abigail, for their never-ending encouragement and patience. Without them onboard from the beginning, this project would have never taken-off. They knew that the time to write this book meant less time for family fun.

Every once in a while each of us is lucky enough to have someone in our corner pulling for us. Barry Render, Ph.D., Consulting Editor, Pearson Press, and Harwood Professor of Operations Management Emeritus, Rollins College Graduate School of Business is the person in my corner. Barry has opened doors and has provided opportunities for me that otherwise may have gone idle. Without Barry's promptings, I may not have started writing books. I am forever grateful for his invaluable guidance and insights.

Jeanne Glasser Levine, Executive Editor, and the others at Pearson/FT Press deserve a huge thank you for accepting my proposal and agreeing to take on this project. Their editorial and publishing expertise is incredible. I am lucky to have such a great team working on my behalf.

I would like to say thank you and give credit to a few of my colleagues who made this book so much better. I would like to thank personally, Annie Wood, Dr. Joseph G. Szmerekovsky, Professor of Management, North Dakota State University, Melissa B. Frye, Ph.D., Associate Professor of Finance, University of Central Florida, Ann Marie Whyte, Ph.D., Associate Professor of Finance, University of Central Florida, Travis L. Jones, Ph.D., Associate Professor of Finance, Florida Gulf Coast University, and Dr. Richard A. Lewin, Associate Professor of International Finance, Rollins College. Without their valuable suggestions and feedback, this book would not have been such a success.

Their subject expertise and mastery of communication has helped me remain focused and consistent in the writing, and to present a coherent storyline from removing jargon and providing intelligible ways to explain difficult concepts.

Thank you everyone!

Steve Leon

About the Author

Steven Leon is a Clinical Professor of Supply Chain and Operations Management in the Marketing Department of the College of Business Administration, University of Central Florida. Prior to his transition to academia, he spent many years in the air transportation industry, particularly in flight operations. Steve is also an accomplished entrepreneur. His research interests include supply chain strategy and financial performance, service operations, behavioral decision-making, and air transportation. He is the author of *Sustainability in Supply Chain Management Casebook: Applications in SCM, Financial Times Press*, and other peer-reviewed academic journal articles. Steve earned his Ph.D. in Transportation and Logistics from North Dakota State University, and his MBA in International Business from Loyola University, Maryland.

1

Introduction

Earnings conference calls are a routine occurrence for executives of public companies. Each quarter, while we listen to the company's CEO, president, CFO, and others recite their prepared remarks about earnings, we may be unfamiliar with the terminology that they use. Of course, we would expect executives to be comfortable speaking about financial information, but what about the rest of us? Shouldn't we be comfortable too? Shouldn't we understand how we affect our organization's economic performance from the decisions and actions we carry out each day?

We can expect that people who work in finance and accounting, and those whose daily responsibilities include financial and accounting work, feel comfortable conversing in financial terms. As an example of this, on a third-quarter 2013 earnings conference call made by Dick's Sporting Goods, Inc., we see common phrases used in most earnings conference calls.

- "Third-quarter earnings of $0.40 per diluted share"
- "We expect non-GAAP consolidated earnings per diluted share to be in the range of $2.62 to $2.65 per share"
- "Total sales for the third quarter of 2013 increased 6.7% to $1.4 billion"
- "Gross profit was $424.9 million or 30.34% of sales"
- "SG&A expenses in the third quarter of 2013 were $333.7 million or 23.83% of sales"
- "Net capital expenditures were $77 million"
- "Gross margins are expected to decline"
- "Operating margin is anticipated to decrease slightly"

These phrases can be overwhelming and somewhat confusing to a nonfinance person, but they don't have to be. Terms and phrases such as earnings, earnings per share, net income, net profit, operating profit, gross profit, gross margins, operating margins, revenue, and sales are common and often are used interchangeably. Revenue, sales, and top line are a perfect example of this. These terms have the same meaning. Another common example of this is net earnings, net income, and bottom line; these mean the same thing. Understanding the meaning of these terminologies will assist supply chain and operations organizations to perform effectively.

For those of us in supply chain and operations management, the tasks we accomplish and the decisions we make every day affect our company's financial performance. The questions are then, how exactly do we affect financial performance and why should we care? It should be our responsibility to know how we affect financial performance to make the best decisions possible. Much of the work we do involves making business cases and persuading executives to replace or add facilities, machinery, materials, and other resources. Obtaining approval depends, in large part, on financial returns. To facilitate these conversations, we ought to feel comfortable using financial terms with CFOs, creditors, owners, and other financial experts; the ability to speak fluently in financial terms makes us more effective. If we want to help our executive leadership demonstrate success during earnings calls, if we want our companies to be profitable, successful, and sustainable, or if we want to create value for our companies, we should know how we contribute to our organizations. If we have any inclination to earn greater responsibility in our companies or to take on executive leadership roles, we need to become knowledgeable in the finance and accounting aspects of organizations.

Financial standing affects our company's ability to move forward in many ways, such as:

1. Borrowing money for working capital
2. Attracting investors and raising funds for growth
3. Finding customers, paying dividends, and paying suppliers
4. Purchasing inventory
5. Innovating
6. Contributing to retirement plans
7. Providing employee growth opportunities

We aren't just talking about reducing costs either; we are talking about implementing projects that add value to our companies, projects that drive revenue growth, deliver positive cash flow well into the future, and deliver satisfactory levels of return on invested capital (ROIC).

What Is Important to the CEO?

Before exploring what we can do in supply chain and operations to help create a profitable, competitive, and valuable company, we need to identify a company's overarching purpose and what is important to CEOs. Primarily, the central purpose of a company is to increase shareholder value. Total return to shareholders (TRS) is frequently used to measure management and company performance. From a CEO's perspective, there is pressure to show returns to shareholders that either meet or exceed shareholder expectations and achieve above-average earnings compared to competitors. If they don't, share price is likely to fall due to unfavorable reviews from financial analysts. CEOs report to numerous audiences, such as:

1. Board of directors
2. Wall Street analysts
3. Shareholders and investors
4. Creditors and banks
5. Stakeholders

Each audience has its own criteria for evaluating success. In addition, many other criteria and financial performance measures are reported and used to gauge company performance. Besides total return to shareholders, other common measures used to evaluate a company and its executive management team include:

1. Earnings before interest taxes depreciation and amortization (EBITDA)
2. Earnings per share (EPS)
3. Earnings before interest and taxes (EBIT)
4. Free cash flow (FCF)
5. Gross margin, return on capital employed (ROCE)
6. Return on investment (ROI)

7. Return on invested capital (ROIC)

8. Return on net assets (RONA)

9. Sales growth

Why these? Quite simply, these measures are what are important to analysts, owners of company stock, and those who invest in or lend money to companies. If it is significant to external constituents, then it is important to the company executives. By no means is this an all-inclusive list. Several other performance measures are considered, but those listed are the most common. No single metric can tell the whole story; however, a core of key performance indicators can provide insight into the financial health of a company.

After exploring the performance measures that interest CEOs, we can ask ourselves how we can help our CEO report company performance in a positive light. In other words, what can we do to make all of the performance measures listed earlier stack up against our competitors and while meeting or exceeding the expectations of our board members, shareholders, analysts, investors, and bankers? Effective supply chain and operations management provides ample opportunity to add firm value and competitive advantage.

Supply Chain and Operations Value Proposition

Although supply chains have garnered more attention in the major business news outlets recently, many executives and up-and-coming managers do not fully grasp how important managing supply chains is to their company's sustained financial health and performance. A high level of emphasis is still placed on top-line growth instead of looking at supply chain and operations. Sales and marketing activities garner much of management's attention, while supply chain and operations are relegated to behind-the-scenes cost savings and cost containment activities. Why is this the case? Because it is much more exciting to report a 15% growth in sales than to cheer about cost savings of an equal amount achieved through supply chain and operations modifications. Although not always celebrated, the understanding of the importance of supply chain management is growing.

Management consulting firms, including many of the top tier firms, recognize the importance of supply chain management. Evidence of this exists in that several firms have established supply chain and operations consulting practices including:

1. Accenture
2. A.T. Kearney
3. Bain and Company
4. Booz & Company
5. Deloitte LLP
6. Gartner
7. KPMG
8. McKinsey & Company
9. PricewaterhouseCoopers (PwC)

In addition to consulting in this area, Gartner publishes a much-referred-to ranking of supply chains called, "The Supply Chain Top 25." This publication provides a ranking of the best supply chains among global manufacturers, retailers, and distributors. Each year, these firms publish many insightful research reports in the supply chain area ranging from managing suppliers, strategies for purchasing commodities, managing risk, sustainability, and the use of big data. The research is important in creating an understanding of the role of supply chain and operations.

The Role of Supply Chain and Operations

Supply chains, for the most part, are focused on delivering products and services to customers at the right price, in the right quantities, to the right places, and at the right time. In doing so, they keep four overarching areas in mind to create value for our organizations:

1. Increasing quality
2. Increasing service
3. Lowering cost
4. Increasing throughput (reducing time)

This is a daunting task considering supply chains are long, complicated, and complex; in addition, consumer preferences change frequently leading to shorter product life cycles along with risk and working capital challenges. In a supply chain, there is no shortage of opportunities for things to go wrong, but these are also opportunities

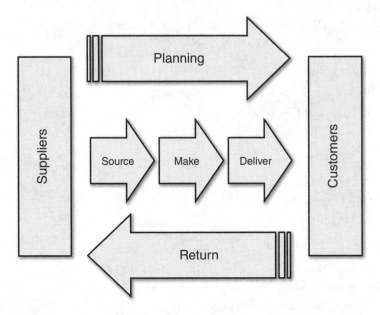

Figure 1.1 SCOR model. (Adapted from Supply Chain Council, Inc.)

for companies to gain a competitive advantage. Execute a supply chain well, and you will leave your competitors behind!

The SCOR model (Figure 1.1), a management tool, attempts to bring structure to many of the areas under the purview of supply chain managers. The SCOR model has been developed to describe the business activities associated with the phases of satisfying customers' demand. It is a process reference model that includes everything from the supplier's supplier to the customer's customer. Each area of the SCOR model, Plan–Source–Make–Deliver–Return, brings opportunity to add value for your organization. Its purpose is to structure the supply chain in a way that allows for identifying and improving supply chain processes. Process improvements are intended to create value for the firm through gaining a competitive advantage in the areas of reliability, responsiveness, agility, cost, and asset management.

In addition to the SCOR model that allows us to identify where value is created throughout the supply chain, Porter's value chain (Figure 1.2) provides an overview of where value is created in an organization. Supply chain and operations are responsible for much of the value creation for an organization. Interestingly, a large percentage of the support value activities and all the primary value activities are comprised supply chain and operations functions.

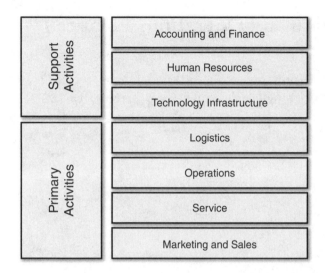

Figure 1.2 Value chain. (Adapted from Michael Porter's Value Chain. Competitive Advantage: Creating and Sustaining Superior Performance, NY: Free Press; 1985.)

Value Chain

Value is created when customers purchase goods or services at prices higher than the cost of performing the value activities. The value activities include primary activities that encompass the physical creation, delivery, and selling of the product or service, while the support activities provide the infrastructure to carry out the primary activities. From a supply chain perspective, we create value by maintaining a cost advantage in each primary and support activity and through the coordination and alignment of each activity.

Porter indicates each firm plays a role in a larger system: a value system.[1] We know this value system as a supply chain where there is supplier value (upstream), firm value, and channel and buyer value (downstream). Taken together, firms create a competitive advantage through the integration and coordination of all members of the value system. Since organizations need to create value for their shareholders, customers, and other constituents, executives and managers are wise to bring supply chain and operations into the boardroom.

---

[1] *On Competition*, Michael E. Porter, Harvard Business School Press; Boston (1996).

Supply Chain and Operations Financial Impact

As the emphasis on supply chain and operations grows, CEOs are beginning to more commonly use supply chain phrases such as:

1. Accountability
2. Collaboration
3. Innovation
4. Operational flexibility
5. Risk mitigation
6. Sustainability
7. Transparency

Why are these ideas so important to CEOs? It is because consumers, shareholders, and government officials demand it. However, the real challenge is in implementing these ideas, moving from discourse to action. Because supply chain and operations is still considered a functional area that exists in silos for many companies, implementing these ideas to achieve true company value is difficult. However, companies that moved their supply chains from functional department to value generator were rewarded. In 2013, PwC did a survey showing leading companies are more than twice as likely to treat their supply chain as a strategic asset.[2]

CEOs continue to grow in their understanding of supply chains and the impact to organizations, thanks in part to news outlets and business publications producing content on the topic. News articles or video segments related to supply chains have several common themes. Some themes that consistently appear are natural disasters and the resulting supply interruptions, the idea that supply chains should be more flexible and agile to meet customers' changing needs, and the need to use technology to manage the flow of information more effectively. Rarely does the conversation entertain ideas about how supply chain activities drive sales, affect revenue targets, impact shareholder value, how the stock price is affected, or the effect on financial ratios. Although these types of conversations are gaining traction, the specifics are generally left out of the dialog surrounding supply chains.

---

[2] http://www.pwc.com/us/en/industrial-products/issues/supply-chain.html

Emerging topics in supply chain today revolve around sourcing goods and services for organizations that directly impact financial performance. The costs of commodities are increasing or are in a constant state of flux. For example, we have a tough time getting our heads wrapped around fluctuating fuel prices. In addition, we see greater instances of companies unable to deliver products and services due to weather interruptions. One prime example is the Northeastern United States from 2012 to 2014. Hurricane Sandy and winter snowstorms crippled transportation systems, resulting in major delivery delays of goods and services. This led to shortages of raw materials coming to production facilities and supply shortages for customers. Of course, this isn't confined to the United States. Tsunamis, hurricanes, and flooding occur globally, affecting companies everywhere. In 2011, floods in Thailand and the earthquake and tsunami in Japan caused massive supply disruptions affecting supplies of raw materials, subassemblies, and finished goods in the computer and automobile industries.

Another important area impacting financial performance is conflict minerals, which has been a topic of discussion for quite some time. These are minerals mined from areas of the world where armed conflict and human rights abuses occur. Recently, this topic has gained special attention. Section 1502 of the Dodd–Frank Act requires certain companies using conflict minerals in their products to disclose the source of these minerals. Even though an estimated 6,000 companies will be directly impacted by this rule, many private companies within the supply chains of those companies will also be affected. The U.S. Securities and Exchange Commission expects the cost of compliance to be substantial for all involved. For primary companies and their suppliers, initial estimates for cost of compliance are between US$3 billion and US$4 billion, with annual costs thereafter of between US$207 million and US$609 million.[3]

A third area of discussion that can affect financial performance is outsourcing. This includes the rights, safety, and health of workers employed by suppliers located in low cost countries. In 2012, the collapse of one Bangladesh factory and a fire in another led to more than a thousand deaths. These tragic events have resurrected the discussion around outsourcing to find the lowest-cost supplier. The backlash retailers face when it is reported that people were treated poorly or put

---

[3] http://www.ey.com/Publication/vwLUAssets/Conflict_minerals/$FILE/Conflict_Minerals_US.pdf

in harm's way can be devastating. Not only are events like these terrible situations for the families that lost loved ones, the companies can suffer a drop in sales, loss of brand value, and reduced stock prices. These are only a few of the many consequences faced by companies using suppliers where human rights are an afterthought.

The examples have been provided for two reasons: (1) to show that supply chain, particularly sourcing has a great deal of responsibility in managing and controlling costs in the face of enormous challenges and (2) to highlight that while knowing how to manage and control costs are essential, it is also important to know how these costs impact the business. What do we need to learn from all of this? Supply chain professionals need to become comfortable explaining how or by how much each of these significant issues can affect your organization. These issues can affect total return to shareholders, earnings per share, free cash flow, return on invested capital, net income, and other financial aspects of the organization. Remember, it is our responsibility to help our CEOs demonstrate success during earning calls.

Supply chains and operations functions are important for organizations. If you ask anyone in a supply chain or operations role, they will tell you that what they do each day is incredibly vital—and it is. Those in the field understand the importance of their roles and can articulate why, usually from the standpoint of operational performance. They can tell you the rate of defects, fill rates, order accuracy, inventory turns, and many other operational performance measures. After all, this is how their performance is measured. What is often missing from their explanations is how their actions directly affect the financial performance of the organization. Other than describing their key economic role in the organization as cost reduction, there is little more financial depth to the explanation. With the information and discussion provided by this book, we can change this.

The majority of supply chain professionals perform well in their functional roles. At the same time, many of these professionals find it difficult to see the company's larger goals or to see how their actions affect other functional areas. Furthermore, supply chain professionals fail to see how their decisions or actions connect to and affect the financial goals and objectives of the firm. Pointing this out is not to degrade supply chain professionals; they are measured by operational performance metrics, which, by all accounts, are plastered on most shop walls. These metrics are what they know and live by. Because the management of supply chains is critical to the long-term prosperity and sustainability of any firm, supply chain professionals who intend to become managers or executives with increasing responsibility must reach a new level of financial aptitude. We will accomplish this from a supply chain and operations perspective. Having this knowledge will help you understand why, how, and what you do every day is important and how it affects the firm's financial performance.

Value from a Different Perspective

If you have a conversation with the finance department or on Wall Street, you will hear different views of what value means. The definition of value from a finance person would include, of course, money. Within this book, we will begin to understand different perspectives on what value means and show how supply chain management and operations affect an organization's financial performance. In the next chapter, we will discuss the monetary value of a firm in greater depth, but for now, taken together, firm value includes ROIC, growth rate, and cost of capital.[4] It is incredibly beneficial for supply chain professionals to understand how these factors are affected by supply chain activities. In the end, you will not only know how operational metrics are affected by your decisions but you will also grasp how financial metrics are influenced by your decisions.

The connection between operations and finance is important. Only looking at a firm's current operational performance does not indicate if it is making any profit at all or that it can remain in business. If we are merely looking at the firm's financial performance, how do we know if it can sustain profitability into the future? We need to measure both financial and operational performance and connect the two to determine if we can generate value for the firm. We do this by looking at what drives value in the firm: ROIC, revenue growth, and cost of capital. Economic value is created whenever the ROIC exceeds the cost of capital (weighted average cost of capital [WACC]).

$$\text{Economic value created} = \text{ROIC} \times (\text{ROIC} - \text{WACC})$$

PwC conducted a study in 2008 that connected supply chain and operations to financial performance using 600 companies that experienced supply chain disruptions. For these companies that experienced disruption, PwC found that shareholder value plunged when compared to their peers. In addition, their stock prices experienced

---

[4] Koller, Chapter 20, *Performance Management*, page 417.

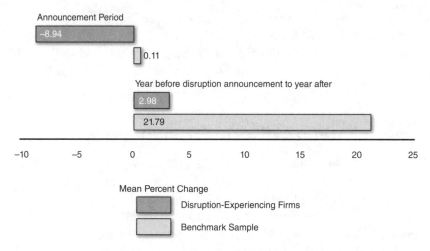

Figure 1.3 How supply chain disruptions affect stock prices. (From PricewaterhouseCoopers, From vulnerable to valuable: how integrity can transform a supply chain; Achieving operational excellence series, 2008.)

greater volatility, and they suffered sharp declines in return on sales and return on assets. Even more, these effects in many cases lasted up to 2 years.[5]

On average, affected companies' share prices (Figure 1.3) dropped 9% below the benchmark group during the day before and the day of the disruption announcement. Two-thirds of affected companies were lagging their peers in stock price performance a year after the disruption. The average stock return of those suffering from disruptions was almost 19 percentage points lower relative to the benchmark group over a 2-year period (i.e., 1 year before to 1 year after the disruption announcement date).

The investment community views disruption-experiencing companies unfavorably, and this uneasiness is likely to spread to employees, consumers, and suppliers. Compared to benchmark stocks, more than half of the affected companies experienced greater volatility for at least 2 years—a sign of diminished confidence among stakeholders. After controlling for normal market movements, the share price

---

[5] From vulnerable to valuable: how integrity can transform a supply chain: achieving operational excellence series, PricewaterhouseCoopers, December 2008.

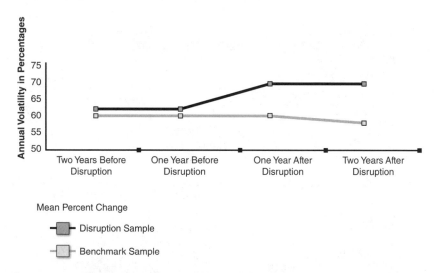

Figure 1.4 How supply chain disruptions affect share price volatility. (From PricewaterhouseCoopers, From vulnerable to valuable: how integrity can transform a supply chain; Achieving operational excellence series, 2008.)

volatility (Figure 1.4) in the year after the disruption of affected firms was around 8 points higher than the benchmark. Two years after the disruption, the affected firms were under performing the benchmark by an even higher 10 points.

Disruptions take a significant toll on profitability as reported by standard accounting measures. More than 60% of affected firms experienced lower returns on assets and sales. After controlling for normal industry and economic effects, the average return on assets (Figure 1.5) for disruption-experiencing firms was found to be down by 5 points.

Return on sales (Figure 1.6) suffered an average drop of 4 points for companies that experienced disruptions. On both measures, the returns of benchmark companies were stable over the 2-year period while those of disrupted companies fell significantly.

Structure of the Book

Throughout this book, you will think about (1) how the decisions you make each day affect the financial performance of your firm, (2) why certain decisions are typically made, and (3) to increase your fiscal aptitude. After reading this book, you will be able to

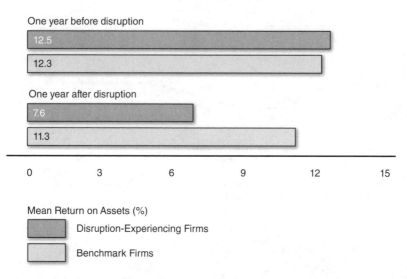

Figure 1.5 How supply chain disruptions affect return on assets. (From PricewaterhouseCoopers, From vulnerable to valuable: how integrity can transform a supply chain; Achieving operational excellence series, 2008.)

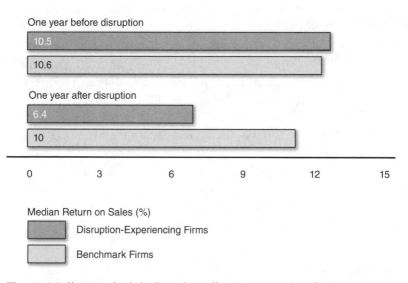

Figure 1.6 How supply chain disruptions affect return on sales. (From PricewaterhouseCoopers, From vulnerable to valuable: how integrity can transform a supply chain; Achieving operational excellence series, 2008.)

speak to finance and operation questions with confidence. Some questions you will be able to address include:

- Why are executives quick to jump on the "reduce cost bandwagon?" Why not focus more on increasing revenues?
- Which financial performance measures are affected by a supply interruption?
- How does a poor project implementation affect net earnings?
- Does poor quality affect gross margins, net earnings, ROIC, or ROA?
- Does cash equal profit?
- Which affects net earnings more, a 10% reduction in the cost of goods sold or a 10% increase in revenue, and why?

To provide you the knowledge to answer such questions, a number of subjects have been identified that will take you on a journey from myopically thinking of operational performance measures to thinking more in financial and value terms. Then you will be able to participate in financial conversations with greater confidence and a strong knowledge base.

The book began by introducing the financial performance measures that are important to company executives and an explanation of why. Then the book explored the idea of value. The remainder of the book will progress in this way.

Financial statements will be discussed, including the balance sheet, income statement, and statement of cash flows. Understanding the aspects of financial statements allows us to identify where pertinent information resides in each statement. This, in turn, helps supply chain managers as we talk about financial ratios, how we affect the ratios with our decisions, and how to calculate them. Financial statements also set the stage for the rest of the book. Once we understand financial statements, we can dive into firm valuation and what comprises value. After developing knowledge of valuation, the final chapters will discuss specific decision areas made by supply chain and operations professionals—projects, network planning, sourcing, managing assets and costs, transportation, logistics, inventory, and forecasting. Finally, we will examine how these areas contribute to value creation (or destruction).

Throughout the book, operational performance measures and their link to financial ratios and financial statements will be introduced and discussed. This will help you see exactly how operations decisions affect financial statements, thus affecting corporate economic goals and objectives. Further, you will see how operations decisions affect the corporation's ability to borrow and attract funds, its ability to reinvest in itself, and its share price and corporate valuation.

Summary

Although we focus on the financial performance of a firm in this book, money is by no means the only extent in which a corporation should be measured. As described in a popular 1992 *Harvard Business Review* article, the balanced scorecard introduced by Robert Kaplan and David Norton shows that financial performance is only one aspect of firm performance. Several other areas must be considered in the overall performance of an organization. For example, qualitative and nonfinancial measures such as environmental and corporate social responsibility measures are equally important. In addition, customer satisfaction, internal business processes, and learning each play important roles in organizations.

Most organizations are in business to create economic value and supply chain and operations greatly contribute to this goal. As such, this book will discuss how supply chain and operations decisions directly affect the financial performance of companies. Throughout the book, you will be exposed to high-level thinking related to financial impact. Then, as you are working toward improving fill rates, reducing lead times, or moving toward JIT inventory, you will understand how these actions affect your organization financially.

Those in not-for-profit or private organizations will also find this book relevant. Executives and managers of nonprofits and private companies are held accountable for raising funds and other revenue generating activities, managing costs and spending, and, just like other companies, nonprofits and private organizations have to bring in more money than they spend to remain viable.

The material in this book will touch on financial and managerial accounting, corporate finance, valuation methods, and other topics. Few other authors have combined these areas into one resource for supply chain and operations professionals. Undoubtedly, as you read this book, you will have additional or alternative viewpoints and experiences, and desire greater depth in particular subjects. If we pique your interest in the topics we cover, and we hope to, entire books have been written in great detail on each of these areas. We encourage you to obtain additional resources and continue learning.

2

Financial Statements Overview

What Are Financial Statements?

Without a formal communication avenue, how can an organization report its financial status? It is important to communicate with current and potential investors, lenders, and management about an organization's financial health, so it is crucial to have an industry standard method for doing so. Chapter 1 addressed many ratios and performance measures used to evaluate the company and management performance, which are calculated using financial statements. Without financial statements, decision makers would have no concrete evidence and would simply have to guess how well firms are performing. Financial statements are instruments to report and analyze company performance.

In some form or fashion, financial statements are prepared for public and private companies, for-profit and not-for-profit organizations, government agencies, sole proprietorships, partnerships, and corporations. The SEC requires public companies to submit financial reports, though most organizations prepare them in order to attract investors or borrow money. Financial statements are also necessary if the company is being acquired.

Financial statements have four components that provide a picture of a company's financial standing. These components include:

- Balance sheet
- Income statement
- Statement of cash flows
- Owner's equity statement

Individually, each piece provides specific information about the finances of a company and can help people make sense of the complexities of a company's financial standing. Annually, public corporations communicate financial information to their stockholders and other stakeholders through annual reports (10-K), quarterly reports (10-Q), and current reports (8-K). However, this picture is not always clear unless one has a thorough understanding of financial statements.

Although the overall look and general flow of financial statements are similar from one company to the next, on many occasions, you will find that account titles differ. Larger companies with several subsidiaries will consolidate their financial statements. From an outsider perspective, this makes it quite challenging to identify how well each subsidiary or affiliate company is performing, and whether or not they are contributing to or draining shareholder value. By all accounts, even if you are within the company, you may still find it difficult to decipher what the financial statements are revealing. The reason being, accountants have to make assumptions and have some discretion as to how they report certain financial activities. This discretion, while legal, has the effect of biasing reported earnings. For example, accountants have the freedom to declare depreciation schedules, but at the same time they do not know how long an asset will last. Accountants also have the liberty to choose an inventory costing method to use. The fact is the asset being depreciated and the actual flow of inventory through the supply chain is the same no matter the depreciation schedule or costing method used. The impact of these choices is reflected in the amount of taxes the company pays and the net income reported.

Financial statements are included in a company's annual report, which may or may not coincide with the calendar year. The fiscal year for The Walt Disney Company begins in October and ends in September. Companies may decide a fiscal year that does not align with the calendar year as more appropriate, considering their industry. Companies may want to remove the negative seasonal effects and end on a high note, where reported revenue is high or when the purchase of inventory is low. As an example, Target Corporation's fiscal year ends on the Saturday nearest January 31. One can infer this is because all the revenue and reconciliation of returned merchandise have been accounted for after the holiday season. Since the busy season is over, the accountants and staff are available to close the books.

The Financial Accounting Standards Board (FASB) has developed standards and practices that make financial reporting consistent with those companies that are required to provide financial statements. These standards and practices are called generally accepted accounting principles (GAAP). U.S. public companies report in accordance with GAAP, but not all countries require GAAP. Other countries have adopted accounting standards developed by the International Financial Reporting Standards (IFRS). Although there are differences between the two standards, they are generally not particularly significant, but the two standards are different. You should be cognizant that these differences are present when comparing companies from various countries. While the goal of GAAP is to promote consistency, differences in account titles and labels between companies and industries are quite common. These differences can lead to additional confusion, but with a little practice and experience, you can clear this hurdle in no time.

Why is it important to know whether companies are reporting in accordance with GAAP or non-GAAP standards? It is important because companies may use accrual or cash basis accounting. These two types of accounting are different in crucial areas. Knowing how the financials are presented helps those in supply chain and operations analyze the reported numbers accurately and make better decisions going forward. GAAP requires accrual basis accounting. In the accrual system, revenue is recognized in the period when it is earned rather than when cash is collected, and expenses are recognized when incurred rather than when paid. The cash basis accounting system records revenue when cash is received and records expenses when cash is paid. Smaller companies might use the cash basis since they do not have large account receivables or account payables; however, cash basis is not in accordance with GAAP standards.

All U.S. public companies report their financials using GAAP standards. GAAP attempts to streamline the reporting and communicating of company financial information. In addition, GAAP standards provide consistency in reporting and communication. Of course, this is easier said than done. Because many companies report their financials conforming to GAAP standards, we need to pay particular attention to all financial statements for a firm. All four components of financial statements are needed to give an accurate depiction of the company. The disparity between when revenue and expenses are recognized in accrual or cash basis accounting highlights this need. To illustrate, the income statement can show revenue earned in December, even though cash is not collected until January. The statement of cash flows will identify when the firm receives cash. You can be misled into believing there is enough cash to pay the bills if only the income statement is used for guidance. Even though the four financial statements seem sufficient, some companies issue additional financial statements.

Be cautious when companies provide pro forma financial statements. Pro forma statements can obscure the true picture of an organization's financial standing. Accountants provide pro forma financial statements, excluding nonrecurring charges or one-time unusual charges, thus showing better results than GAAP-conforming statements. As an example of when this practice would be used, a company may have an unusually large cache of obsolete inventory on its balance sheet in a fiscal year, so the accountants decide to remove this inventory from the balance sheet. The company considers this a one-time extraordinary charge and prepares pro forma financial statements along with its GAAP-conforming financial statements. Why are pro forma statements provided? Management has determined that this type of situation will not happen again and, thus, pro forma statements will provide a clearer picture of the company going forward. One issue with such practices, however, is managerial competence. Could this situation of having an extraordinarily large cache of inventory truly not happen again? Maybe, maybe not. The company did pay to acquire this inventory, and its impact could be long lasting. The SEC has warned companies that if they try to defraud investors through the use of pro forma statements, the SEC will investigate.

This is not to say there are no legitimate reasons to provide pro forma statements. One-time extraordinary charges are reasonable and expected to occur when a company restructures or merges. In some industries, it is standard practice, such as those with routine operating losses. For example, you might see where goodwill, depreciation, and amortization are written off as one-time unusual expenses. If done correctly and in the right context, these are legitimate cases of when to display pro forma financial statements. Remember, when a company reports pro forma statements, it should be attempting to provide a clearer and more accurate financial and operational picture of the company. But, of course, some will try to muddy the picture instead.

What Are Financial Statements Used For?

Simply put, financial statements are used to make decisions. The types of decisions made and the analysis of financial statements can be challenging. While you, as a supply chain and logistics professional, may not perform financial analysis using financial statements, others will. Thus, your decisions today will affect their decisions tomorrow.

From an accounting perspective, firms conduct three principal business activities. These include financing activities, investing activities, and operating activities. Accountants are tasked with identifying, collecting, measuring, processing, and reporting the company's business activities. Financing (obtaining money) can be in the form of borrowing money from a bank (lender) in which the loan is repaid with interest. Another form of financing is to trade equity (ownership) in the company for the money received from an investor. Investing activities vary from one organization to another. Companies can invest their money in other companies, in securities, and in property, plants, and equipment. And companies that are not traditional banks may even provide loans to other companies and consumers to earn interest on the loan principal. Finally, operating activities (applying the money and things of value to produce goods and services) are those in which a company produces and sells its products and services. For instance, for a sporting goods manufacturer who produces football helmets, operating activities would include buying raw materials for the helmet, the transportation of the raw materials to the factory, the manufacturing of the helmet, the wages paid to employees making the helmets, and the transportation of the helmets from the manufacturing facility to the distribution center. The principal business activities all affect the finances of an organization.

Data are collected and compiled from the three principal business activities. The data are used by internal users to manage the company (managerial accounting) and by external users to make investment and credit decisions (financial accounting).

Internal users need to understand the financial data to make informed decisions about the best use for funds. Management uses this information for decisions related to:

1. Finance—paying dividends, mix of debt and equity to fund operations, paying down debt early, and buying back stock.

2. Human resources—paying competitive wages and wage increases, staffing levels, employee benefits, and implementation of new training programs.

3. Marketing—promotion and advertising, product and service mix, markets served, and pricing.

4. Supply chain and operations—outsourcing, asset utilization, inventory management, commodity purchasing, supplier relationships, and distribution.

External users include tax authorities, government regulators, banks, investment firms, portfolio managers, analysts, investors, suppliers, and many others.

External uses of information include decisions related to:

1. Tax authorities—are companies paying their taxes?
2. Government regulators—are companies committing fraud?
3. Banks—companies' creditworthiness, companies' ability to pay back loans, and loan approvals.
4. Investment firms, portfolio managers, analysts, other investors—buy, sell, and hold stock.
5. Suppliers—payment terms, contract terms, relationships, process integration, and sharing information.
6. Customers—purchasing based on corporate social responsibility, environmental, and human rights practices.

A Closer Look at the Elements of Financial Statements

Balance Sheet

The balance sheet (Table 2.1) reports the financial position and condition of the firm at a point in time, on a specific date. It shows what assets the firm holds and who owns them. The three parts of the balance sheet are as follows:

1. Assets
2. Liabilities
3. Stockholders' equity

Assets

Assets are the things of value: resources owned by the company that provide future services and economic benefits. They are going to be used to carry out a company's operational activities, such as the production and the sale of goods and services. Assets come in two forms: tangible and intangible. Tangible assets consist primarily of operating assets, such as inventory, receivables, and plant, property, and equipment (PP&E). Intangible assets consist of copyrights, goodwill, patents, and trademarks. Essentially, if a company resource can be turned into cash, then it is an asset.

Table 2.1 Balance Sheet PepsiCo (Data Obtained from SEC.gov)

Balance Sheet
December 28, 20xx
In Millions (USD $), unless otherwise specified

Assets

Cash and cash equivalents	$ 9,375
Short-term investments	303
Accounts and notes receivable, net	6,954
Inventories	3,409
Prepaid expenses and other current assets	2,162
Total Current Assets	22,203
Property, plant and equipment, net	18,575
Amortizable intangible assets, net	1,638
Goodwill	16,613
Other nonamortizable intangible assets	14,401
Nonamortizable intangible assets	31,014
Investments in noncontrolled affiliates	1,841
Other assets	2,207
Total Assets	77,478
Liabilities and Equity	
Short-term obligations	5,306
Accounts payable and other current liabilities	12,533
Income taxes payable	—
Total Current Liabilities	17,839
Long-term debt obligations	24,333
Other liabilities	4,931
Deferred income taxes	5,986
Total Liabilities	53,089
Commitments and contingencies	
Preferred stock, no par value	41
Repurchased preferred stock	–171
PepsiCo Common Shareholders' Equity	
Common stock, par value 1 2/3¢ per share (authorized 3,600 shares, issued, net of repurchased common stock at par value: 1,529 and 1,544 shares, respectively)	25
Capital in excess of par value	4,095

(Continued)

Table 2.1 (*Continued*)

Balance Sheet
December 28, 20xx
In Millions (USD $), unless otherwise specified

Retained Earnings	$ 46,420
Accumulated other comprehensive loss	–5,127
Repurchased common stock	–21,004
Stockholders' equity attributable to parent	24,409
Noncontrolling interests	110
Total Equity	24,389
Total Liabilities and Equity	77,478

Assets are further classified as current or noncurrent (long-term) assets, separated only by the time the company thinks it will hold the asset. You can also think of this in the following way, how liquid is the asset? Current assets are held for 1-year or less. These include cash, inventory, and receivables. Noncurrent or long-term assets are held longer than 1 year. Long-term fixed assets, such as plant, property, and equipment (PP&E), have three common characteristics:

1. They have a physical presence (you can touch them).
2. They are used in the operation of the business.
3. They are not intended to be sold to customers.

Examples of PP&E are land, factories, distribution centers, tools, machinery, trucks and other vehicles, and furniture. Having assets are crucial to a company to offset liabilities.

Liabilities

Liabilities, also known as debts and obligations, are considered claims creditors have against assets. In other words, who do we owe? Liabilities arise when a company borrows money, when goods and services are purchased on account, when it owes employee wages, real estate taxes, sales taxes, utilities, and even when it collects money from customers and has yet to deliver the product or service. Like assets, companies have current and long-term liabilities. Current liabilities are debts payable within 1 year, whereas long-term liabilities are debts payable beyond 1 year.

It is important to understand the types of liabilities in each category. Typical current liability account titles include accounts payable, accrued expenses, income taxes payable, and deferred/unearned revenue. Common long-term liability account labels—some of which look very similar to current liability account labels—include long-term debt, pension benefits, deferred income taxes, deferred/unearned revenue, and notes payable. The long-term portion of the debt, held longer than 1 year, would be classified as a long-term liability. Remember, a company's liabilities are claims against its assets.

Stockholders' Equity

Stockholders' equity, also known as owners' equity or shareholders' equity, is the difference between total assets and total liabilities. It represents the claims against assets held by the owner(s). Taking the assets the company owns and subtracting what it owes, determines the company's value to its owners. This is stockholders' equity.

Stockholders' equity has two components:

1. Owners' contributions
2. Retained earnings, the earnings retained from profitable operations retained in the business

Other names are commonly seen on the balance sheet as a replacement for owners' contributions. You might see names, such as owner's capital, contributed capital, and capital stock, which all mean essentially the same. Although there are many names, the multiplicity does have a purpose. Depending on how the firm is organized (i.e., private, public, and partnership), the different labels help distinguish between the equity positions of individuals, partners, and shareholders. Contributed capital (owners' contributions) is an owners' equity account title that reports the asset contributions of owners. Owners' contributions are the investments made by the original owners to start the company and by subsequent investors. Investors obtain an equity stake or ownership in the company through the purchase of common and/or preferred stock. Contributed capital can be further separated into two accounts: capital stock and additional paid-in capital. Capital stock has two components: common stock and preferred stock. The contributions made to a company are an important part of understanding stockholder's equity; however, it is also important to look at the earnings.

Retained earnings are the money kept in the business from profitable operations. Specifically, it is an account title that reports earnings that are retained from profitable operations in the business. It is an aggregate number that represents cumulative net income less any cumulative net losses and asset withdrawals. Net income from the income statement is the primary driver of a change in retained earnings. Revenue increases net income, thus increasing retained earnings, while expenses and dividend payouts will reduce retained earnings. As a note, the components of financial statements are interconnected. The income statement links to the balance sheet through net income and retained earnings.

Cash earned by the company from profitable operations can be returned to stockholders and owners in the form of dividends. If the money is not paid to its stockholders and owners, it is held back as retained earnings and used for other purposes such as research and development, innovation, entering new markets, and other growth initiatives. A dividend policy is set by management and can certainly be the source of debate. For instance, Apple has long been accumulating massive amounts of cash as shareholders, investors, and hedge fund managers have been pressuring the company to return some of the cash to its shareholders.

The balance sheet provides the asset, liability, and owners' equity position of the company at a point in time. Income statements provide revenue end expense information for a specified time period.

Income Statement

The income statement reports performance and operating results of the firm for a specific time period, for example, from January 1 through December 31. Typical time periods for income statements are monthly, quarterly, and yearly. Contrast this with the balance sheet, as the balance sheet is a snapshot at a specific point in time on a particular date. The income statement demonstrates the profitability of the company. The income statement concludes with net income (or net loss), sometimes referred to as the "bottom line." Net income can be easily confused with the amount of cash the company has collected. Net income, net profit, and net earnings, all mean the same thing and tend to imply that net income is the amount of cash the company received during this time period. However, nothing can be further from the truth. Even a company that shows it is profitable on the income statement can be in peril of running out of cash, being unable to pay its bills, and ceasing operations. On the contrary, a company can show a net loss and still have plenty of cash. Keep this in mind: net income represents an excess of revenues over expenses. At the same time, a limitation of net income is that it does not exactly portray profit. Taxes and depreciation affect net income.

The income statement (Table 2.2) is also referred to as the earnings statement, profit and loss statement (P & L), and statement of operations. The income statement is essentially divided into four sections:

1. Revenue—dollar amount sold in the time period
2. Cost of goods sold—cost to make the items sold in the time period
3. Operating expenses—expenses incurred that supported sales and production in the time period
4. Other—other income, expenses, and taxes

Thus, net income is calculated as:

$$\text{Net income} = \text{Revenue} - \text{Costs} - \text{Expenses}$$

Or more fully explained as:

$$\text{Net income} = \text{Revenue} - \text{COGS} - \text{Operating expenses} - \text{Noncash items} - \text{Interest} - \text{Taxes}$$

Table 2.2 Income Statement PepsiCo (Data Obtained from SEC.gov)

Income Statement 12 Months Ended December 28, 20xx In Millions (USD $), except Per Share data, unless otherwise specified	
Net revenue	$66,415
Cost of sales	31,243
Selling, general, and administrative expenses	25,357
Amortization of intangible assets	110
Operating Profit (EBIT)	9,705
Interest expense	–911
Interest income and other	97
Income before income taxes	8,891
Provision for income taxes	2,104
Net Income	6,787
Less: Net income attributable to noncontrolling interests	47

(Continued)

Table 2.2 (*Continued*)

Income Statement 12 Months Ended December 28, 20xx In Millions (USD $), except Per Share data, unless otherwise specified	
Net Income Attributable to PepsiCo	<u>$6,740</u>
Net Income Attributable to PepsiCo per Common Share	
Basic	$4.37
Diluted	$4.32
Weighted-Average Common Shares Outstanding	
Basic	1,541
Diluted	1,560
Cash Dividends Declared per Common Share	$2.24

Revenue

Instead of using the term revenue, one could also use sales, but a more correct term would be net revenue or net sales. In some conversations, you will hear "top line growth," referring to sales and revenue growth. This figure ultimately represents the dollar amount of revenue less any sales incentives, discounts, returns, or allowances. Revenue can come from the sale of goods and/or services.

How is revenue documented on the income statement? Accountants use the principle of revenue recognition to answer this question. Revenue is recognized in the period in which it was earned. Revenue is recognized and earned when a sale is made—not when an order is received or even when cash is received. A company can earn revenue and show this on the income statement even though it has not been paid yet. Then one might question, "What is considered a sale?" A sale can be identified when the product is shipped to the customer, and the customer is intending to pay for the product. In a service-oriented company, a sale is recognized when the service is performed, and the customer is intending to pay for the service.

To better understand revenue as a whole, it is important to consider these points. Recognizing revenue on the income statement is not the same as when cash changes hands and sales are not the same as orders. It is entirely possible to take an order, and then ship the product the following week, but not receiving payment for 30 days, 60 days, or even later after the product was shipped.

The following passage from PepsiCo's Annual Report, 2013, p. 41 explains when they recognize revenue.

Our products are sold for cash or on credit terms. Our credit terms, which are established in accordance with local and industry practices, typically require payment within 30 days of delivery in the U.S., and generally within 30 to 90 days internationally, and may allow discounts for early payment. We recognize revenue upon shipment or delivery to our customers based on written sales terms that do not allow for a right of return.

It is important to realize, too, that revenues are not the same as assets. Revenue is earned through the disposition of assets or sale of an asset. Although revenues may enter the company in the form of an asset, such as cash or accounts receivable, revenue represents an increase in owners' equity not an increase in an asset.

Cost of Goods Sold

Companies record the cost of producing items for sale through the cost of goods sold (COGS). Other labels used instead of COGS include cost of sales (COS) and cost of revenue (COR). Service-oriented companies use COS or COR more frequently than manufacturing companies, but this is not universally applied. For example, PepsiCo uses cost of sales (COS) in their income statement. COGS (an expense) are considered product costs. Product costs can be directly connected to producing goods and services and include direct materials, direct labor, and manufacturing overhead costs that enable the company to produce goods for sale. These costs will show up as COGS when the goods are actually sold. Before the sale, all the direct production costs are tallied and stored on the balance sheet as inventory. In its annual report, Pepsi includes in COS (PepsiCo *Annual Report*, 2013, p. 73):

- Raw materials
- Direct labor
- Plant overhead
- Purchasing and receiving costs
- Costs directly related to production planning
- Inspection costs
- Raw materials handling facilities

Expenses

The expense category on the income statement is referred to as selling, general, and administrative expenses, commonly labeled SG&A. These expenses are grouped and classified as operating expenses and support the generation of revenue, but are not connected directly to the production of the goods for sale. PepsiCo includes in its SG&A, the indirect costs of moving, storing, and delivering finished product and the costs related to advertising and marketing activities. SG&A expenses include officers, office staff, and sales salaries, in addition to commissions, advertising and store displays, delivery expenses, office supplies, and business licenses. Expenses can also include noncash expenses, such as depreciation expense. Further, manufacturers find cost allocation especially difficult. For example, a plant manager directly supervises the manufacturing of the firm's products. However, the manager is also responsible for managing the administrative staff. Is the plant manager's salary included in COGS, SG&A, or both? Particular attention should be placed on allocating production overhead (COGS) and administrative operating expenses (SG&A) equitably.

As with revenue recognition, there is also expense recognition. Accountants generally follow the matching principle: let the expenses follow the revenues. If revenue is earned, expenses associated with earning the revenue are recognized too. Expenses incurred by the company that are not related directly to earning revenue—but do in an indirect way, such as office salaries and utilities—are generally recorded in the period that the expense occurs and not matched with revenue recognition. Thus, these costs are considered period costs. Prepaid expenses, such as rent and insurance where the expense might be paid for an entire year upfront, are considered assets until the prepaid services are used over time, then they become expenses on the income statement. As discussed earlier, revenue increases retained earnings; however, there is an opposite effect with expenses. Expenses represent a decrease in retained earnings of owners' equity.

To recap, expenses are the cost of assets consumed or services used in the process of earning revenue. An asset is used up or a liability is incurred as a result of an operating activity. Expenses represent the cost of goods or services used up or consumed to produce revenue.

Statement of Cash Flows

Of each of the financial statements, the statement of cash flows (Table 2.3) seems to receive the least amount of attention. Knowing and managing cash flows are important though. Without adequate cash, companies could not pay their obligations on time, fund operations, or company growth. The statement of cash flow is quite useful since it provides information as to the actual movement of cash; how much and where the cash is being spent. The statement of cash flows reports cash position of a company during a specific period of time. The statement does so by classifying each cash inflow (receipt) and each cash outflow (payment) into operating, investing, and financing activities. Is this not what the cash account on the balance sheet is for? Well, not exactly. Remember, the balance sheet captures a picture of the company's financials on a specific date and time. In contrast, the statement of cash flows shows the movement of cash in and out of the business over a certain time period and differentiates between the sources of cash. The statement of cash flows only reports cash movements, whereas the balance sheet and income statement report both cash and noncash transactions.

Table 2.3 Statement of Cash Flows PepsiCo (Data Obtained from SEC.gov)

Statement of Cash Flows
12 Months Ended December 28, 20xx
In Millions (USD $), unless otherwise specified

Operating Activities	
Net income	$6,787
Depreciation and amortization	2,663
Stock-based compensation expense	303
Merger and integration costs	10
Cash payments for merger and integration costs	−25
Restructuring and impairment charges	163
Cash payments for restructuring charges	−133
Restructuring and other charges related to the transaction with Tingyi	—
Cash payments for restructuring and other charges related to the transaction with Tingyi	−26
Noncash foreign exchange loss related to Venezuela devaluation	111
Excess tax benefits from share-based payment arrangements	−117
Pension and retiree medical plan contributions	−262
Pension and retiree medical plan expenses	663

(Continued)

Table 2.3 (*Continued*)

<table>
<tr><td colspan="2" align="center">**Statement of Cash Flows**
12 Months Ended December 28, 20xx
In Millions (USD $), unless otherwise specified</td></tr>
<tr><td>Deferred income taxes and other tax charges and credits</td><td>$–1,058</td></tr>
<tr><td>Change in accounts and notes receivable</td><td>–88</td></tr>
<tr><td>Change in inventories</td><td>4</td></tr>
<tr><td>Change in prepaid expenses and other current assets</td><td>–51</td></tr>
<tr><td>Change in accounts payable and other current liabilities</td><td>1,007</td></tr>
<tr><td>Change in income taxes payable</td><td>86</td></tr>
<tr><td>Other, net</td><td>–349</td></tr>
<tr><td>Net Cash Provided by Operating Activities</td><td>9,688</td></tr>
<tr><td>**Investing Activities**</td><td></td></tr>
<tr><td>Capital spending</td><td>–2,795</td></tr>
<tr><td>Sales of property, plant, and equipment</td><td>109</td></tr>
<tr><td>Acquisition of WBD, net of cash, and cash equivalents acquired</td><td>—</td></tr>
<tr><td>Investment in WBD</td><td>—</td></tr>
<tr><td>Cash payments related to the transaction with Tingyi</td><td>–3</td></tr>
<tr><td>Other acquisitions and investments in noncontrolled affiliates</td><td>–109</td></tr>
<tr><td>Divestitures</td><td>133</td></tr>
<tr><td>**Short-Term Investments, by original maturity**</td><td></td></tr>
<tr><td>More than 3 months maturities</td><td>—</td></tr>
<tr><td>Three months or less, net</td><td>61</td></tr>
<tr><td>Other investing, net</td><td>–21</td></tr>
<tr><td>Net Cash Used for Investing Activities</td><td>–2,625</td></tr>
<tr><td>**Financing Activities**</td><td></td></tr>
<tr><td>Proceeds from issuances of long-term debt</td><td>4,195</td></tr>
<tr><td>Payments of long-term debt</td><td>–3,894</td></tr>
<tr><td>Debt repurchase</td><td>—</td></tr>
<tr><td>**Short-Term Borrowings, by original maturity**</td><td></td></tr>
<tr><td>More than 3 months proceeds</td><td>23</td></tr>
<tr><td>More than 3 months payments</td><td>–492</td></tr>
<tr><td>Three months or less, net</td><td>1,634</td></tr>
<tr><td>Cash dividends paid</td><td>–3,434</td></tr>
<tr><td>Share repurchases common</td><td>–3,001</td></tr>
</table>

Table 2.3 (*Continued*)

Statement of Cash Flows
12 Months Ended December 28, 20xx
In Millions (USD $), unless otherwise specified

Share repurchases preferred	$ –7
Proceeds from exercises of stock options	1,123
Excess tax benefits from share-based payment arrangements	117
Acquisition of noncontrolling interests	–20
Other financing	–33
Net Cash Used for Financing Activities	–3,789
Effect of exchange rate changes on cash and cash equivalents	–196
Net Increase/(Decrease) in Cash and Cash Equivalents	3,078
Cash and Cash Equivalents, Beginning of Year	6,297
Cash and Cash Equivalents, End of Year	$ 9,375

Information within the statement of cash flows is useful for current and potential investors and creditors because it can help answer questions such as:

1. Where did the cash come from, what was the cash used for, and what was the change in cash balance during the period?
2. What are the reasons for differences between net income and cash flow?
3. Is the company able to meet its obligations or pay dividends?

The information presented in the statement of cash flows helps answer these questions. Essentially, the statement of cash flows begins with how much cash the company has at the start of the period, adds any cash received, subtracts cash spent, and is then left with cash on hand at the end of the period. In developing the statement of cash flows, items from the balance sheet and income statement are used and then organized by operating, investing, and financing activities.

Much of the supply chain and operations activities fall into the operating activities, and include cash outflows for payables, inventory and materials, COGS, overhead, and prepaid expenses. Cash inflows include accounts receivable and sales revenue. Noncash expense accounts such as depreciation and amortization are included in operating activities. In short, typical operating activities consist of collecting cash from customers, paying cash for merchandise and inventory, and paying cash for leased space and salaries.

Investing activities include the purchase and proceeds from fixed assets such as PP&E. Financing activities include those activities where cash is accumulated from investors who buy company stock, from lenders who loan the company money or from lenders who extend a line of credit. Of course, when dividends are paid and the company pays off the loan, cash will leave the company.

Relationship between Financial Statements

As mentioned earlier, all four financial statements should be consulted for an accurate picture of the company. Each statement alone cannot clearly depict the company's current state of affairs. Compiling the information provides a meaningful and distinct view of the company. If we want to identify what amount owned or owed at a particular point in time, the balance sheet is an excellent representation. To know which operations have contributed to the firm's profit or loss in a given period, the income statement provides this information. Finally, to know the amount of cash flowing into and out of the business over time, the statement of cash flows holds the answer.

Business activities affect each financial statement in some way. As an example, a chemical manufacturing company sold $10,000 worth of chemicals on credit to a construction company. The sale earned revenue and it is recorded on the income statement. Presumably, the chemical company incurred expenses making chemicals to sell. For the sake of example, in this case, the COGS is $2,500, and with this sale, the COGS increases as well. As the buyer intends to pay in the future, the chemical company will see accounts receivable increase by $10,000 on the balance sheet, while at the same time, the inventory assets will decrease by $2,500. These actions have adjusted the balance sheet and income statement, but still no cash has changed hands, so the statement of cash flows remains unchanged. Finally, retained earnings on the balance sheet will adjust according to the revenue earned, expenses incurred, and taxes paid generated from the sale of chemicals. If the $10,000 sale is higher than the sum of expenses incurred and taxes paid, retained earnings will increase from the additional net income. If not, a net loss is incurred, which will reduce retained earnings.

1. Income statement
   - Revenue $10,000+
   - COGS $2,500+
2. Balance sheet
   - *Current assets*
     - o Accounts receivable $10,000+
     - o Inventory $2,500–
   - *Retained earning*
     - o Revenue > expenses and taxes+
     - o Revenue < expenses and taxes–
3. Cash flow
   - Unchanged

Now consider this situation from the construction company's perspective, as the buyer. The construction company has gained inventory assets, chemicals worth $10,000 that will provide a future economic benefit for the company. It has also incurred a liability, accounts payable, since it now owes the chemical company $10,000. The chemical company has a claim against the construction company's chemical assets of $10,000. Does the construction company's statement of cash flow change? Not yet, as it has not paid any cash yet. Once it does, then the statement of cash flow will change. Has the income statement changed yet? Not yet. There are three factors in play in this situation. First, determine if the chemicals are directly or indirectly related to the revenue being generated by the construction company. Second, allocate the expenses to either COGS if directly related, or SG&A if indirectly related. Third, the timing of the expense allocation is determined. COGS expenses are allocated at the time revenue is realized on the income statement. SG&A expenses are recorded on the income statement when the asset, chemicals, is used.

Finally, understanding how each financial statement is not only related to each other, but connected to each other is important. Looking back to Tables 2.1 to 2.3, or viewing the modified financial statements (Table 2.4), the connection between the financial statements through certain line items is clear. Notice that "ending cash" on the cash flow statement is equal to "cash" on the balance sheet. "Net income" on the income statement is equal to the "net income" on the statement of cash flows. Net income from the income statement is added to retained earnings on the balance sheet, and thus stockholders' equity increases, though this transaction is not quite as apparent.

Table 2.4 Modified Financial Statements

Balance Sheet
December 28, 20xx
In Millions (USD $), unless otherwise specified

Assets	
Cash and cash equivalents	$ 9,375
Short-term investments	303
Accounts and notes receivable, net	6,954
Inventories	3,409
Prepaid expenses and other current assets	2,162
Total Current Assets	22,203
PepsiCo Common Shareholders' Equity	
Retained Earnings	**$46,420**
Accumulated other comprehensive loss	–5,127
Stockholders' equity attributable to parent	24,409
Noncontrolling interests	110
Total Equity	24,389
Total Liabilities and Equity	77,478

Income Statement
12 Months Ended December 28, 20xx
In Millions (USD $), Except Per Share Data, unless otherwise specified

Net Income	$ 6,787

Statement of Cash Flows
12 Months Ended December 28, 20xx

Operating Activities	
Net Income	$ 6,787
Cash and Cash Equivalents, beginning of year	6,297
Cash and Cash Equivalents, end of year	$ 9,375

Summary

This chapter focused on financial statements, giving a description of financial statements and how they are used to communicate important financial information. Next, an explanation about what financial statements are used for and how they are used was provided. Further, each component of a financial statement (1) balance sheet, (2) income statement, and (3) statement of cash flows was described in detail, ending with the interrelationship between the three financial statements.

3

Financial Statement Primer Essentials

Introduction

Chapter 2 covered basic information related to financial statements. In this chapter, more in depth information related to financial statements will be presented. To gain additional insights into the topics of subsequent chapters, particularly ratio analysis, it is necessary to examine the finer details of financial statements. This chapter focuses on how the figures that appear in the financial statements are calculated. Figures that are covered include:

1. Value of assets
2. Inventory costing
3. Depreciation and Amortization
4. Revenue recognition
5. COGS
6. Leases

As employees and managers, we truly want to know if our actions are assisting the company to gain more solid financial footing or detracting from this effort. Understanding financial statements in detail allows for more informed decision-making by supply chain and operations managers. Financial topics such as determining inventory cost or how depreciation and amortization impact the numbers are particularly important for understanding a company's financial position. Ratio analysis is especially useful in evaluating company performance; however, they need to be interpreted with caution.

The next chapter will discuss financial ratio analysis. To truly understand what ratios imply, it is necessary to know what components comprise the ratios and how they are calculated. Additionally, it is crucial to understand how each component of the ratio is determined and from where this information comes. This is the basis for this chapter; to introduce how the figures in the financial statements are calculated so reasonable inferences from ratio analysis can be made. Accountants and executives make assumptions about reported information, which is perfectly legal; however, the assumptions can make financial analysis and ratio analysis more difficult. Financial analysis and ratio analysis can and should be performed using information from different sections of the financial statements.

Rarely, all of the information needed for analysis is made obvious on the balance sheet, income statement, or statement of cash flows. Instead, it may require closer examination to find the necessary information. The numbers reported in the financial statements may not be exactly what is needed for financial analysis and day-to-day decision making by those in supply chain and operations because of the assumptions made by a company's financial experts. Accountants have the liberty to make assumptions based on historical trends when preparing financial statements. Examples of these assumptions include the amount of accounts receivable will not be collected, or what liabilities exist, such as tax, pension, and legal liabilities. Accountants also make assumptions about how to value tangible assets, how to value brand and intangible assets, and an amount to allocate to goodwill. As a result of these assumptions, financial results can vary widely.

The following passage from PepsiCo's 2013 Annual Report explains its use of assumptions.

> The preparation of our consolidated financial statements in conformity with generally accepted accounting principles requires us to make estimates and assumptions that affect reported amounts of assets, liabilities, revenues, expenses and disclosure of contingent assets and liabilities. Estimates are used in determining, among other items, sales incentives accruals, tax reserves, stock-based compensation, pension and retiree medical accruals, amounts and useful lives for intangible assets, and future cash flows associated with impairment testing for perpetual brands, goodwill and other long-lived assets.

Footnotes and comments are widely used throughout financial reports and explain many important details needed to more fully understand the company's financial and operational position. As long as the company remains consistent (consistency principle) in its assumptions, then the analysis, decision making, and inferences about the company remain fairly straightforward. When the assumptions change from year to year or when one begins to compare companies, then financial analysis becomes more difficult. To best understand a company's financial reports, it is crucial to pay attention to the notes and comments.

PepsiCo includes sections in its 10K report (annual report) that highlights its accounting policies. The 10K report provides insight as to how *PepsiCo* documents and reports its numbers, providing valuable information from which to learn.

For instance, *PepsiCo* provides the following notes in their financial statements:

1. Revenue recognition: "We recognize revenue upon shipment or delivery to our customers based on written sales terms that do not allow for a right of return . . . Similarly, our policy for certain warehouse-distributed products is to replace damaged and out-of-date products."

2. Cost of sales: Raw materials, direct labor, and plant overhead, as well as purchasing and receiving costs, costs directly related to production planning, inspection costs, and raw material handling facilities are included in cost of sales. The costs of moving, storing, and delivering finished product are included in selling, general, and administrative expenses.

3. Distribution costs: "Distribution costs, including the costs of shipping and handling activities, are reported as selling, general, and administrative expenses."

4. Inventories: "Inventories are valued at the lower of cost or market. Cost is determined using the average: first-in, first-out (FIFO) or last-in, first-out (LIFO) methods."

5. Property, plant, and equipment: "Property, plant, and equipment are recorded at historical cost. Depreciation and amortization are recognized on a straight-line basis over an asset's estimated useful life. Land is not depreciated and construction in progress is not depreciated until ready for service."

With detailed information such as provided by *PepsiCo*, financial analysis can provide a clearer picture of a firm's financial position as it takes into account assumptions made in reporting. Understanding assumptions allows supply chain and operations professionals to make informed inferences and judgments about how day-to-day actions of the company are being presented to management, shareholders, and analysts.

Value of Assets

Accountants use various methods of asset valuation. The method chosen to value an asset influences what is stated within the categories on the balance sheet. For this reason, it is necessary to know which valuation method is used before any inference from financial analysis can be made. Assets are typically valued at cost or fair market value. Simply put, cost is how much the company paid to acquire the asset, which includes all the costs related to purchasing an asset. Contrastingly, fair market value is how much the company could receive if the asset is sold.

From a supply chain and operations perspective, cost is the most common valuation method. This is largely due to the asset categories associated with supply chain and operations. For example, inventory is typically valued at acquisition cost or replacement cost; property, plant, and equipment (PP&E) are also valued at acquisition cost. Other asset categories often use a different valuation method. Fair market value is often used when assets are actively traded, such as investments in stocks, marketable securities, and accounts receivables.

Knowing that cost is regularly used as the valuation method in supply chain and operations, one may question why fair market value is not used. On the surface, it may make more sense to use fair market value, since that would be the amount received if the asset was sold; however, fair market value is quite subjective. Determining or estimating fair market value is time-consuming and costly because it needs to be verified. As an example of determining fair market value in a corporate setting, consider the Target Corporation. Target estimates fair market value goods to sell, doing so by obtaining market appraisals, valuations from third party brokers, or other valuation techniques. Completing this estimation is costly. Therefore, without great expense, fair market value cannot be readily verified; however, acquisition cost can be verified. In the acquisition of goods, there is documentation of a monetary exchange and proof of goods' cost. For these reasons, cost is a more commonly used valuation for supply chain and operations.

Recall that valuing an asset using the cost method is equal to historical acquisition cost. This includes all the costs related to purchasing and getting the asset ready for operation in the desired location. Applicable costs include, transportation, storage, taxes, tariffs, duties, insurance, legal, testing, and installation. Comparatively, fair market value is a subjective measure related to the amount a company would receive if the asset is sold. To more clearly understand the cost valuation method, consider the following examples.

Property Example

Land, of course, is typically purchased as a physical location for buildings, stores, distribution centers, or warehouses in order for the business to operate. The total cost of the land includes the cash price for the land, closing and title costs, taxes, real estate broker commissions, and costs related to readying the property for use. Preparing the land can include activities such as grading, clearing, draining, removing underground gas tanks, adding parking lots, and adding roads or access to the land.

Reporting the cost of land can be affected by many factors, including time. An example using the land cost method, assume that the Target Corporation purchased land for $500,000 5 years ago. In those 5 years, the land appreciated to a fair market value of $1,000,000. Despite the fair market value of the land, the balance sheet would report the cost of the land at $500,000. The difference in the cost affects how analysts perceive the company's performance. The company actually has land that is more valuable than is reported.

Cost of land example:

+ Cash price of property

+ Net removal cost of a warehouse currently located on the parcel

+ Attorney's fees

+ Real estate broker's commission

= Cost of land

Plant and Building Example

Plant and building costs are similar to land purchases. There are costs such as cash price for the building, closing and title costs, taxes, real estate broker commissions, and cost related to preparing the property ready for use. Preparation costs can include remodeling, plumbing, electrical work, painting, and interest payments related to financing the building during the time period of construction. Again, the company could have plants and buildings that are more or less valuable than is reported on the balance sheet.

Equipment

Equipment includes assets used in the operation of the business, such as factory machinery, delivery trucks, office furniture, and computers. On top of purchase price, equipment costs must also consider sales taxes, freight charges, and insurance during shipping, assembly, installation, and testing. Because of these additional factors, equipment cost must be calculated to provide the true cost of any equipment. Calculation examples are:

Factory machinery example:

+ Cash price

+ Sales taxes

+ Insurance during shipping

+ Installation and shipping

= Cost of factory machinery

Delivery truck example:

+ Cash price

+ Sales taxes

+ Painting and printing

= Cost of delivery truck

To understand the true financial position of the company, knowing how assets are valued is worthwhile. It should be apparent that the reported asset balances do not necessarily match current market conditions or fair value. Further, knowledge about cost methods provides insights about how asset acquisition costs can be lowered.

Noncash Transactions

Tangible Assets and Depreciation

Over time fixed or long-term assets become worn, obsolete, or their production capability is reduced. In short, their ability to generate revenue decreases over time. To account for an asset's reduction in usefulness, the asset is depreciated over its useful life. An asset's useful life can be determined by time, number of units produced, number of cycles, or some other measurement that defines when the asset is no longer useful. Software may have a useful life of 3 years, where landing gear or an airframe on an airplane may have a useful life of 25,000 cycles (takeoffs and landings). An airplane's engine may have a useful life of 15,000 flight hours. Of course, routine and preventive maintenance will have an impact on whether or not the airplane components' useful life is shorter or longer than the estimates.

Not all assets are depreciated, though. Knowing this then begs the question, "What assets are depreciated?" With the exception of land, those assets classified as PP&E are depreciated. Land improvements, buildings, and equipment are depreciated; however, land itself is not. Land does not have a useful life; rather, it has an unlimited life, and in many cases, land becomes more useful as less land is available. Land tends to continue to produce revenue for a company. Note that depreciation is used to allocate cost; it does not determine an asset's value. Eventually, a fully depreciated asset may show a book value of zero dollars but its fair market value, what you could sell the asset for, may be much higher.

Typically, fixed assets are valued on the balance sheet at historical acquisition cost less accumulated depreciation. Consider this example: a company acquires manufacturing equipment for $12,000, estimates the salvage value will be $2,000, and determines that the useful life for this equipment is 5 years. Over the next 5 years, a portion of the asset's cost is converted to an expense on the income statement. Assume the asset depreciates $2,000 per year, so this $2,000 per year is allocated as a depreciation expense until all $10,000 (from $12,000 – $2,000) is used up. On the balance sheet, the actual historical asset value does not decline, it is still $10,000; however, a percentage or dollar amount of the historical cost value is reduced through a balance sheet account called accumulated depreciation. Accumulated depreciation is a running total of the amount of depreciation a company has considered an expense for tax purposes. In this example, accumulated depreciation increased by $2,000 per year. Since depreciation reduces gross profit through the depreciation expense account on the income statement, a company will pay fewer taxes per year. Less income earned means fewer taxes paid, which is why recording depreciated is beneficial. In the Target Corporation balance sheet (Table 3.1), assets are reduced by the amount of accumulated depreciation of $14,402. As seen in their income statement (Table 3.2), a depreciation and amortization expense of $2,223 reduces taxable income.

After considering the example of depreciating manufacturing equipment and examining the Target Corporation example, it is clear that a company is not actually paying out $2,000 every year, though the depreciation is listed as an expense. No cash is changing hands; the company is showing a noncash expense. Even though the gross profit shows a $2,000 decline on paper, no cash has changed hands. Another question that may arise is, "Can the equipment still be used after 5 years?" Absolutely, there is no reason that a company cannot

Table 3.1 Target Asset Section of Balance Sheet

Target Corporation **Balance Sheet, Millions (USD $)** **February 1, 20XX**	
Assets	
Cash and cash equivalents	695
Credit card receivables, held for sale	—
Inventory	8,766
Other current assets	2,112
Total Current Assets	11,573
Property and equipment	—
Land	6,234
Buildings and improvements	30,356
Fixtures and equipment	5,583
Computer hardware and software	2,764
Construction-in-progress	843
Accumulated depreciation	−14,402
Property and equipment, net	31,378
Other noncurrent assets	1,602
Total Assets	44,553

Source: Target Corporation's 2013 Annual Report.

continue to use the equipment; however, the company cannot allocate any more depreciation expense to reduce taxes.

Company management can choose to use various depreciation methods including straight-line, units of activity, declining balance, and accelerated depreciation. In choosing a method, management must consider the advantages and disadvantages of each method. For example, the straight-line method is most common and easiest to use, which is advantageous; though, a disadvantage is the assumption that the asset's usefulness remains constant over its useful life, which tends to maximize net income. The straight-line method expenses depreciate the same amount each year of the asset's useful life, whereas accelerated depreciation methods depreciate assets to a greater degree early on and to a lesser degree over time.

Companies have the freedom to choose the depreciation method used to prepare financial statements and which method is used to complete tax obligations. The two methods can be different, so accelerated

Table 3.2 Target Income Statement

Target Corporation **Income Statement, Millions (USD $) 20XX**	
Sales	72,596
Credit card revenues	—
Total revenue	72,596
Cost of sales	51,160
Selling, general, and administrative expenses	15,375
Credit card expenses	—
Depreciation and Amortization	2,223
Gain on receivables transaction	–391
Earnings before interest expense and income taxes	4,229
Net interest expense	1,126
Earnings before income taxes	3,103
Provision for income taxes	1,132
Net Earnings	**1,971**

Source: Target Corporation's 2013 Annual Report.

depreciation methods are often used for tax returns because doing so minimizes taxes in the short term. Interestingly, regardless of which depreciation method is used for tax returns, over the long term, the taxes paid and effects on income are nearly identical. However, in the short term, there are significant differences on income and taxes paid dependent on which depreciation method is used.

The amount a company depreciates an asset is called depreciable cost. This is determined by the cost of the asset less its salvage value. Salvage value is an estimate of the value of the asset after its useful life. In the previous example, if the cost of the equipment is $12,000 and the estimated salvage value is $2,000 for the equipment after its useful life of 5 years, then this equipment can be depreciated by $10,000 or $2,000 per year (Table 3.3). To clearly illustrate straight-line depreciation for this example, consider the following:

Straight-line depreciation method example:

Cost of equipment = $12,000

Salvage value = $2,000

Useful life = 5 years

Book value = Cost – Accumulated depreciation

Table 3.3 Depreciation Schedule

Year	Depreciable Cost ($)	Annual Depreciation Expense ($)	End of Year Accumulated Depreciation ($)	Book Value ($)
2015	10,000	2,000	2,000	10,000
2016	10,000	2,000	4,000	8,000
2017	10,000	2,000	6,000	6,000
2018	10,000	2,000	8,000	4,000
2019	10,000	2,000	10,000	2,000

Annual reports demonstrate how companies depreciate their assets. Looking at a real-world example, the Target Corporation's Annual Report states that it depreciates its property and equipment using the straight-line method over the estimated useful lives or lease terms, if shorter. For income tax purposes, accelerated depreciation methods are generally used. To further clarify their depreciation methods, they provide the following guidance for useful life of the assets' depreciation:

Estimated useful lives—Life (years)

Buildings and improvements—8 to 39

Fixtures and equipment—2 to 15

Computer hardware and software—2 to 7

How does a company decide whether or not it should classify a particular asset-related expense as an operating or depreciation expense? When a company incurs ordinary and recurring costs to maintain or operate an asset, the costs are allocated as an operating expense on the income statement against revenue. If an asset is acquired, upgraded or improved in someway that allows the company to generate additional revenue, these costs would be classified as capital expenditures. Capital expenditures are shown as an increase in assets and accumulated depreciation on the balance sheet, and as a depreciation expense on the income statement. Capital expenditures are typically fixed, physical, nonconsumable assets, such as buildings and equipment. These costs are generally nonrecurring and significant in amount.

Net Fixed Assets

After considering the valuation of different categories of assets, it is important to understand aggregating fixed assets. Net fixed assets is the value of all fixed assets held by a company plus any improvements to the assets, less any accumulated depreciation, permanent decline in the value of the assets, and the total of any liabilities against the assets.

Net fixed assets example:

+ Fixed asset purchase price
+ Subsequent additions to existing assets
− Accumulated depreciation
− Accumulated asset impairment
− Liabilities associated with the fixed assets
= Net fixed assets

Nontangible Assets and Amortization

Amortization is identical to the concept of depreciation, except that the assets in these instances are not physical assets, but are assets that cannot be touched. These assets may include copyrights, patents, trademarks, franchises, licenses, and customer lists. Certain intangible assets lose value over time and are amortized over time, just as physical assets are depreciated over time. The amortization process, just as the depreciation process, reduces income on paper and requires the company to pay fewer taxes.

Another nontangible asset is goodwill. Goodwill is a collection of favorable intangible attributes that are not grouped with other assets. Items grouped in the goodwill category include desirable locations, exceptional skill or talent, positive customer relations, or healthy union relationships. These items may justify paying more for an acquisition in excess of fair value when acquiring a company. In addition, goodwill is not amortized because the useful life for goodwill cannot be pinpointed. When a company is acquired, the difference between the purchase price and net assets is goodwill. Goodwill is therefore, only recorded when an acquisition is completed but is tested for impairment annually. Goodwill may be reduced over time as the reasons for paying more than fair market value in the first place erode.

Inventory Costing and Cost of Goods Sold

Besides fixed assets, managing inventory is one of the greatest concerns for supply chain and operations professionals. At the end of a reporting period, a company must determine how much inventory remains and needs to be reported as an asset on the balance sheet. It also has to determine the amount of inventory sold during the same period and thus reported as an expense on the income statement as cost of goods sold (COGS). Understanding how inventory is valued and presented on the balance sheet and translated to COGS on the income statement is of utmost importance to supply chain and operations professionals. Although there are many inventory tracking and costing practices, not all are explained here; however, the explanations provided throughout the book will offer a sufficient overview.

Inventory is classified differently for retail companies, merchants, and manufacturers. Retailers classify their inventory as merchandise inventory, the merchant owns it and it is ready for sale. Contrastingly, manufacturers and assembly plants categorize their inventory as raw materials, work-in-process, and finished goods. Manufacturers and assemblers classify inventory this way to indicate the condition of the inventory and if it is ready for sale. For example, prior to assembly of an aircraft, an aircraft manufacturer would classify components of the airplane such as tires, wiring, and hydraulic pumps as raw materials. These materials are directly used in production. As soon as assembly starts, the manufacturer would then classify the components as work-in-process. Work-in-process is inventory costs related to direct materials, direct labor, and manufacturing overhead. A completed aircraft ready for sale would be classified as finished goods. As a reminder, all inventories are combined and reported on the balance sheet.

Inventory is typically valued at cost and reported on the balance sheet in this way. If the market value of the inventory is less than the actual cost of the inventory, then companies may reduce the inventory amount to the lower of cost or market value. Inventory costs include the amount to acquire the product plus the costs related to placing it in the location and condition ready for sale. This includes costs related to purchasing, transporting, and storing inventory. Purchasing costs decline by the amount of purchase returns, allowances, and discounts received. Further, manufacturers and assemblers add direct costs of production, such as labor and overhead, to the COGS.

It is important to note that manufacturing overhead consists of all manufacturing costs other than direct materials and direct labor that is related to production and included in the COGS. Overhead includes factory supplies used and labor not directly identified with the production of specific products. It also includes general manufacturing costs such as depreciation, maintenance, repairs, property taxes, insurance, and utilities. Additionally, a reasonable share of the managerial costs associated with production, other than those relating solely to the selling and administrative functions of the business, can be considered overhead.

Companies use inventory account balances to determine COGS on the income statement.

$$(\text{Beginning inventory} + \text{Purchases}) - \text{Ending inventory} = \text{Cost of goods sold}$$

Since the balance sheet demonstrates a point in time, ending inventory is portrayed on the balance sheet for the current period, while the last period's inventory would be classified as beginning inventory. Stated another way, if one period ends with $1.5 million in inventory, the next period begins with $1.5 million in inventory.

Difficulty determining COGS arises when a company buys inventory at different times and at different costs. For example, a company purchases three hydraulic pumps at different times and at different prices with the intent to resell the pumps to its customers. In this case, how do they know what the value of the inventory will be when one of the pumps is sold? Assume that the pumps were bought for $1,000, $1,100 and $1,200; now the company sells one pump. This situation raises several questions:

- What is the value of inventory?
- Which one should be sold first?
- Which one did it sell?
- Does it matter?
- Is the value of remaining inventory $2,100, $2,200, or $2,300?

When companies have limited inventory, it is fairly easy to match the item bought with the item sold; however, with many more SKUs, this becomes more difficult.

A few methods of costing inventory to determine COGS have been developed due to the impracticality of matching items that are bought and later sold. These methods do not assume the flow of goods matches the flow of costs. This means that in the hydraulic pump example, the $1,000 pump could have been bought first, but it could have been sold first or last. Regardless, the cost allocated to the first pump sold could be $1,200. So, how do managers decide how to cost their inventory and does it really matter?

Inventory costing methods include FIFO, LIFO, and average inventory. Management chooses the method that suits their company's objectives best. At this point, it is necessary to restate that a company will perform costing of the inventory to assign a dollar amount for ending inventory on the balance sheet. In addition, this allows the company to assign a COGS amount on the income statement. The company is not deciding in what order to sell the physical inventory as there is no requirement to match costs to the actual physical flow of the inventory. When inventory is sold, the cost is moved from the inventory asset account to the COGS expense account. The overarching idea you should remember: inventory costs and COGS are affected by the costing method chosen by management and accountants. Two identical companies buying, producing, and selling inventory can have very different inventory and COGS amounts presented on their respective financial statements because of the costing method used.

FIFO assumes that the goods bought first are the first ones sold. Thus, the costs of the goods bought last are used to calculate ending inventory cost. LIFO assumes that the costs of the goods bought last are the first ones sold. Thus, the costs of the goods bought first are used to calculate ending inventory cost. The average inventory method allocates costs based on a weighted average unit cost. An example of FIFO and LIFO ending inventory and COGS calculations is provided next. See Tables 3.4 to 3.6.

On January 1, Machine Works, a distributor of water pump parts started the year with 100 units of a particular water tube in inventory. They subsequently purchased more water tubes throughout the year. At the end of the year, on December 31, the company had 120 units on hand. They sold 400 units during the year. We want to know what the ending inventory is and what the COGS will be at the end of the year.

The COGS formula is COGS = (Beginning inventory + Purchases) – Ending inventory.

Table 3.4 Purchase Data

Date	Purchases (units)	Unit Cost ($)	Purchase Cost ($)
January 1	100	10	1,000
May 11	200	11	2,200
August 14	100	12	1,200
September 18	120	15	1,800
Total	520		6,200

Table 3.5 FIFO Ending Inventory and COGS

FIFO			
Purchased Date	**Remaining (units)**	**Unit Cost ($)**	**Cost ($)**
September 18	120	15	1,800
Ending inventory cost			1,800
COGS = ($1,000 + $5,200) − $1,800 = $4,400			

As there are three methods to choose from, three factors often determine which method a company chooses. The factors include balance sheet effects, income statement effects, and tax effects. Since prices usually increase over time, the balance sheet will show a more accurate inventory balance during periods of inflation if FIFO is used, whereas inventory balance during periods of inflation using LIFO will be understated. Since the ending inventory on the balance sheet can be different based on the chosen inventory costing method, so too will COGS be different on the income statement based on the chosen method. Ending inventory is used to calculate COGS, which also affects the dollar amount of COGS on the income statement. COGS directly impacts gross profit and, subsequently, earnings and the amount of taxes to be paid. Net income is usually higher in periods of inflation when FIFO is used, where LIFO reduces net income. Thus, FIFO produces a higher tax bill. However, if LIFO is used and COGS goes up, this reduces income before taxes. Overall, this will produce a lower income tax bill.

The following narrative explains Target Corporation's inventory and COGS policy.

> "Inventory and cost of sales: We use the retail inventory method to account for the majority of our inventory and the related cost of sales. Under this method, inventory is stated at cost using the last-in, first-out (LIFO) method as determined by

Table 3.6 LIFO Ending Inventory and COGS

LIFO			
Purchased Date	**Remaining (units)**	**Unit Cost ($)**	**Cost ($)**
January 1	100	10	1,000
May 11	20	11	2,200
Ending inventory cost			3,200
COGS = ($1,000 + $5,200) − $3,200 = $3,000			

applying a cost-to-retail ratio to each merchandise grouping's ending retail value. The cost of our inventory includes the amount we pay to our suppliers to acquire inventory, freight costs incurred in connection with the delivery of product to our distribution centers and stores, and import costs, reduced by vendor income and cash discounts. The majority of our distribution center operating costs, including compensation and benefits, are expensed to cost of sales in the period incurred. Since inventory value is adjusted regularly to reflect market conditions, our inventory methodology reflects the lower of cost or market. We reduce inventory for estimated losses related to shrink and markdowns. Our shrink estimate is based on historical losses verified by physical inventory counts. Historically, our actual physical inventory count results have shown our estimates to be reliable. Markdowns designated for clearance activity are recorded when the salability of the merchandise has diminished."

Operating Leases and Off-Balance Sheet Transactions

Operations managers may prefer operating leases (rentals) rather than the purchase of assets. Operating leases provide favorable tax treatment and financing options, and offer operational flexibility. Operating leases keep assets and liabilities (debt) from appearing on balance sheets, putting operating expenses on the income statement instead. Unfortunately, some managers will use this technique to keep the transactions off the balance sheet to improve the appearance of the company's financial position. An operating lease has the effect of increasing return on assets and asset turnover ratios, and reducing the debt to equity ratio, making them appear favorable. For this reason, operating lease disclosure requirements are in place and compel companies to provide information about how they are using operating leases.

A second type of lease exists: a capital lease. It simulates ownership and forces the company to show the asset on the balance sheet through the asset and liability accounts. A company using a leased asset tries to have the lease classified as an operating lease rather than as a capital lease to keep the lease obligation off the balance sheet. Certain criteria must be met before a company can classify a lease as an operating lease. Although this is beyond the scope of the book, it is worth noting since accountants and executives often struggle with the criteria. Essentially, these criteria relate to ownership and title transfer, in addition to how long the company leases the equipment or property compared to the useful life of the property. If the lease agreement transfers ownership of the leased asset from the lessor to the lessee, then the capital lease is used.

Each company has its own approach to leases. The Target Corporation explains their handling of leases in the following narrative:

> "We lease certain retail locations, warehouses, distribution centers, office space, land, equipment and software. Assets held under capital leases are included in property and equipment. Operating lease rentals are expensed on a straight-line basis over the life of the lease beginning on the date we take possession of the property. At lease inception, we determine the lease term by assuming the exercise of those renewal options that are reasonably assured. The exercise of lease renewal options is at our sole discretion. The lease term is used to determine whether a lease is capital or operating and is used to calculate straight-line rent expense. Additionally, the depreciable life of leased assets and leasehold improvements is limited by the expected lease term."

Net Accounts Receivable

Many suppliers and merchants sell goods and services on account, and there is an expectation that these companies will receive payment from those who owe them cash. Realistically though, companies that extend credit or financing terms for payment do expect that there will be instances when payment will become uncollectable. The asset account on the balance sheet, accounts receivable, is adjusted to show what is owed less any payments that the company thinks it will not collect or any sales returns before cash being collected from the customer.

When a payment owed is not collected, the amount not collected shows up on the income statement as bad debt expense (or by another similar name), thus reducing net income. In such cases, companies have a choice of which method to use when valuing receivables and computing bad debt expense. One method, the direct write-off method, functions in this way: When the actual loss occurs, that is, when the company knows that it will not get paid, it reduces accounts receivable and increases bad debt expense. This method shows actual losses. However, a more common and useful method, the allowance method, estimates uncollectable amounts at the time of sale (matching principle). Then it adjusts the account receivables allowance balance to reflect a more accurate depiction of how much cash the company believes will be collected.

Net accounts receivable example:

+ Accounts receivables

– Allowance for uncollectable (doubtful) accounts

= Net receivables

How do companies estimate the amount of uncollectible receivables? They will use a percentage of sales or a percentage of receivables. Both methods use historical information to create an estimate. For the percentage of sales method, a percentage of total or net credit sales is calculated. The percentage of receivables method applies differing percentages to receivables based on the length of time they have been unpaid. The longer a payment is left unpaid or uncollected, the less likely it will be collected.

Net Revenue

Revenue (sales) shown on the income statement is revenue less any returns, discounts, or allowances for damaged or missing goods. In addition, the revenue on the income statement subtracts freight costs if this cost was added to the customer invoice. In the end, net revenue is reported on the income statement.

Net sales revenue example:

+ Gross sales revenue

– Sales returns

– Sales allowances

– Sales discounts

= Net sales revenue

Although gross sales make a company appear profitable, it is not reasonable to expect that a company will retain all of its sales revenue. It is not uncommon for goods to be returned or that services rendered are not satisfactory; in these cases, customers receive refunds or credit. Inevitably, the company will give some of its sales revenue back to its customers. Net sales provide a better picture of how much revenue the company expects to receive and keep. After goods have been returned, customers have received refunds, allowances for damaged or missing goods are accounted for, and discounts are given to customers, net sales are what remain.

Companies have different approaches to recognizing sales revenue, incentives, and discounts. For example, the Target Corporation explains how they recognize sales revenue:

> "Sales include merchandise sales, net of expected returns, and gift card breakage. Revenues are recognized net of expected returns, which we estimate using historical return patterns as a percentage of sales. Revenue from gift card sales is recognized upon gift card redemption. Our gift cards do not expire. Based on historical redemption rates, a small and relatively stable percentage of gift cards will never be redeemed, referred to as 'breakage.' Estimated breakage revenue is recognized over time in proportion to actual gift card redemptions and was not material in any period presented."

PepsiCo explains how they recognize sales incentives and discounts:

> "We offer sales incentives and discounts through various programs to customers and consumers. Total marketplace spending includes sales incentives, discounts, advertising and other marketing activities. Sales incentives and discounts are primarily accounted for as a reduction of revenue and totaled $34.7 billion in 2013 and 2012, and $34.6 billion in 2011. Sales incentives and discounts include payments to customers for performing merchandising activities on our behalf, such as payments for in-store displays, payments to gain distribution of new products, payments for shelf space and discounts to promote lower retail prices. It also includes support provided to our independent bottlers through funding of advertising and other marketing activities."

Net Credit Sales

Although companies do not usually report credit sales, it is still important to recognize the importance of credit sales. Selling on credit is the basis for accounts receivables and for uncollected payments.

Just because a company sells its products and services, fully expecting to be paid, the reality is that it may not receive payment.

Net credit sales are revenues from credit sales less sales returns and sales allowances. If a company ships goods of poor quality or that do not meet the customer's specifications, it typically has two choices to immediately rectify the situation. It can allow the customer to return the products, in which case all revenue from this sale is lost. Another option is to provide a reduction in the price charged to the customer, thus salvaging a portion of the revenue the company expected to collect from the sale.

Net credit sales example:

+ Sales on credit
− Credit sales returns
− Credit sales allowances
− Credit sales discounts
= Net credit sales

Foreign Exchange

Revenue

As companies conduct business across the globe, foreign exchange rates can have an effect on revenue reporting in both positive and negative ways. Fluctuations in revenue may be the result of the company's home currency gaining strength or weakening, and not at all due to pricing power or greater number of units sold. As the U.S. dollar weakens against foreign currency, companies will see higher revenues. On the other side of the coin, a stronger U.S. dollar translates to less revenue. The reasons for revenue fluctuation are explained next.

If a U.S. company is selling a good or service to a buyer in another country and agrees to receive currency in other than U.S. dollars, it is likely that the foreign currency will fluctuate in value prior payment. If the foreign currency depreciates (U.S. dollar appreciates in comparison) between the time goods or services are sold for a certain price and the time the customer pays, their payment will actually convert into fewer U.S. dollars. In this case, the company loses money.

In the example below, a company agrees to a payment of 100,000 Euros, worth $130,000 U.S. dollars with the exchange rate of 1.30 at the time of the agreement with the buyer. Then the Euro appreciates

Table 3.7 Foreign Exchange

Currency	Exchange Rate	Amount	Gain (Loss)
Euro at the time of purchase = $130,000			
Euro	1.30	€100,000	
USD	1.00		
Euro appreciates (rises in value) = $135,000			
Euro	1.35	€100,000	
USD	1.00		$5,000
Euro depreciates (falls in value) = $125,000			
Euro	1.25	€100,000	
USD	1.00		($5,000)

so the exchange rate becomes 1.35. This situation requires the buyer to pay 100,000 Euros, which converts to $135,000 U.S. dollars. Alternatively, if the Euro depreciates to an exchange rate of 1.25, then the company will receive $125,000 U.S. dollars instead of the original $130,000 U.S. dollars expected at the time of the purchase agreement.

Of course, the uncertainty of the exchange rate goes both ways. For example, if a U.S. company pays a vendor in the vendor's currency, which then devalues against the U.S. dollar, the U.S. company pays less money for its purchases because the obligation to the vendor is satisfied with fewer U.S. dollars. Contrastingly, if the vendor's currency appreciates against the U.S. dollar, the U.S. company will end up paying more for the purchase because more U.S. dollars are required to satisfy the obligation to the vendor. In short, fluctuating exchange rates can affect a company's revenue reporting.

Inventory Purchases

Previously, purchases and the effect on inventory and COGS were explained. Global purchasing introduces foreign exchange risk, which occurs when purchases of goods and services are in denominations other than the home country currency. Inventory and COGS amounts are adjusted based on exchange rates. As an example, on June 1, a U.S. company buys raw materials from a German supplier in the amount of €100,000 EUR with payment due on July 1. On June 1, the exchange rate is $1.30 per EUR. Stated another way, this would be €0.7692 EUR per $1.00 USD. On July 1, when payment is due, the exchange rate has changed. On this day, the U.S. company would have to buy €100,000 EUR at an exchange rate of $1.35 per EUR instead of $1.30 per EUR. This would in turn be €0.7407 EUR per $1.00 USD. To calculate how many EUR per USD, take 1/current exchange rate.

On June 1, the U.S. company would have had to pay €100,000/€0.7692 = $130,005. However, since the exchange rate changed, on July 1, the U.S. company now has to pay €100,000/€0.7407 = $135,007. Of course, the U.S. company could have made the payment before July 1 and saved $5,000, but the company did not know which way the exchange rate would move or by how much. The fluctuation of the exchange rate can either benefit or negatively affect a company's payment. If the exchange rate had been $1.25 USD per EUR, the U.S. company would have had to pay only €100,000/€0.80 = $125,000. Fortunately, there are some foreign exchange rate risk mitigation techniques, such as hedging contracts, buying and selling in the home currency, buying from and selling to in the same foreign country without the need to convert to the home currency, and conducting business in stable currency markets. Purchasing foreign inventory can be risky because of the fluctuating exchange rates; however, the mitigation techniques allow companies to operate globally with less risk to a company and its stockholders.

Stockholders

Even for those well versed in business terms, remembering the various stockholder accounts and terminology can be quite confusing. This section will reduce confusion by reviewing some of the more common terms and phraseology. When investors contribute capital (money) to a corporation, they become owners of the corporation. Typically, these owners receive stock (equity) in the corporation through the ownership of common or preferred company stock. Common stock carries voting rights in corporate affairs and the right to share in company profits through dividend payouts. Common stockholders might vote on board of directors' elections and other actions that require stockholder votes at annual meetings. Preferred stock holders do not usually have voting rights, but they do have preferred status along with access to dividends and assets when a company is going out of business.

Additional paid in capital is an account that shows how much more cash has been collected (invested by owners) by the company in excess of par value for its common and preferred stock. Par value is an arbitrary dollar amount assigned to each share of common or preferred stock used to calculate common stock or preferred stock dollar of its own stock. Finally, when treasury stock is listed on the balance sheet, it represents the dollar amount of stock the corporation has bought back to take out of circulation. Corporations buy back stock for various reasons including,

- Reissuance to executives and managers for bonuses and compensation
- Employee stock ownership programs
- To reduce the number of shares outstanding to increase earnings per share
- To signal the market that management thinks the value of its stock is undervalued.

Dividends are a distribution of a portion of a company's earnings to its shareholders. Dividends are paid to preferred stockholders (preferred dividends) first, then to common stock holders. Management communicates to preferred stock holders with statements such as Preferred Stock Dividends Declared, that the company intends to pay them a certain amount of money for each preferred share they own.

Shares can be categorized in a few more ways. Outstanding shares or common shares outstanding indicate the number of shares that are held by all investors including officers, employees, and the public, but excluding any shares that were bought back or repurchased by the company. Undiluted and diluted shares further categorize shares. Undiluted shares exclude stock options, whereas fully diluted shares are the total number of shares that would be outstanding if all possible sources of stock were converted and exercised, including stock options. Identifying diluted shares provides a more accurate financial picture of a corporation by showing what could happen if all options were exercised.

Summary

This chapter explained some of the finer details of financial statements. It started with an explanation of asset valuation. Assets included property, plant, and equipment (PP&E) because they are the most

commonly considered assets from a supply chain and logistics perspective. Then, noncash transactions were discussed. This included
as tangible assets and depreciation along with nontangible assets and
amortization and how this affects the financial statements. Next, the
writing examined how the cost of inventory and cost of goods sold
(COGS) are determined. Fourth, operating leases and off–balance
sheet transactions and how managers use these financial documents
were covered. Then, the chapter provided further details showing
how net revenue, net accounts receivable, and net credit sales are
determined, along with how foreign exchange rates impact revenue,
inventory, and COGS. Finally, a discussion of dividends and stockholder balances ended the chapter.

4

Ratio Analysis with Financial Statements

Understanding ratio analysis is foundational to making sense of financial and operations ratios. An organization's successes and areas in need of attention from management are highlighted by performance ratio analysis. Ratios are used to evaluate the performance of an organization, an industry, and management personnel.

Financial statements were explained in detail in Chapter 3, providing a foundation to understand ratio analysis. This chapter will introduce many of the common financial performance ratios that executives and analysts use. In addition, the chapter will explain how to compute ratios, what information the ratios offer for decision making, and how to consider multiple factors that are critical to fully understanding the ratios. In subsequent chapters, how operations and supply chain ratios affect and influence financial ratios will be examined. Operations ratios, after all, are used to ensure that financial performance meets the expectations of creditors, investors, and executives. Ultimately, these ratios provide information about an organization's financial health and ability to continue operations.

Before financial ratios are discussed in detail, a general introduction to ratio analysis is provided first. How might ratio be defined anyway? A ratio is a relationship or comparison between two numbers. It is a statement of how two numbers compare to each other. It compares the size of one number with the size of another number. It is the quantitative relation between two amounts showing the number of times one value is contained within the other.

Once it is understood that ratios tell a story about how a company is performing, decisions must be made regarding the number of and which performance ratios to use. Considering too many measures can burden an organization as it collects and analyzes a vast amount of data; excessive data can lead to decision paralysis. Focusing on too few ratios, though, will not provide a comprehensive picture of organizational performance. It is difficult to prescribe the ideal number of ratios to review, but as a general rule, organizations should use as few as necessary. The right number of ratios is one that provides an accurate depiction of the company's performance.

Consider the following scenario. As the manager of inventory for your company, you are told to improve inventory effectiveness by your managing director. Because you are familiar with inventory ratios and performance measures, you do not ask any additional questions. You have identified and selected the following inventory ratios and performance measures for examination:

- Average inventory
- Cycle time
- Order accuracy
- Order fulfillment time
- Percent inventory cost reduction
- Perfect orders

Each of these performance measures is related to inventory in some way or another and provides good information. However, are all of them necessary to review for this scenario? After all, it does take time and effort to collect, analyze, and interpret data. If all of the performance measures are used, what is the likelihood of being able to improve all of them at the same time? If each measure is being evaluated concurrently, it is likely that frustration will set in because it is unlikely that you can improve each measure at the same time. Working through this scenario demonstrates the need to first identify what is most important to the organization. Is it response time, cost, order accuracy, or some other objective? Identifying the goals and objectives of the company drives which measures are selected.

Once the objectives and goals are determined the most useful performance measures can be selected. A useful conceptual model, the supply chain strategy framework (Figure 4.1) adapted from the Supply Chain Council, can assist in the selection and placement of the most suitable performance measures. The framework provides a logical flow for developing a supply chain. Once the supply chain is developed, performance measures are implemented to communicate how well the supply chain is operating based on stated objectives and goals.

The framework starts with identifying the corporation's business unit strategy. Once this strategy is identified, the corporation is ready to design the supply chain strategy, leading to the design of the supply

Figure 4.1 Supply chain strategy framework. (Adapted from Supply Chain Council)[1]

chain network. Next, the model implements the processes needed to sustain the supply chain network. Finally, it determines the resources that need to be allocated to operate the processes developed in the other phases.

To be successful, the model requires that each phase be carefully thought out before generating the next one. After each phase has been implemented, they act together to accomplish the corporation's business unit strategy. Feedback is provided throughout the system from the use of appropriately selected performance measures and ratios. These performance measures communicate how well each stage is executing.

Continuing with the previous example, if it is determined that the business unit strategy is to compete through high customer service levels, then the supply chain is constructed to accommodate this. Further, improving inventory management should revolve around increasing customer service levels. For instance, speed of delivery and perfect orders would be more important than solely focusing on reducing average inventory. If the inventory manager instead used measures that focus on reducing costs through reducing average inventory and safety stock, it is unlikely that speed of delivery and perfect orders will improve. Using metrics that are not aligned with the business unit strategy creates an environment where supply chain managers are unable implement changes to improve performance.

Benchmarking

Producing financial statements require a company to invest a significant amount of time, effort, and resources. Thus, it is crucial for the statements to be accurate and informative. Executives, managers, investors, lenders, and others use a company's financial statements to

---

[1] Supply Chain Council. 22012 SCW SEA M4SC Program Overview, 5, September 29, 2011.

conduct analysis and due diligence through the use of financial and operating ratios and then benchmark the results. Benchmarking is (1) comparing a company against their competitors and (2) a company comparing its own performance over time.

Typically, analysis and due diligence identify how the organization or business unit has performed in the past. Although past performance is not necessarily an indication of future performance, it does provide meaningful information and guidance. Historical data provide information that helps companies decide where to focus their attention and resources to improve the business. More importantly, data can offer information about the organization's trajectory. If management and company performance have historically been mediocre, why would there be an expectation for it to improve? To obtain an accurate picture of management and organizational performance, it is important to view performance over time. One data point is not enough to provide an accurate account of organizational performance. Trend information guides decision making and reduces the chance that an organization will overreact to a positive or negative report.

Considering only a company's own performance is not enough. The industry landscape must also be taken into account by looking at a company's performance compared to the performance of its competitors, industry averages, and top-performing organizations. Unless a company compares itself to its competitors and industry averages, it will never know if it is an average company or worse. Average companies can expect average returns or worse, for its stockholders. Comparing a company to other firms provides at least three insights:

1. Reveals areas for improvement—a company that is lagging behind its competitors can recognize the need to improve.
2. Reveals public perception—comparison provides information about how others perceive the organization, as a formidable competitor, insignificant, or a target for acquisition.
3. Reveals ranking within the field—knowing how high or low performing a company is compared to others informs what actions are necessary to remain competitive.

Benchmarking is conducted with the use of ratios and other performance measures. Without understanding ratio and ratio analysis, benchmarking is a futile exercise.

Ratio Analysis

Comprehensive ratio analysis requires not only the knowledge of how to compute ratios but also what the ratios indicate and how the numbers can be manipulated by a variety of factors, all of which will be explained in this chapter. Computing the ratio is only the beginning of ratio analysis. The numbers offer a starting point to understand what is happening within the business and what information the ratios reveal about the organization. Closer examination of the data can explain more about the company's performance in a particular area. Reviewing the ratios also provides insight on how the numbers are being affected by the company's actions in addition to any industry phenomena that are influential.

Ratios contain two parts: a numerator and a denominator. This is no surprise to anyone, but what many fail to recognize is that a change in either component will affect the ratio. This is important for two reasons:

1. When analyzing a ratio, both parts need to be considered to make informed decisions.
2. When making decisions based on ratios, it is critical to understand the components that make up the ratio.
3. When making decisions based on ratios, it is critical to understand the factors that may have changed that caused a change in the ratio.

Improvements to a company's finances or operations based on a ratio can be accomplished in three ways:

1. Improving the numerator
2. Improving the denominator
3. Improving both at the same time

To highlight the importance of understanding the components of a ratio, consider a simple operation's ratio related to workplace safety. The ratio is injury rate, or how many injuries per month the company records. Last year, the company reported 100 injuries for October, this year the company reported 125 injuries for October. Looking at the numbers only, without considering any other factors may not provide an accurate picture. It is crucial to ask a number of questions before passing judgment on the injury rate. Has the company changed how it records injuries? Have any barriers to reporting injuries been removed? Was there an increase or decrease the number of hours employees are working? If hours have been increased, could fatigue be a factor? Answers to these questions will guide future workplace safety decisions, impacting safety policies and how resources are allocated. As this example demonstrates, many factors need to be considered to fully understand why a ratio changed over time.

Caveats to Ratio Analysis

Before discussing the calculations of the forthcoming ratios, it is important to address a few caveats. First, when comparing firms, it is necessary that the firms be in the same industry. Even then, precautions should be taken. As seen in Table 4.1, industries take on certain characteristics related to the profit margins they earn, to the levels of assets they carry, and to their efficiency in using their assets. Because of these differences, it is impossible and meaningless to compare companies from different industries. For instance, service companies vary considerably from manufacturing companies; as such, it would not make sense to compare utility companies to retailers to airlines. The industries are simply too different in the way they operate and compete. Their mix of debt and equity, their cost structure, inventory levels, and pricing power vary greatly.

Second, companies need to be cautious when comparing themselves to who they think their competitors are, considering a number of variables. Would it make sense to compare Target Corporation to Nordstrom? These companies, while both retailers, cater to different consumer segments and use different strategies. Because of this, comparison is difficult and impractical. Even comparison between high and low margin retailers is not worthwhile because ratios such as inventory turnover are quite different. Despite the difference, each type or retailer is likely satisfied with its own ratio.

Further, it is imperative to understand that accountants have a significant level of discretion and make assumptions as they produce financial statements. Thus, making direct comparisons between similar companies from the same industry are difficult. Even knowing about the assumptions, comparing conglomerates is not easy. Two examples of how accounting latitude influences ratio comparison are as follows:

1. The depreciation schedule is used.
2. How the cost of inventory is determined.

Table 4.1 Select Performance Measures Across Industries

	Airlines	Oil and Gas Exploration	Personal Care Products Manufacturing	Restaurants	Retail	Semiconductor and Electronic Component Manufacturing	Transportation Services Sector
Gross margin	52.70%	68.90%	35.10%	66.70%	23.80%	39.60%	56.90%
Net income percent of revenues	0.70%	3.90%	3.20%	1.30%	0.70%	2.50%	1.40%
Accounts receivable percent of total assets	12.60%	9.60%	18.90%	5.10%	14.00%	25.10%	15.00%
Inventory percent of total assets	1.60%	1.20%	22.40%	2.40%	36.70%	15.80%	1.40%
Property, plant, and equipment percent of total assets	53.30%	13.10%	15.40%	52.50%	19.10%	11.70%	48.70%
Financial Ratios							
Quick ratio	1.18	1.13	0.9	1.03	0.8	1.34	1.44
Current ratio	1.68	1.46	1.93	1.52	2.06	2.04	1.84
Current liabilities to net worth	39.00%	44.90%	63.60%	30.70%	71.80%	65.60%	41.70%
Days accounts receivable	36	93	73	10	17	67	43
Inventory turnover	×37.58	×9.69	×2.75	×27.33	×6.31	×5.23	×38.18
Total assets to sales	80.30%	263.40%	109.60%	50.80%	33.20%	73.00%	78.50%
Working capital to sales	9.60%	26.20%	29.10%	3.90%	11.40%	24.40%	12.10%

(Continued)

Table 4.1 (*Continued*)

	Airlines	Oil and Gas Exploration	Personal Care Products Manufacturing	Restaurants	Retail	Semiconductor and Electronic Component Manufacturing	Transportation Services Sector
Accounts payable to sales	7.40%	22.10%	10.60%	2.50%	4.60%	10.40%	4.40%
Pretax return on sales	1.10%	6.30%	5.20%	2.20%	1.10%	4.10%	2.20%
Pretax return on assets	1.30%	2.40%	4.70%	4.30%	3.40%	5.60%	2.90%
Pretax return on net worth	3.00%	4.90%	10.50%	8.90%	7.50%	11.50%	6.50%
Interest coverage	×1.27	×1.60	×128.26	×2.39	×2.81	×5.16	×1.89
EBITDA to sales	4.90%	16.80%	8.70%	7.40%	2.50%	7.70%	11.40%
Capital expenditures to sales	3.10%	11.50%	5.90%	5.40%	1.30%	3.10%	7.80%
Company count	3,012	10,637	550	213,740	493,148	2896	159,794

Note: Data as of march 2014, x = times.

Two identical companies can have different financial performance ratios due to nothing more than the choice of depreciation and inventory accounting methods.

A fourth caveat is related to how ratios are computed. Some are computed using only the balance sheet or only the income statement, while others require the use of both: the balance sheet and income statement. When both the balance sheet and the income statement are used to calculate a ratio, it is important to be aware of the reporting period. It bears repeating that the balance sheet represents a point in time and the income statement represents a time period. By only taking a point in time for the balance sheet items, anything that occurred earlier in the quarter or year is neglected. Given this fact, using averages for balance sheet asset and liability items can offer greater clarity. Using the average smooth's highly seasonal numbers or accounting schemes may not represent the entire year. Computing averages can be done using the following representative equation for average total assets. Table 4.2 shows *PepsiCo's* ending total assets for years 2012 and 2013. The two values are used to compute average total assets.

Average total assets = (Beginning total assets + Ending total assets)/2
$$\$76{,}058 = (\$74{,}638 + \$77{,}478)/2$$

In this chapter, for the sake of simplicity, balance sheet accounts have not been averaged. In practice, though, averages should be used.

Finally, a point to clarify is that a ratio may have more than one name, but mean the same thing. It is common to hear the words earnings, income, and profit, which are all synonymous. It is important to understand what is being referred to exactly. To make matters worse, when profits are used, is the term referring to gross profit, operating profit, or net profit? In short, accurate ratio analysis requires clarity so that comparisons can be made. The items mentioned in this section should all be considered when analyzing ratios because they can create confusion.

Financial Ratios

Although the information in this chapter is highly technical, it lays the foundation for operations and supply chain managers to develop a greater understanding of how their role influences a company's finances. The financial ratios discussed next are the ratios that interest executives and investment community. These common ratios have long been used by financial experts and provide meaningful, useful,

Table 4.2　*PepsiCo* Balance Sheet

Balance Sheet
In Millions (USD $), unless otherwise specified

	December 28, 2013 ($)	December 29, 2012 ($)
Assets		
Cash and cash equivalents	9,375	6,297
Short-term investments	303	322
Accounts and notes receivable, net	6,954	7,041
Inventories	3,409[a]	3,581[a]
Prepaid expenses and other current assets	2,162	1,479
Total Current Assets	22,203	18,720
Property, plant, and equipment, net	18,575	19,136
Amortizable intangible assets, net	1,638	1,781
Goodwill	16,613	16,971
Other nonamortizable intangible assets	14,401	14,744
Nonamortizable intangible assets	31,014	31,715
Investments in noncontrolled affiliates	1,841	1,633
Other assets	2,207	1,653
Total Assets	77,478	74,638
Liabilities and Equity		
Short-term obligations	5,306	4,815
Accounts payable and other current liabilities	12,533	11,903
Income taxes payable	—	371
Total Current Liabilities	17,839	17,089
Long-term debt obligations	24,333	23,544
Other liabilities	4,931	6,543
Deferred income taxes	5,986	5,063
Total Liabilities	53,089	52,239
Commitments and contingencies		
Preferred stock, no par value	41	41
Repurchased preferred stock	–171	–164
PepsiCo Common Shareholders' Equity		
Common stock, par value 1 2/3¢ per share (authorized 3,600 shares, issued, net of repurchased common stock at par value: 1,529 and 1,544 shares, respectively)	25	26

Table 4.2 (*Continued*)

Balance Sheet
In Millions (USD $), unless otherwise specified

	December 28, 2013 ($)	December 29, 2012 ($)
Capital in excess of par value	4,095	4,178
Retained Earnings	46,420	43,158
Accumulated other comprehensive loss	–5,127	–5,487
Repurchased common stock (337 and 322 shares)	–21,004	–19,458
Stockholders' equity attributable to parent	24,409	22,417
Noncontrolling interests	110	105
Total Equity	24,389	22,399
Total Liabilities and Equity	77,478	74,638
Preferred stock, shares issued	803,953	803,953
Preferred stock, dividends paid	–1	–1
PepsiCo **Common Shareholders' Equity**		
Repurchased stock	–171	–164
Common stock, shares issued	1,529	1,544
PepsiCo **Common Shareholders' Equity**		
Repurchased stock	–21,004	–19,458

Note: Data obtained from SEC.gov.
[a]Approximately 3%, in both 2013 and 2012, of the inventory cost was computed using the LIFO method. The differences between LIFO and FIFO methods of valuing these inventories were not material.

understandable information. In addition, computing them is fairly straightforward.

Financial ratios calculated from financial statements primarily fall into the following five categories:

1. Liquidity
2. Profitability
3. Valuation
4. Asset management
5. Debt management

Refer to *PepsiCo* balance sheet (Table 4.2) and *PepsiCo* income statement (Table 4.3) as the financial ratio calculations are explained.

Table 4.3 *PepsiCo* Income Statement

Income Statement 12 Months Ended		
In Millions (USD $), Except Per Share Data, unless otherwise specified	**December 28, 2013 ($)**	**December 28, 2012 ($)**
Net revenue	66,415	65,492
Cost of sales	31,243	31,291
Selling, general and administrative expenses	25,357	24,970
Amortization of intangible assets	110	119
Operating profit (EBIT)	9,705	9,112
Interest expense	−911	−899
Interest income and other	97	91
Income before income taxes	8,891	8,304
Provision for income taxes	2,104	2,090
Net income	6,787	6,214
Less: Net income attributable to noncontrolling interests	47	36
Net income attributable to *PepsiCo*	6,740	6,178
Net Income Available to Common Stockholders'	6,732	6,171
Net income attributable to *PepsiCo* per common share		
Basic	4.37	3.96
Diluted	4.32	3.92
Weighted-average common shares outstanding		
Basic	1,541	1,557
Diluted	1,560	1,575
Cash dividends declared per common share	2.24	2.13

Data obtained from SEC.gov.

Notes: (1) Preferred dividends paid: $1M in 2012 and 2013; redemption premium $6M in 2012 and $7M in 2013. (2) Depreciation, net $2,472 in 2013.

Liquidity Ratios

Liquidity ratios are used to identify whether or not a company can meet its short-term obligations. For instance, can the company pay its bills in the coming year? Can the company pay its suppliers? Can it pay its employees? Because this is related to paying off debts in the near term, the numbers for calculation are drawn from current assets and liabilities indicated on the balance sheet. Recall that current assets are assets that should be used up within 1 year of being acquired. In this way, they are the most liquid of all assets. They are most likely to be used to pay the bills and include cash, account receivables, and inventory. Current liabilities, then, are debts that need to be paid within the coming year. Typically, this includes accounts payable, short-term notes payable, income taxes payable, and accrued expenses. For example, using these values from the *PepsiCo* balance sheet, the current ratio can be calculated.

Current Ratio

$$\text{Current ratio} = \text{Current assets/Current liabilities}$$
$$= \$22,203/\$17,839 = 1.24 \text{ times}$$

What does the ratio indicate? *PepsiCo* has 1.24 times as many current assets as it has current liabilities. For every dollar of current liabilities, *PepsiCo* has $1.24 of current assets indicating that *PepsiCo* could pay their debts if the debts were due today. What this particular liquidity ratio does not specify is the mix of current assets. Using just the current ratio, it is difficult to know if their current assets are made up mostly of cash or tied up in inventory or receivables. The *PepsiCo* example demonstrates a company that can more than meet its short-term obligations, which is not the case for every company. A current ratio of 1.0 indicates that the company can exactly meet its short-term obligations, whereas a ratio less than 1.0 means that a company cannot meet those obligations.

Knowing that ratios can vary, what ratio should a company target? The answer to this question is that it depends. A higher current ratio is better than a lower one; however, a ratio that is too high is not desirable. In general, a current ratio of 1.5 to 2.0 meets with approval, though this does vary depending on the industry. To better understand a current ratio, it should be considered in the context of the company's industry and history. For the sake of example, say *PepsiCo's* current ratio of 1.24 is higher than the industry average. It is also higher than its historical current ratio. With this information, it becomes clearer that 1.24 can be considered a good current ratio for *PepsiCo*.

Extremely high current ratios call for closer examination. What if *PepsiCo's* current ratio was 4.24? With such a high ratio, it is possible that the company has an excess of cash and a look at the balance sheet would be warranted. Another investigation could be made into whether or not *PepsiCo* is reinvesting in research and development, or innovation of products, services, and processes to create such a high current ratio. A real-world example of this comes from both Microsoft and Apple. These companies have been criticized for holding onto cash, which results in frustrated shareholders. If cash is not reinvested into the company's operations, then shareholders expect that the cash would be returned to them. Similarly, if excess cash is sitting in the bank, it is considered an inefficient use of capital. Other scenarios resulting in high current ratios might be related to excess inventory or elevated receivables. Without further investigation, neither situation is considered ideal.

Low current ratios are also not desirable. They signify a less efficient use of assets or other operational problems. A current ratio of less than 1.0 is a cause for concern. It indicates that the company may not be able to pay its debts if they became due today. Companies that are unable to pay off debts with current assets might be increasing current liabilities at a faster rate through bank loans or holding onto payables longer. A current ratio of less than 1.0 however, does not mean the company is about to collapse and is insolvent. Short-term funding can be obtained to pay off debts, which could buy time for now, but is not a long-term strategy. In addition, a current ratio that is less than the industry average calls for examination.

Industries vary as to what is a normal or acceptable current ratio. Some industries routinely operate at current ratios of less than 1.0. For example, Brinker International, Inc. (EAT), operator of Chili's Grill & Bar and Maggiano's Little Italy brands, had a current ratio of 0.58 during the quarter ending December 25, 2013. Restaurants generally have low current ratios but are solvent.

Quick Ratio

Quick ratio = (Current assets – Inventories)/Current liabilities
= ($22,203 – $3,409)/$17,839 = 1.05 times

The quick ratio, sometimes called the acid test ratio, is similar to the current ratio, except that inventories are removed from the calculation. Without considering inventory, the quick ratio becomes more conservative than the current ratio. Inventory is the least liquid of current assets and is much more difficult to turn into cash than marketable securities or receivables. One factor to consider with the quick ratio is whether or not the company included prepaid expenses in its current assets. Some companies might not include prepaid expenses in the numerator as a current asset. Prepaid expenses are current assets; cash has been spent to pay some of the bills already, but the service paid for has not been used up yet. Prepaying for 1 year of insurance is an example of a prepaid expense.

Knowing if a company can pay its debts without having to rely on selling its inventory is important in understanding its liquidity. If the market turns down or customers are not purchasing merchandise, inventory may sit idle for a time. Idle inventory does not bring in cash nor does it pay the bills, creating financial problems for the company.

Liquidity ratios help determine if the company can pay its short-term obligations. However, more analysis is required to ascertain whether or not the firm is actually solvent. Using liquidity ratios only may lead to inaccurate conclusions. Companies with liquidity ratios below 1.0 can be solvent (remember the example of Brinker International, Inc.). Cash flow analysis, including the amount of cash and particularly the timing of the cash flow are also important considerations.

Operating Cash Flow Ratio

$$\text{Operating cash flow ratio} = \text{Operating cash flow/Current liabilities}$$
$$= \$9,688/\$17,839 = 0.54$$

Operating cash flow ratio can also be called cash flow from operations to current liabilities ratio. It provides information to determine a firm's solvency through a cash flow point of view. Since debts are paid with cash, it is useful to see what a company's cash position is from its operations. This ratio shows whether or not a company is generating enough cash from its operations to pay current debts. Operating cash flow, obtained from the statement of cash flows (Table 4.4), shows how cash from operations is moving through the company over a period of time (not at a point in time like current assets from the balance sheet do). A higher value, preferably greater than 1.0, indicates that the firm generates enough cash from its operations to cover current liabilities. A value lower than 1.0 implies that there is a higher risk of the company not being able to pay its current debts. In such instances, a company may need to sell assets, borrow money, issue stock, or slow the rate of spending to meet short-term debt obligations.

Low operating cash flow ratios can be problematic; however, closer examination of the ratio is necessary. For example, *PepsiCo* has an operating cash flow ratio of 0.54, which is low. Before rushing to judgment, recognize that this ratio must be viewed in context. It is possible to identify a number of reasons why a low operating cash flow ratio might be acceptable.

1. Some industries, such as capital-intensive industries, historically have lower operating cash flow ratios.

2. A company may be undertaking projects and building infrastructure, to increase future cash flows.

3. Like other ratios, it is best to view the trend of the ratio.

4. The company may have deferred revenue as a current liability. In this case, the company has to perform a service and deliver a good, instead of paying a debt.

As described in later chapters, cash flow plays an important role in determining company valuations, capital budgeting, and project selection.

Table 4.4 *PepsiCo* Abbreviated Statement of Cash Flows (Operating Activities)

12 Months Ended December 28, 2013 In Millions (USD $), unless otherwise specified	
Operating Activities ($)	
Net income	6,787
Depreciation and amortization	2,663
Stock-based compensation expense	303
Merger and integration costs	10
Cash payments for merger and integration costs	–25
Restructuring and impairment charges	163
Cash payments for restructuring charges	–133
Restructuring and other charges related to the transaction with Tingyi	
Cash payments for restructuring and other charges related to the transaction with Tingyi	–26
Non-cash foreign exchange loss related to Venezuela devaluation	111
Excess tax benefits from share-based payment arrangements	–117
Pension and retiree medical plan contributions	–262
Pension and retiree medical plan expenses	663

Table 4.4 (*Continued*)

**12 Months Ended December 28, 2013
In Millions (USD $), unless otherwise specified**

Operating Activities ($)	
Deferred income taxes and other tax charges and credits	−1,058
Change in accounts and notes receivable	−88
Change in inventories	4
Change in prepaid expenses and other current assets	−51
Change in accounts payable and other current liabilities	1,007
Change in income taxes payable	86
Other, net	−349
Net cash provided by operating activities	9,688

Profitability Ratios

Many people use the terms profit, earnings, and income inter-changeably. Adding to the confusion, consider the words gross, operating, and net as they relate to profit. The multitude of terms is challenging. When discussing finances, it is expected the terms net profit, net earnings, net income, operating profit, operating income, operating margin, gross profit, gross income, and gross margin will be used. What is more important to remember is that profit, earnings, and income have the same meaning. Three other terms to know are gross profit, operating profit, and net income, which all are part of the income statement. Gross profit is located toward the top of the income statement, whereas operating profit is located further down the statement, and net is located near the bottom.

Starting from the top of the income statement and working down, gross profit refers to the place within the income statement where COGS reduce revenues. Gross profit is an important number because if the company cannot earn enough from a product line to cover its direct costs, it will not be able to remain in business. Notice *PepsiCo* uses COS instead of COGS (Table 4.3). This, too, is a matter of preference.

$$\text{Revenues} - \text{COGS} = \text{Gross profit}$$

Operating profit is often referred to as earnings before interest and taxes (EBIT). It is the profit when revenue is reduced by COGS (the number calculated as gross profit) and by operating expenses (SG&A), but before interest and taxes are subtracted.

Gross profit – Operating expenses (SG&A) = Operating profit (EBIT)

Finally, net profit is the bottom line. After all costs, expenses, interest, and taxes have been deducted from revenue the net profit remains. Typically, when "profit margin" is specified, it refers to "net profit margin." Use net income (net profit, net earnings) in the ratio calculation.

Operating profit (EBIT) – Interest – Income taxes = Net profit

Profitability ratios are used to measure management's effectiveness in generating returns on sales and return on stockholder financing. Information from the income statement is used to calculate these ratios and they are typically represented as percentages.

Profit Margin

The profit margin on sales, also called return on sales or net profit margin, is an important foundational concept. Looking at the equation, remember that net income (in the numerator) is also known as profit or net earnings. Sales revenue is the denominator; however, revenue or sales could be used instead.

$$\text{Profit margin on sales} = \text{Net income available to common stockholders/Sales revenue}$$

$$= (\$6{,}732)/\$66{,}415 = 10.1\%$$

$$\text{Net income available to common stockholders} = \text{Net income} - \text{Preferred dividends requirements}$$

Once dividends are paid out to preferred stockholders, the remaining is net income available to common stockholders. To determine the amount of net income that is available to common stock holders, we must first remove any income that is due to preferred stockholders.

As an example of dividends being paid out to preferred stockholders first, see the income statement, Table 4.3, Note 1: *PepsiCo's* dividends paid to preferred stockholders and redemption premium totaled $8M period ending 2013. $6,740 – $8 = $6,732. Thus, $6,732 is net income available to common stockholders.

Profit margin on sales indicates the profit (net income) per dollar of sales the company is earning. In other words, how much of every dollar is kept after everyone else has been paid. After paying all of the costs (COGS) and operating expenses (SG&A), including interest expense, taxes, depreciation, and amortization, the amount that remains compared to what was sold is revenue. A profit margin of 10.1% tells *PepsiCo* that for every dollar it earns in sales, it keeps 10 cents after everyone else is paid.

Supply chain and logistics managers greatly influence the profit margin in several ways. First, inventory purchasing influences COGS and manufacturing expertise directly related to producing goods and services. SG&A is influenced by the efficiencies and effectiveness of processes in running the business each day, but not directly related to the manufacturing of products and services. Next, interest expense is influenced by the company's debt burden. A company financed with more debt would have higher interest payments. Further, a tax efficient supply chain can improve profits, while a supply chain not optimized for taxes could see a larger portion of its earnings paid to tax authorities. Finally, depreciation and amortization expenses, often left to the judgment of accountants, also weigh down profits, but also can reduce a company's tax burden.

Operating Profit Margin Ratio

Operating profit margin = Operating profit (EBIT)/Sales revenue
= $9,705/$66,415 = 14.6%

Operations managers rarely have any influence or control over the company's taxes and interest charges. Thus operating profit (EBIT) is a more accurate ratio to measure the performance of managers and to identify how well the business is operated. Operating profit margin, or operating margin, focuses on pricing effectiveness and revenue management. It also measures how costs and expenses are managed when producing and delivering products while managing overhead (SG&A). A downward trend in this ratio shows that costs and expenses are increasing faster than sales. An upward trend in this ratio shows that sales are increasing faster than costs and expenses. Looking at the example calculation above, the 14.6% rate indicates that before paying interest and taxes, *PepsiCo* keeps 14.6 cents of every dollar it earns in sales.

Gross Profit Margin Ratio

$$\text{Gross profit margin} = (\text{Sales revenue} - \text{COGS})/\text{Sales revenue}$$
$$= \text{Gross profit/Sales revenue}$$
$$= (\$66,415 - \$31,243)/\$66,415 = 52.96\%$$

Gross profit margin ratio, also called gross profit ratio or gross margin, demonstrates the sales revenue after direct costs (COGS) are subtracted. The gross margin must also pay for other expenses, interest payments, and taxes. The calculation provided here shows that *PepsiCo* has 53 cents left over to pay for all other expenses and to make a profit. The ratio also indicates that 47 cents of every dollar are direct costs showing up as COGS.

Gross margin trends indicate what direction pricing power and COGS are headed. In *PepsiCo's* case, gross margins are headed in the preferred direction from 52.22% in the previous year to 52.96% in the latest year from improvements in both sales revenue and COGS.

Basic Earnings Power Ratio

$$\text{Basic earnings power} = \text{EBIT/Total assets}$$
$$= \$9,705/\$77,478 = 12.5\%$$

Basic earnings power (BEP) ratio is used for two reasons. One, it is used to measure the earnings power of a company's assets. In other words, it answers the question, how many dollars has the company earned from operations per dollar of asset employed? Second, since taxes and debt financing have a direct effect on profit margin on sales, BEP is useful in distinguishing between companies with different tax and debt structures. *PepsiCo* brings in 12.5 cents in operating profit for every dollar it has in total assets.

Return on Total Assets Ratio

$$\text{Return on total assets (ROA)} = \text{Net income available to common stockholders/Total assets}$$
$$= (\$6,740 - \$8)/\$77,478 = 8.7\%$$

Return on assets (ROA) measures the amount earned per dollar of total assets the company owns. ROA shows how effectively management employs the company's assets (balance sheet) to generate a profit (income statement). Assets such as cash, inventory, plants and factories, stores, offices, and vehicles are used to generate sales and earn profits. As the above equation indicates, *PepsiCo* brings in 8.7 cents in net profit for every dollar it has in total assets.

Assets have two components: (1) how they are bought and financed, and (2) how efficiently they are operated. When measuring manager's use of assets to generate a profit, it is beneficial not to include how the assets were financed. Dollars earned (net income) for ROA is an after interest and tax amount. To remove the interest and tax impact, use the basic earnings power (BEP) ratio.

To reiterate, since accountants have some liberty in the way assets are valued on the balance sheet, discretion is necessary when comparing companies.

Return on Equity Ratio

Return on common equity (ROE)
= Net income available to common stockholders/
Common stockholders' equity
= ($6,740 − $8)/$24,409 = 27.6%

Stockholders invest in companies expecting to earn a return on their investment in the company. The return on common equity (ROE) ratio measures what that return is to the stockholders. Comparing similar companies in the same industry may show considerably different ROE numbers. ROE depends on the mix of debt and equity financing. Because of this, one company may show higher ROE simply because it has chosen to finance with more debt and less equity. Continuing to look at *PepsiCo*, the equation shows that *PepsiCo* returned nearly 27 cents in net profit for every dollar stockholders invested in the company.

Notice the difference in *PepsiCo's* ROA (8.7%) and ROE (27.6%). The difference is due to financial leverage.

Financial leverage = Equity multiplier = Total assets/Common equity

Leverage is another word for debt. How can debt be used advantageously? Remember that companies finance assets and operations with a mix of debt and equity. Debt helps companies earn a greater return for shareholders than if they used only their own money (equity). Consider this example of how financial leverage can be helpful: You want to live in a house that you cannot afford. Few people can buy a house outright, or without taking on some form of debt. For a small down payment, say 10% of the home price, you can borrow money from a bank and live in a house that you would otherwise not be able to afford. Not only can you live in the house but you can also save and earn money from home ownership. Tax laws allow you to reduce your tax bill by deducting the long-term interest (mortgage interest). Further, your house may appreciate, so when you sell your home and pay back the remaining loan balance, you get to keep what is left over. You have decreased your tax bill and earned additional money—all from borrowing money.

To make a connection between a personal home purchase and a company taking on debt, in essence, the company is increasing the return for its stockholders (company owners) with money from nonowners. This is accomplished through an increase in net income while at the same time not increasing common stockholders' equity. If the equity multiplier increases, the firm is using more debt to finance its assets.

Valuation Ratios

The market value of a firm is a reflection of what investors think of the company's past performance and future outlook. This perception is portrayed through valuation ratios. Company stock prices fluctuate based on investor sentiment; thus stock prices are generally higher when investors arc plcascd with the company's past performance and future prospects. Valuation ratios generally include the number of company shares available and stock prices.

To best understand the valuation ratios, it is important to also understand the concept of diluted shares. Companies that issue stock may have a certain amount of stock in reserve. When companies report diluted shares, they are including shares that stockholders already own plus stock options that stockholders could own if they exercised their stock options. Thus, earnings per share is diluted because of the extra shares included in the calculation. Reporting diluted shares provides the investment community a "what if scenario" to understand what would happen if the stock options were exercised.

Earnings per Share (EPS)

EPS = (Net income – Preferred stock dividends declared)/
        Common shares outstanding

EPS = ($6,740 – $8)/1,541 = $4.37

Earnings per share (EPS) is a widely used metric found on all the financial websites and touted all over the financial news outlets. Executives are held accountable for EPS performance. After all, stockholders want a return for their money. Here, it is calculated that *PepsiCo* earned $4.37 for each share.

Again, by removing preferred stock dividends declared, net income available to common stockholders remains. EPS comparisons between firms or industry averages are meaningless since there is significant variability in the number of common shares outstanding among firms. It is best to use EPS as an internal measure of performance. Because EPS is so popular on Wall Street and executives are held accountable for it, there is incredible pressure to make EPS appear positive in the short term. A risk of this, though, is it can cause executives to make decisions in the short term to manipulate and prop up net income. The focus on the short term can hinder long-term performance of the organization.

Price-to-Earnings (P/E) Ratio

Assuming the market price for *PepsiCo* common stock is $85.00, the price-to-earnings (P/E) ratio is given below:

$$\text{Price-to-earnings (P/E)} = \text{Market price per share/Earnings per share}$$
$$= \$85/\$4.37 = 19.45 \text{ times}$$

Price-to-earnings (P/E) ratio indicates how much investors are willing to pay per dollar of profits. Investors are often willing to pay more per dollar of profits for high growth companies, companies with higher future cash flows, and for companies that are less risky. In this example, investors are willing to pay $19.45 for every dollar the company earned. P/E ratios can be compared to competitors and the industry average; however, be cautious, as high P/E ratios can be a sign of overvaluations.

Price/Cash Flow Ratio

$$\text{Price/Cash flow} = \text{Price per share/Operating cash flow per share}$$

First, it is critical to calculate *operating cash flow per share*.

$$\text{CFPS} = (\text{Net income} + \text{Depreciation} + \text{Amortization})/\text{Common shares outstanding}$$
$$= (\$6,732 + \$2,472 + \$110)/1,541 = \$6.04$$

With this number, the price-to-cash-flow ratio can be determined as:

$$= \$85/\$6.04 = 14.07 \text{ times}$$

Many investors are particularly interested in a company's cash flow and find that the price-to-cash-flow ratio is more useful and reliable than the price-to-earnings ratio. Investors realize that net earnings take into account many noncash charges such as depreciation and amortization that reduce net earnings. Since stock prices fluctuate based on future cash flow projections, this ratio measures stock investment attractiveness. Since investors value companies based on future cash flows, the discussion in later chapters will concentrate on firm value and cash flow.

Here, the example shows that *PepsiCo* investors are willing to pay $14.07 for every $1.00 of cash flow per share. This tells investors and management that there is some appeal for this stock at this price.

Market/Book (M/B) Ratio

Market/book (M/B) = Market per share price/Book value per share

First, *book value per share* needs to be calculated. Book value per share indicates how much each share would receive if all assets were sold at book values and if all creditors were paid in full.

$$\text{Book value per share} = \text{Total common stockholders' equity/} $$
$$\text{Common shares outstanding}$$
$$= \$24,409/1,541 = \$15.84$$

Knowing this, compute the M/B ratio as follows:

$$= \$85/\$15.84 = 5.37 \text{ times}$$

The market-to-book ratio provides another indication of how investors view the company. Since assets are based on historical costs, plus certain assets and nontangible items are not captured on the balance sheet, the balance sheet rarely reflects an accurate value of the company. The market-to-book ratio depicts the difference between the book value and what the market values the company. Are investors willing to pay more for a stock than the accounting book value? A company's market capitalization is the total number of shares multiplied by share price. Book value, on the other hand, is the value of equity shown on the balance sheet.

Companies that have higher rates of return on equity generally will show higher market-to-book ratios. When the book value exceeds the market value, some in the investment community might see this as an opportunity for an acquisition. In *PepsiCo's* instance, investors are willing to pay 5.37 times more for the company's stock than its book value.

Dividend Yield

Dividend yield = Cash dividends per share/Market price per share
= $2.24/$85 = 2.64%

Investors hold stock in companies because they are interested in a return on their investment. The return could come from dividends paid to the stockholder or from appreciation in the market value of the stock. Dividend yield is the ratio of the dividend paid per common share to the market price per common share. This gives investors some idea of the rate of return they will receive in cash dividends from their investment. Low dividend yield companies generally keep a large portion of net income funding growth and expansion. Many well-known high tech companies do not pay dividends for this very reason to fund growth and expansion.

Dividend Payout Ratio

Dividend payout = Cash dividends per share/Earnings per share
= $2.44/$4.37 = 55.83%

The dividend payout ratio shows how much of the company's earnings are paid out in dividends. Growth investors would like this ratio to be a small percentage, while investors who prefer dividends would like this to be a large percentage. Companies that are in industries with stable earnings typically have higher payout ratios and can maintain these payouts over time. Companies in industries with fluctuating earnings tend to have lower dividend payouts.

As an alternative, the dividend payout ratio can be used to show how much the company retains instead of paying out. This is calculated as 100% – (Dividend payout) = Retained earnings: 100% – 55.83% = 44.17% retained earnings.

Asset Management Ratios

Investors, lenders, and management are concerned with a company's asset base. Does the firm have too many assets or too few assets? Are the assets employed to generate an appropriate return for stockholders? Not having the ideal amount of assets, either too many or too few, negatively affects cash flow and stock price. Companies strive to have an ideal amount of assets given their expectation of future sales. Too few assets and firms lose sales; too many assets and firms incur unnecessary costs. Asset management ratios evaluate how efficiently a company uses its various resources.

Inventory Turnover Ratio

$$\text{Inventory turnover} = \text{COGS/Inventory}$$
$$= \$31,243/\$3,409 = 9.16 \text{ times}$$

One of the most commonly used ratios is the inventory turnover ratio. It indicates how many times inventory sold out and then a company bought new inventory to replenish stock for a given time period. It conveys how efficiently the company purchases, produces, and sells its inventory.

Some financial reporting agencies and companies use sales in the numerator, while others use COGS. COGS has an advantage over sales since sales are reported at market prices; COGS and inventories are both reported at cost. Using sales has the effect of overstating the inventory turnover ratio, making it seem better than it really is. Also, inventory costs and COGS are directly related to which inventory costing system is place. The use of FIFO or LIFO impacts this ratio.

On income statements, sales and COGS are reported for an entire time period, while inventories are reported at a point in time on the balance sheet. Because of these challenges, many analysts will use average inventory when calculating the inventory turnover ratio. Using average inventory allows the analyst to adjust for changing inventory levels, which may be due to seasonal effects, trends, or even wild swings in consumer or company purchasing behavior. Different methods can be used to average inventories.

In general, a higher number of inventory turns is more desirable. This indicates that the firm is selling its inventory faster, thus earning revenue and a generating a return on its investment more quickly. A lower number indicates that the firm is holding onto inventory for longer periods of time, signaling poor sales. In addition, the longer inventory is held the greater the chance that the inventory will become obsolete, damaged, or stolen. In addition, the cost of holding inventory increases over time.

By reducing average inventory through just-in-time (JIT) practices, companies have increased the inventory turnover ratio. Do not misinterpret this as reducing inventory and not meeting demand. By reducing inventory levels, demand is met by purchasing inventory more frequently. Idle inventory ties up a company's capital, so operations managers want to move the inventory through the supply chain and through the company more quickly.

An important caveat for this ratio is the ways in which it can be manipulated. Other ratios can be manipulated as well, but the inventory turnover ratio is common and used frequently. For example, on way to manipulate the ratio would be to delay the purchasing of inventory until the next reporting period, artificially showing a better inventory turn for the current period. A manipulative practice such as this will eventually catch up to the company, though.

Interestingly, one can also artificially elevate the ratio through increasing COGS. This may not necessarily be done on purpose. For example, if the person in charge of purchasing became an ineffective buyer, or the direct costs for production and transportation increased, these changes would result in a higher inventory ratio.

Days in Inventory

Days in inventory = 365 days/Inventory turnover ratio
= 365/9.16 = 39.85 days

Days of inventories on hand, average holding period, and days inventory unsold are all common labels for days in inventory. This ratio indicates how long unsold inventory is kept and not sold. The ratio is a more intuitive way of showing how long inventory is held. The goal is to reduce this number because there is a direct relationship between the number of inventory turns and the number of days inventory is held. Continuing with *PepsiCo* as an example, the inventory turnover of 9.16 multiplied by its average holding period of 39.85 days equals 365 days in 1 year.

Accounts Receivable Turnover Ratio

Accounts receivable turnover = Net credit sales/Net accounts receivable

$$= \$66,415/\$6,954 = 9.55 \text{ times}$$

The accounts receivable turnover ratio indicates how quickly a firm converts its receivables to cash. It indicates relative frequency of which the receivables account is turned into cash. A higher accounts receivable turnover ratio means that a company is successfully collecting cash from its credit sales. Rarely do companies state or divulge credit sales, so this is more of an internal metric. However, net credit sales can be replaced with sales revenue to calculate a rough estimate. A higher ratio is more desirable, meaning that the company will have quicker access to its cash. This ratio can indicate if customers are buying more on credit and if customers are taking longer to pay. From a supply chain perspective, delivering products and services on time, without defects and to specifications increases the rate at which receivables are converted to cash.

Days Sales Outstanding

Days sales outstanding (DSO) = Receivables/Average sales per day

$$= \text{Receivables/(Annual sales/365)}$$

$$= \$6,954/(\$66,415/365) = 38.22 \text{ days}$$

Or

$$= 365 \text{ days/Accounts receivable turnover ratio}$$

$$= 365/9.55 = 38.22 \text{ days}$$

Note: Analysts might use 360 days or some other number for the sake of simplicity; however, 365 days is common.

Days sales outstanding (DSO), also called average collection period, is another ratio that evaluates receivables. It represents the number of days it takes to collect cash from receivables. DSO can be more intuitive to understand than the A/R turnover ratio.

This is the average duration a firm waits to collect cash from customers after the sale of goods or services. It is common for suppliers to offer terms to their customers. It is also an attractive way to gain additional customers. In essence, when offering terms to customers, the company becomes a bank, financing purchases for them. In most cases, companies are not collecting any interest from the loans provided.

If DSO is higher than the terms typically offered, the company will need to investigate why customers are paying late. Are they struggling financially, or are they taking advantage of a lax attitude toward on-time payment? Either way, high DSO is a cause for concern. The longer a customer takes to pay, the less likely full payment will be received.

There is a connection between DSO and A/R turnover ratio, just as there is a connection between inventory turns and days in inventory. *PepsiCo's* DSO of 38.22 days times the number of A/R turns of 9.55 is equal to 365 days in 1 year.

Fixed Asset Turnover Ratio

$$\text{Fixed asset turnover} = \text{Sales revenue}/\text{Net fixed assets}$$
$$= \$66,415/\$18,575 = 3.58 \text{ times}$$

Fixed asset turnover ratio evaluates how efficiently management uses fixed assets. Remember fixed assets include those with long useful lives, such as property, plant, and equipment that are used in the production of goods (PP&E). As shown here, *PepsiCo* generates just more than $3.50 for each dollar it has in fixed assets.

As with other ratios, careful interpretation is required. Property, plant, and equipment (PP&E) is typically recorded on the balance sheet at cost. This could be misleading when compared to fixed asset turnover between similar companies. For instance, compare two identical companies; however, one is older than the other. The only difference between the two companies is when each company purchased its PP&E. Since inflation affects the purchase price of PP&E, the older company records its fixed assets at a value lower than the younger company, which recently purchased fixed assets. Comparing the fixed asset turnover of these two companies, it would appear that the older company more efficiently uses fixed assets, when in fact this may not be the case at all.

Total Assets Turnover Ratio

$$\text{Total assets turnover} = \text{Sales revenue}/\text{Total assets}$$
$$= \$66,415/\$77,478 = 0.86 \text{ times}$$

Total assets turnover ratio measures how efficiently management generates sales given the total asset base provided. A low ratio would suggest that the company is not generating enough volume or revenue considering the amount of assets owned. This would suggest that the company should consider its capacity requirements by selling assets, reducing inventory, or generating additional sales. A combination of all three would also be beneficial. How can sales be increased? Several short-term tactics may immediately come to mind—decreasing prices, providing incentives, and offering discounts—but these suggestions are short lived and are counterproductive. Instead, companies should consider long-term solutions such as improving distribution systems, e-commerce websites, and sales processes. Each of these tactics allows customers to purchase products with greater ease.

Debt Management Ratios

Debt management ratios, also known as leverage ratios, show the extent to which a company is financed with debt. Companies that are financed with debt, rather than equity, must pay principal and interest on the debt at regular time periods. If they are unable to pay back these loans on time, creditors can force the firm to accelerate repayment or force it into bankruptcy. In many instances, loan covenants require companies to maintain certain ratio targets or go into default of the loan. Most long-term debt obligations contain covenants related to secured debt levels.

Tax laws favor debt financing, but debt financing increases the financial risk for the company. Interest on long-term debt is tax deductible, whereas dividend payouts are not. Companies try to find an optimal mix of debt and equity financing to provide favorable returns for their common stockholders while minimizing financial risk.

Debt management ratios are important to creditors. Before extending loans to companies, creditors need to know if the company can pay back the loan principal plus interest. The debt management ratios help determine this.

Debt Ratio

The debt ratio, sometimes called total debt ratio or debt-to-assets ratio, shows how much of the company's funds come from sources other than equity.

$$\text{Debt ratio} = \text{Total liabilities/Total assets}$$
$$= \$53,089/\$77,478 = 68.52\% \approx 69\%$$

A debt ratio of 69% indicates that lenders have supplied more than half of the company's funds. Creditors and lenders prefer lower debt ratios, much like mortgage officers do when a homebuyer applies for a mortgage. The less debt a homebuyer has, the less likely the homebuyer will default on the loan. Similarly, a lower debt ratio for a company lessens the likelihood of default.

High debt ratios will likely prohibit the company from acquiring any new debt financing from lenders. In such cases, it will need to rely on equity sources instead. If they could obtain debt financing, it would likely be more costly to borrow the funds. Lenders will increase the borrowing interest rate to offset the higher risk of non-repayment.

Debt-to-Equity Ratio

The debt ratio is similar to the debt-to-equity ratio.

Debt-to-equity ratio

$$= \text{Debt-to-assets}/(1 - \text{Debt-to-assets})$$
$$= 0.6852/(1 - 0.6852) = 2.18 \text{ or } 218\%$$

Or

$$= \text{Total liabilities}/(\text{Total assets} - \text{Total liabilities})$$
$$= \$53,089/(\$77,478 - \$53,089) = 2.18 \text{ or } 218\%$$

Debt-to-equity ratio reveals the amount of assets that is provided by creditors for each dollar of assets being provided by the owners of a company. Look at *PepsiCo*. Creditors are providing *PepsiCo* $2.18 cents of assets for every $1.00 of assets being provided by stockholders. Seeing this, one may wonder if 2.18 is a concerning or not. Different people will have different points of view on this. Just like the debt-to-assets ratio, creditors prefer lower debt-to-equity ratios; however, the industry a company operates within is a factor. The different industries give creditors different levels of assurance that they will be repaid. Low debt-to-equity ratios signal the possibility of a leveraged buyout, where investors use debt to buy up stock of the company. Common stockholders, however, prefer higher ratios since they benefit more from assets being provided by creditors through financial leverage, as discussed in the "Profitability Ratios" section. Too high of a debt ratio can highlight an increased risk of bankruptcy. Each industry has its own mix of debt to equity averages, so again, it is important to compare like companies from the same industry.

Times Interest Earned

Times interest earned (TIE) ratio = (Net income + Interest
expense + Income tax
expense)/Interest expense

= EBIT/Interest expense

= \$9,705/\$911 = 10.65 times

Times interest earned (TIE) ratio, also known as interest cover-age, measures the degree to which a company is able to pay its inter-est obligations. Specifically, it shows how much operating income could decline before the company is unable to pay its interest costs. A declining TIE toward 1.0 is concerning. Since interest is paid with pretax earnings, earnings before interest and taxes (EBIT) are used for this ratio. The lower the ratio, the greater the risk of defaulting on the loan covenants. Consider the calculation above: for every \$1.00 of interest expense, *PepsiCo* has \$10.65 of operating profit. At this point of time, *PepsiCo* is able to repay their loan interest.

There are some concerns when relying on the TIE ratio. Compa-nies have other debts to pay beyond paying interest payments, such as loan principal and bond payments. In addition, EBIT does not coin-cide with cash flow. Revenue may have been earned and recognized thus increasing EBIT, but the company may not have collected any cash yet. Even though, cash is needed to pay debts and interest. Con-sidering these concerns, an alternative ratio to consider is the debt service coverage ratio.

Debt Service Coverage Ratio

Debt service coverage ratio = Cash flow from operations before
interest and tax payments/(Interest
payments + Principal payments +
Other debt payments)

This ratio provides insight into whether or not the cash generated by the company's operations is sufficient to repay interest, principal, and other debt obligations. Other debt obligations may include early retirement of debt and lease payments. The information to complete this ratio comes from the statement of cash flows. As this ratio is regularly changed to fit the user's particular circumstance, you may find still that EBIT or a whole host of other variables are used in the numerator, but still we include all debt obligations in the denominator.

Summary

Companies and management are evaluated on many outcomes and operations functions can directly impact a company's financial performance. Companies are evaluated on their ability to pay current bills, profitability, management of assets and debts, and the valuation of the company. Operations and supply chain managers have a significant impact on a company's cash flow, profitability, debt burden, utilization of assets, and its ability to remain in business. Operational decisions and actions will be reflected on a company's financial statements and subsequent performance ratios. Table 4.5 provides a summary of the performance ratios that were introduced in this chapter.

Table 4.5 Summary of Ratios

Ratio	Formula	Calculation
Liquidity Ratios		
Current ratio	Current assets/Current liabilities	= $22,203/$17,839 = 1.24 times
Quick ratio	(Current assets – Inventories)/Current liabilities	= ($22,203 – $3,409)/ $17,839 = 1.05 times
Operating cash flow ratio	Operating cash flow/ Current liabilities	= $9,688/$17,839 = 0.54
Profitability Ratios		
Profit margin on sales	Net income available to common stockholders/ Sales revenue	= ($6,740 – $8)/$66,415 = 10.1%
Operating profit margin ratio	Operating profit (EBIT)/ Sales revenue	= $9,705/$66,415 = 14.6%
Gross profit margin ratio	(Sales revenue – COGS)/ Sales revenue	= ($66,415 – $31,243)/ $66,415 = 52.96%
Basic earnings power (BEP) ratio	EBIT/Total assets	= $9,705/$77,478 = 12.5%
Return on total assets ratio	Net income available to common stockholders/ Total assets	= ($6,740 – $8)/ $77,478 = 8.7%

(Continued)

Table 4.5 (*Continued*)

Ratio	Formula	Calculation
Return on equity ratio	Net income available to common stockholders/ Common stockholders' equity	= ($6,740 – $8)/$24,409 = 27.6%
Valuation Ratios		
Earnings per share (EPS)	(Net income – Preferred stock dividends declared)/ Common shares outstanding	= ($6,740 – $8)/1,541 = $4.37
Price to earnings (P/E) ratio	Market price per share/ Earnings per share	= $85/$4.37 = 19.45 times
Price/Cash flow ratio	Price per share/Operating cash flow per share	= $85/$6.04 = 14.07 times
Market/Book (M/B) ratio	Market per share price/ Book value per share	= $85/$15.84 = 5.37 times
Dividend yield	Cash dividends per share/ Market price per share	= $2.24/$85 = 2.64%
Dividend payout ratio	Cash dividends per share/ Earnings per share	= $2.44/$4.37 = 55.83%
Asset Management Ratios		
Inventory turnover ratio	COGS/Inventory	= $31,243/$3,409 = 9.16 times
Days in inventory	365 days/Inventory turnover ratio	= 365/9.16 = 39.85 days
Accounts turnover ratio	Net credit sales/Net accounts receivable	= $66,415/$6,954 = 9.55 times
Days sales outstanding (DSO)	Receivables/Average sales per day	= $6,954/($66,415/365) = 38.22 days
	Or	Or
	365 days/Accounts receivable turnover ratio	= 365/9.55 = 38.22 days
Fixed asset turnover ratio	Sales revenue/ Net fixed assets	= $66,415/$18,575 = 3.58 times
Total assets turnover ratio	Sales revenue/ Total assets	= $66,415/$77,478 = 0.86 times
Debt Management Ratios		
Debt ratio	Total liabilities/ Total assets	= $53,089/$77,478 = 68.52% ≈ 69%

Table 4.5 (*Continued*)

Ratio	Formula	Calculation
Debt-to-equity ratio	Debt-to-assets/(1 – Debt-to-assets)	= 0.6852/(1 – 0.6852) = 218%
	Or	
	Total liabilities/(Total assets – Total liabilities)	= $53,089/($77,478 – $53,089) = 218%
Times interest earned (TIE)	(Net income + Interest expense + Income tax expense)/Interest expense	= $9,705/$911 = 10.65 times
Debt service coverage ratio	Debt service coverage ratio = Cash flow from operations before interest and tax payments/(Interest payments + Principal payments + Other debt payments)	

5

Company Valuation

Executives focus on the valuation of their companies, some almost obsessively so. Particularly, since those executives who are responsible for public companies are scrutinized. The investment community continually assesses the valuation or stock price of companies. The valuation is based on management skill and missteps, the environment in which the business operates and competes, and how well executives run their companies. Returns to investors are also important; often an executive's tenure and compensation rests on his or her ability to maximize investor returns. Another consideration, if companies are planning to sell or to be acquired by another company or investment firm, a higher valuation means a higher return for the sellers, owners, and stockholders. In addition, employees should be concerned about their companies' valuation. For some employees, retirement plans contain company stock or they may be part of an employee stock ownership program (ESOP). In such situations, the employee owns part of the company through shares of stock; thus, the valuation of the company and resultant stock price directly affects retirement and investment account balances. Though executives are often the ones who bear the weight of a company's valuation, all those within the organization should be interested in the valuation.

Supply chain and operations professionals have numerous opportunities to affect the valuation of organizations. Earlier chapters have discussed value. Supply chain and operations create value for customers by delivering quality products, providing excellent and timely service while keeping costs manageable. Managing each of these areas increases the financial value of a company. Remember that valuation ratios indicate market value of the company. This chapter will examine valuation more closely and explain why valuation is important, how investors and buyers value companies, and how supply chain and operations managers affect a company's valuation.

Value

Many valuation techniques are employed in the industry. While it is interesting to understand the details of these techniques, this chapter's focus is to connect how supply chain and operations decisions affect a company's valuation. Investors and valuation experts differ on the merits of the various valuation techniques and when each is most appropriate to use. There are several resources that can provide additional information for you.

What is value? Value can be defined in different ways. There are those who might classify value in the short term in two main categories: book value and market value. A company's financial statements determine its book value. The book value of assets and stockholder's equity can be ascertained from the balance sheet. Recall from earlier chapters that stockholder's equity is the difference between assets and liabilities. Market value, commonly referred to as market capitalization, is calculated by taking the number of shares outstanding times the share price. Market value changes multiple times per day, every day. When concentrating on the number of shares and share price, this refers to a company's market value of equity.

To further complicate matters, adding debt and other obligations back into the equation can modify book and market values. Items such as short- and long-term debts, capital lease obligations, and non-operating liabilities matter when finding the true value of a company. Further, the valuation of a company varies based on whether or not a company continues over a period of time or is set to liquidate. Companies that continue to operate typically are valued higher than those set to liquidate because their assets will continue to produce revenues for extended periods of time. Conversely, liquidation values are seldom more than book value. They typically substantially less due to the level of obsolescence, coupled with the relatively specialized nature of such surplus equipment.

Contrastingly, value creation can be looked at over long periods of time. The long-term approach that Koller et al. (2010) take when describing value creation is the primary reference source for this chapter.[1] Companies that compete on long-term value tend to treat all stakeholders better. They tend to treat current and past employees better, create more employment opportunities over time, and they are more focused on corporate social responsibility than their shortsighted peers. Moreover, they are concerned with their suppliers abiding by fair labor and the safety laws; they are concerned about whether or not the materials used in their products are safe for consumption; and they are concerned about not harming the environment. The long-term value includes tradeoffs and is more complex than simply maximizing sales and minimizing costs.

Since competition in the market place can erode one's competitive advantage, thus eroding going-concern value, companies need to continually evolve as competitors and the market place change. The long-term value depends on a company's evolution. Because companies must adjust, a conflict can arise between achieving short-term gains that can appeal to Wall Street and the need for a long-term value creating strategy. It is possible that long-term value enhancing strategies can erode short-term financial performance; however, over the longer term, the expectation is that the company will be in an advantageous position to create value and achieve higher rates of return for its stakeholders over a longer period of time. Companies that aim only for short-term gains often find themselves in precarious competitive positions and are not as strong over the long term.

Using assets and resources more efficiently and effectively to generate cash flows at higher rates than competitors tend to result in a company being valued higher (Figure 5.1). Essentially, those companies that invest the capital they have raised from investors to generate future cash flows that are growing at rates higher than the cost of capital, create value. Cost of capital is viewed as the required risk-adjusted rate of return investors require. A company's value is driven by its ability to generate cash flow from revenue growth and return on invested capital (ROIC) relative to its cost structure. ROIC measures how efficiently a company uses the money it collects from investors and lenders. It shows the amount of profit a company generates from its core operations by showing how many dollars a company earns for each dollar it brings in from investors and lenders. If ROIC is greater than the cost of capital, the company is generating value. As an example, if a company has an ROIC of 15% and cost of capital of 10%, the company is making $0.05 for every $1.00 it collects from investors and lenders.

To recap, return on invested capital and revenue growth is the principal drivers of company valuations. Companies with higher ROIC and growth, as long as higher ROIC is above cost of capital, are valued more highly in the stock market. Over the long term, higher ROIC and

---

[1] Koller T, Goedhart M, and Wessels D. *Valuation: Measuring and Managing the Value of Companies*. 5th ed. Hoboken, New Jersey: John Wiley & Sons, Inc.; 2010.

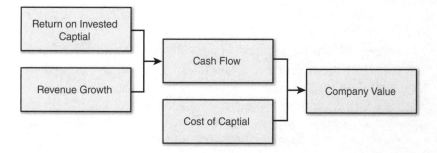

Figure 5.1 Value drivers. (Adapted from Koller T, Goedhart M, and Wessels D. *Valuation: Measuring and Managing the Value of Companies*, 5th ed. Hoboken, New Jersey: John Wiley & Sons, Inc.; 2010:16.)

growth lead to higher total return to shareholders in the stock market. From a management perspective, if a company has a high ROIC from the outset, it will benefit more from revenue growth. If a company has a low ROIC from the outset, it will benefit more from increasing ROIC.

Competitive Advantage

Companies strive to gain an advantage over their competitors from a combination of marketing and operations. Some companies earn higher margins on sales; they are able to charge more for the same item or service that a competitor sells. They do this through being reliable, providing consistent quality, implementing systems that remove barriers for customers to purchase from them, and developing innovative products, services, or business methods. For example, Delta Airlines earns more money per seat mile than other air carriers through brand equity, reliability, and a network of flights that meet passenger needs. Companies can achieve a competitive advantage and increase profits, too, by maintaining or becoming efficient with capital and costs. Some examples include:

- Growing or scaling capacity with minimal marginal cost
- Economies of scale and scope
- Access to and using materials that are superior or unique from their competitors
- Implementing systems that are efficient but difficult for competitors to copy

Production, logistics, and customer interaction systems go a long way to providing customer satisfaction and return customers. Business systems have the ability to increase margins and reduce costs raising barriers to competitors.

Growth in revenues is important for value creation. Increasing growth comes from projects, acquisitions, and new customers; however, each brings additional costs. Growth is not without cost. Operations and supply chain facilitate growth. By implementing efficient and appropriate systems while increasing capacity with minimal marginal costs, free cash flow can grow, thus increasing ROIC and valuations.

Reorganizing Traditional Financial Statements

Many attempt to evaluate companies using traditional financial statements; however, the main purpose of financial statements is for reporting historical financial information, not necessarily analysis. Balance sheets combine operating and nonoperating assets along with sources of financing for companies. Income statements mix operating profits with financing costs, such as interest expense. To truly examine and evaluate a company's operation, performance, and value, traditional financial statements need to be reorganized into three separate categories: operating, nonoperating, and sources of financing. Through this reorganization, three important concepts come to light that assist in determining the value of a company. The three concepts, which cannot be found directly on financial statements are as follows:

- Net operating profit less adjusted taxes (NOPLAT)
- Return on invested capital (ROIC)
- Free cash flow (FCF)

To move forward, it is important to understand these key concepts and how they are calculated. With this knowledge, one can connect how supply chain and operations actions affect these key value drivers. The process of finding the information and computing the calculations can be confusing; however, recognizing the pieces of the calculations creates a greater understanding of how supply chain and operational actions may affect the outcomes.

To calculate ROIC and FCF, the balance sheet is reorganized to find invested capital and the income statement is reorganized to find NOPLAT. The terms in the following equations are defined as ROIC is the return a company earns on each dollar invested in the business. NOPLAT is the after-tax profit generated from a company's core operations. Invested capital is the cumulative amount a company has invested in its core operations and is mainly composed of PPE and working capital, without regard for how the capital is financed. Free cash flow is the cash flow generated by a company's core operations after removing investments in new capital. Net investment is the difference in invested capital from 1 year to the next.

ROIC = NOPLAT/Invested capital

FCF = NOPLAT + Noncash operating expenses
– Investment in invested capital

Or

FCF = NOPLAT – Net investment

The previous formulas will be further explained throughout the chapter. To sum up what has been described so far though, companies that can increase ROIC or maintain a steady trajectory of increasing ROIC above the cost of capital will generate value. As an example in mathematical form:

Value = FCF (1 + g)/WACC – g

The perpetuity growth method assumes that the company will continue its historic business and generate FCFs at a steady state forever. Value for a company is driven by the amount of its invested capital, ROIC, growth in revenue, and its cost of capital (WACC). WACC is weighted average cost of capital or the cost to the company for the capital it obtained from stockholders and lenders (equity and debt holders) and g is the growth rate of future FCFs.

NOPLAT

Net income differs when comparing two companies with identical operating performance that carry different amounts of debt. The company with more debt would show a lower net income. Remember that net income is the profit only available to equity holders.

Operating profit (EBIT) then places both companies on an equal footing by measuring the difference in the amount of money the company receives from operations and the amount of money it spends on operating expenses. It excludes costs and benefits of debt financing and income taxes.

Net operating profit less adjusted taxes (NOPLAT), sometimes referred to as net operating profit after tax (NOPAT), is the after-tax operating profit—profit generated from a company's core operations, excluding any gains from nonoperating assets or financing expenses. NOPLAT is used in calculating free cash flow and is a measure of management's operations performance. It shows how effective managers are in their operations through a comparison of the company's economic performance to its cost of capital. In addition, NOPLAT identifies the profit for all investors, which includes all equity owners and all debt providers.

Table 5.1 provides an example of how NOPLAT is found. NOPLAT is $2,400M and income available to investors is $2,426M after adding back in after-tax nonoperating income.

Table 5.1 Abbreviated Income Statement, NOPLAT, and Income Available to Investors

Abbreviated Income Statement ($USD, in Millions)		NOPLAT	
	Current Year		**Current Year**
Revenues	14,500	Revenues	14,500
Operating costs	(11,000)	Operating costs	(11,000)
Depreciation	(300)	Depreciation	(300)
Operating profit	3,200	Operating profit	3,200
		Operating taxes	(800)
Interest	(250)	NOPLAT	2,400
Nonoperating income	35		
Earnings before taxes	2,985		
		After-tax nonoperating income	26
		Income available to investors	2,426
Taxes	(746)		
Net income	2,239		
		Reconciliation with Net Income	
		Net income	2,239
		After-tax interest expense	187
		Income available to investors	2,426

Source: Adapted from Koller T, Goedhart M, and Wessels D. *Valuation: Measuring and Managing the Value of Companies*, 5th ed. Hoboken, New Jersey: John Wiley & Sons, Inc.; 2010:135.

The income statement is used to calculate NOPLAT. Take operating profit (EBIT), earnings before interest and taxes, and then adjust EBIT for the impact of taxes. Analysts often adjust operating income further; however, for our purposes, the following equation suits us well:

$$\text{NOPLAT} = \text{Operating profit} \times (1 - \text{Tax rate})$$
$$\text{NOPLAT} = \$3,200 \times (1 - 0.25)$$
$$= \$2,400 \text{ (assuming a 25\% tax rate)}$$

Recall that taxes are calculated on operating income less interest expense. In the previous example, the interest expense is removed before calculating taxes. Taxes reported and calculated on a normal income statement would be based on $2,985M after interest expense and nonoperating income were accounted for. Now, when the income statement is reorganized, taxes reported and calculated are based on $3,200M. This change increases the tax amount for the purposes of computing NOPLAT. However, the tax burden is not changed. Because of the focus on operations only, the income statement must be reformatted to remove interest expense and any nonoperating income.

Invested Capital

Consider invested capital, another term necessary to find ROIC. First remember that operating assets consist of receivables, inventory, and PPE, while operating liabilities are noninterest bearing and consist of accounts payable, accrued expenses (such as salaries), and income taxes payable. In addition, equity consists of common stock, preferred stock, and retained earnings. Using a balance sheet, Table 5.2 provides an example of how invested capital is found.

For the current year, Net operating working capital (NOWC) = Operating current assets – Operating current liabilities

$$\text{NOWC} = \$3,100 - \$1,900 = \$1,200$$

Total operating capital = NOWC + Operating long-term assets (PPE)
Total operating capital = $1,200 + $4,650 = $5,850

If equity investments are counted as operating assets, then total funds invested are:

Total invested capital = $1,200 + $4,650 + $150 = $6,000

This shows the amount of capital used for operations and the financing provided by investors for operations.

Table 5.2 Abbreviated Balance Sheet and Invested Capital

Abbreviated Balance Sheet ($USD, in Millions)			Invested Capital		
	Current Year	**Prior Year**		**Current Year**	**Prior Year**
Assets			**Assets**		
Inventory	3,100	3,500	Inventory (operating current assets)	3,100	3,500
Net PP&E	4,650	4,550	Accounts payable (operating current liabilities)	(1,900)	(2,100)
Equity investments	150	300	Net operating working capital	1,200	1,400
Total assets	7,900	8,350			
			Net PP&E	4,650	4,550
			Total operating capital	5,850	5,950
Liabilities and Equity					
Accounts payable	1,900	2,100			
Interest-bearing debt	3,450	2,800	Equity investments	150	300
Common stock	800	700	Total funds invested	6,000	6,250
Retained earnings	1,750	2,750			
Total liabilities and equity	7,900	8,350			
			Reconciliation of Total Funds Invested		
			Interest-bearing debt	3,450	2,800
			Common stock	800	700
			Retained earnings	1,750	2,750
			Total funds invested	6,000	6,250

Source: Adapted from Koller T, Goedhart M, and Wessels D. *Valuation: Measuring and Managing the Value of Companies*, 5th ed. Hoboken, New Jersey: John Wiley & Sons, Inc.; 2010:134.

Reconciling the calculations provides this insight:

Invested capital = Debt + Equity
Invested capital = $3,450 + $800 + $1,750 = $6,000

The current year's invested capital is $6B and the previous year's invested capital is $6.25B.

For an accurate perception of invested capital, it is important to know how certain assets are treated on the balance sheet and then on the income statement through a depreciation expense. When a company obtains tangible assets such as PP&E, the asset is capitalized on the balance sheet and depreciated over time. Intangible assets such as a brand name, a distribution network, or a patent are expensed in whole on the income statement immediately. Companies with significant amounts of intangible assets will find that their invested capital will be underestimated, leading to an artificially high or overstated ROIC.

Return on Invested Capital

Return on invested capital (ROIC) is a preferred measure by many to understand a company's financial and operational performance, rather than the use of return on assets (ROA) or return on equity (ROE). This is because ROIC focuses solely on the company's operations. ROA has a limitation in that it includes nonoperating assets and ignores the benefits of accounts payable and other operating liabilities. Together these reduce the amount of capital required from investors. Further, since assets depreciate over time, the asset base also changes. ROE mixes operating performance with capital structure, making peer group and trend analysis less meaningful.

A company's ROIC can be disaggregated so the root causes for key drivers in ROIC can be identified. ROIC can be expressed as:

ROIC = (1 – Operating cash tax rate) × (EBITDA/Revenues) ×
(Revenues/Invested capital)

The above equation can identify what drives ROIC. Is it profitability expressed as EBITDA/revenues (operating margin)? Is it capital turnover expressed as revenues/invested capital? Is it the ability to minimize operating taxes? This can be examined further (Figure 5.2) and put into an operations context, showing how

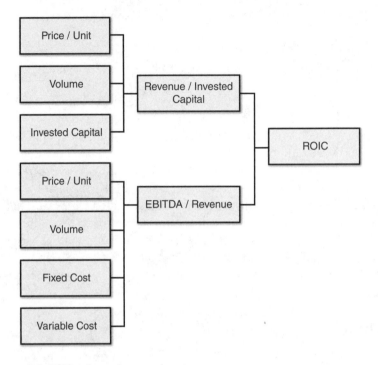

Figure 5.2 ROIC, price, volume, and costs.

profit is affected by price, fixed, and variable expenses along with volume.

$$\text{Profits} = (\text{Price} \times \text{Volume in units}) - \text{Fixed costs} - (\text{Variable cost per unit} \times \text{Volume in units})$$

The equation reveals how price and cost drive ROIC. Units were used in the explanation, which might imply a goods or manufacturing perspective; however, units can be applied to many situations. For instance, units can be the number of transactions processed, the number of calls answered, or the number of hours billed. From this equation, one can see that supply chain and operations decisions play a significant part in achieving high ROIC. Costs can be reduced, capital can be used more productively, and through efficient and effective processes, supply chain and operations professionals can achieve greater price per unit. The ability to purchase materials, manage inventory and transportation, manage projects, and to use building, plants and equipment effectively and efficiently are of chief importance to a company's competitiveness and value.

Operationally, the effect of supply chain actions on ROIC is obvious. However, what is the effect of keeping assets off the balance sheet through operating leases, discussed in Chapter 3? When a company borrows money to purchase an asset, the asset is capitalized or placed on the balance sheet along with its associated debt. Then the interest is expensed on the income statement. When a company rents or leases an asset instead, it is using an operating lease, which allows the company to expense the rent money on the income statement, thus keeping assets and debt off the balance sheet. In doing so, many financial and operational ratios are affected, typically in a way that is advantageous to the company. ROIC is no different. This results in high capital efficiency because the asset is not placed on the balance sheet, and this creates an artificially high ROIC. Industries such as the airline industry that have large and easily transferable assets tend to use operating leases more often.

Free Cash Flow

High or increasing FCF is often a sign of a healthy company. Investors tend to search for companies that have high or increasing FCF but undervalued share prices, expecting that the share price will increase as inherent value is discovered in the market. This is because investor sentiment plays a predominant role in the short term, whereas true competitive position and intrinsic value being generated by the firm is reflected in the longer term. Free cash flow measures a company's ability to generate cash flow, which is a fundamental basis for stock pricing and company valuation. Free cash flow can be more telling about a company than just about any other financial measure, including the popular earnings per share (EPS) measure. Share prices change in the short term for a variety of reasons; however, cash flows determine the long-term share value for a company. EPS does not take into account any changes to fixed assets or working capital, both of which can absorb large amounts of cash. Even though CEOs and CFOs know that EPS is not the most accurate measure, they tend to use it anyway to guide decisions because of Wall Street's focus on EPS. Management has a great deal more control over the EPS denominator through share buybacks and issuance than the competitive dynamics that determine the numerator.

Just as NOPLAT identifies the profit for all investors, which includes all equity owners and all debt holders, free cash flow essentially does the same. FCF is the after-tax amount of cash flow, taking into account capital expenditures, such as buildings or equipment, which is available to all investors, stockholders, and creditors. Consequently, managers can make the company more valuable by increasing free cash flow.

Unlike the cash flow from operations on an accountant's statement of cash flows that is found in an annual report, free cash flow is independent of financing and nonoperating items. If a company reports a significant gain or loss that is not directly related to the company's normal core business, such as a one-time gain on the sale of equipment, this amount should be excluded from the free cash flow calculation for an accurate picture of the company's normal cash-generating ability. Thus, FCF depends on sales revenue, operating costs and taxes, and required investments in operations.

FCF is, of course, used in a company's valuation, but the cash itself is used for such things as paying interest or repaying debt holders, paying dividends to shareholders, to repurchasing stock from stockholders, or buying nonoperating assets. FCF generally isn't used to buy operating assets since FCF already takes into account the purchase of operating assets needed to support growth.

As a reminder, FCF is the amount of cash flow a company generates after taking into account capital expenditures such as building or equipment. Since companies have some leeway about what is considered a capital expenditure, FCF can be affected.

FCF is calculated as:

$$\text{FCF} = (\text{Operating profit} \times [1 - \text{Tax rate}] + \text{Depreciation}) - \text{Capital expenditure} - \text{Change in net operating working capital}$$

Alternatively, (Operating profit × [1 – Tax rate] + Depreciation) can be expressed as

$$\text{Operating cash flows} = \text{EBIT} - \text{Taxes} + \text{Depreciation}$$

The change in net operating working capital is expressed as the change in operating current assets – the change in operating current liabilities.

To simplify the above equation, think of it as:

$$\text{FCF} = \text{NOPLAT} + \text{Noncash operating expenses} - \text{Investments in invested capital}$$

Table 5.3 provides an example of how free cash flow is found. Free cash flow is $2,100M and cash flow available to investors is $2,276M.

Table 5.3 Abbreviated Cash Flow Statement and Free Cash Flow

Abbreviated Cash Flow Statement ($USD, in Millions)		Free Cash Flow	
	Current Year		**Current Year**
Net income	2,239	NOPLAT	2,400
Depreciation	300	Depreciation	300
Decrease (increase) in inventory	400	Gross cash flow	2,700
Increase (decrease) in accounts payable	(200)		
Cash flow from operations	2,739		
		Decrease (increase) in inventory	400
		Increase (decrease) in accounts payable	(200)
Capital expenditures	(800)	Capital expenditures	(800)
Decrease (increase) in equity investments	150	Free cash flow	2,100
Earnings before taxes	(650)		
		After-tax nonoperating income	26
		Decrease (increase) in equity investments	150
Increase (decrease) in debt	650	Cash flow available to investors	2,276
Increase (decrease) in common stock	100		
Dividends	(455)		
Cash flow from financing	295		

Source: Adapted from Koller T, Goedhart M, and Wessels D. *Valuation: Measuring and Managing the Value of Companies*, 5th ed. Hoboken, New Jersey: John Wiley & Sons, Inc.; 2010:136.

Cost of Capital

Previously, the weighted average cost of capital (WACC) was discussed. Remember that it is the cost to the company for the capital obtained from stockholders and lenders (equity and debt holders). Since obtaining funds or capital is not free, it is necessary to know what the cost is when a company obtains these funds. This cost will affect free cash flow, which, of course, will affect a company's valuation. When buying a home or a car, a person might borrow money from a mortgage lender or bank. If so, the lender will provide the loan at a certain interest rate, and that rate determines the cost for borrowing money. Thus, when money is borrowed, the total cost of buying the home or car includes the price for the home or car plus the interest expense.

For investors, lenders, and debt holders, WACC is the opportunity cost faced when investing money in one company versus another company or investing money in a different opportunity entirely.

A company's WACC is not exactly stated or observable, so it becomes an estimated value. Each of the three WACC components, cost of equity, the after-tax cost of debt, and the company's target capital structure (mix of debt and equity), needs to be estimated.

Performance Trees

Performance trees disaggregate financial and operational performance. There are a number of performance trees such as the DuPont model, ROIC, and value trees that are used in the industry. By disaggregating measures, such as ROIC and value, performance trees are useful in determining how changes in operations affect ROIC, revenue growth and company value. In addition, the DuPont model, ROIC, and value trees can be used as a method of conducting sensitivity analysis and risk analysis. Inserting new values or expected changes in the values provide instant feedback about the changes in ROIC, revenue, and value. ROIC trees build off of the financial ratios that are based on a specific company's operations. The value tree in Figure 5.3 depicts the connection between marketing and manufacturing and their overall impact to company value creation (or destruction). From the value tree, you can identify where and how fixed and variable costs, price per unit, and production volume affect company value. Of course, value trees are constructed based on industries and will look differently depending on the industry.

Summary

Company executives strive to increase company value. Companies with higher ROIC and revenue growth are valued more highly in the stock market and over the long term lead to higher total return to

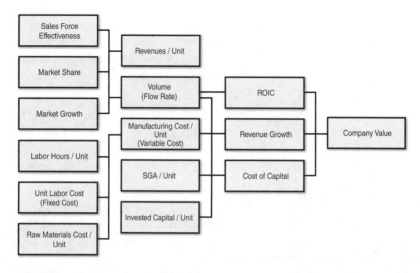

Figure 5.3 Company value tree.(Adapted from Koller T, Goedhart M, and Wessels D. *Valuation: Measuring and Managing the Value of Companies*, 5th ed. Hoboken, New Jersey: John Wiley & Sons, Inc.; 2010:421.)

owners and stockholders. A company's value is driven by its ability to generate cash flow from revenue growth and return on invested capital (ROIC) relative to its cost structure. ROIC measures how efficiently a company uses the money it collects from investors and lenders and shows how much profit a company generates from its core operations. Companies that use their assets and resources more efficiently and effectively to generate cash flows better than their competitors do tend to be valued higher. Growth in revenues is important for value creation. Increasing growth comes from projects, acquisitions, and new customers. Operations and supply chain make the growth happen. Implementing efficient and appropriate systems and increasing capacity with minimal marginal costs, companies can increase free cash flow, thus increasing ROIC and valuations.

6

Decision-Making Tools

Introduction

Businesses spend money to make money. Since companies do not have unlimited access to cash, some of the most important business decisions surround capital expenditures. Capital expenditures are the allocation of money to undertake projects to generate future cash flows for the company. Typically, these are long-term projects and are expensive. It is important that the management of a company select projects with the highest payoffs and the greatest chance of success. Capital budgeting encompasses evaluating, comparing, and selecting projects.

Historically, supply chain and operations managers have been asked to reduce costs wherever possible. Therefore, it is no surprise that we are traditionally classified as a cost center. In one aspect, we do have influence over cost containment and cost savings, however, we also have influence over revenue generation. Although we might not be classified as revenue centers, the work of supply chain and operations managers influence profit margins from both the revenue and cost perspectives. Yes, sales people will sell products, but the supply chain then has to deliver. If a salesperson sells 1000 electric generators but they are not delivered to the customer or the generators are of poor quality, no revenue is collected. In the end, the organization has to perform all of its functions. Services or products must be delivered for a company to be paid.

As supply chain and operations personnel, we are responsible for projects of all types. Our expertise is called upon for implementing new processes that help the organization become more productive, more efficient, and more effective in its dealings with employees, suppliers, and customers. We are responsible for carrying out projects that help the organization perform at a higher level. But, how do we know which projects and process improvements to undertake? This also begs the question, how do we know if the process improvements and changes are beneficial to the organization financially?

For many supply chain and operations experts, it is not necessarily the calculations performed that provide the most insight about how the business is being affected by their decisions. Instead, the information gathering and thought processes used to develop models initially will offer a greater depth of understanding. Thinking through business challenges, estimating initial investment dollars, estimating cash flows, and considering project risk increase understanding of the likelihood of success. Research and thoughtful consideration also deepen understanding of the competitive environment in which a company operates.

In practice, once an output is provided from each of the tools introduced in this chapter, it will raise additional questions. These questions are the first step toward greater understanding. Many questions are "what if" questions, such as, what if we drop the price of our jet engines by 10%, and how would the demand and cash flows be affected? Another example: If we change suppliers, how will our cost of raw materials and cash flows be affected? Asking such questions is actually scenario and sensitivity analysis. By doing scenario and sensitivity analysis, supply chain and operations personnel can identify various outcomes based on changes to the inputs. The different inputs can lead to both best-case and worst-case scenarios. The tools discussed next are useful for understanding how supply chain and operational decisions affect a company's finances.

This chapter discusses some of the common tools financial experts and others use to make supply chain and operations decisions. The tools help inform decisions as well as communicate how the company is affected financially. After reading this chapter, you will be able to apply the tools and communicate more clearly.

DuPont Model

The DuPont model is useful in communicating how operations affect the company financially. It helps bridge the gap between operations, finance, and accounting. The DuPont model also known as the DuPont equation shows how the return on assets (ROA) and return on equity (ROE) are influenced by business decisions. ROE is a closely watched ratio and is considered a good measure of how well a company's management creates shareholder value. Just like all ratios, it is important to identify what is driving the ratio. Simply looking at ROE at a point in time or its trend may not provide the information needed about the company. In short, ROE can be misleading; however, the DuPont model uncovers what is truly driving ROE.

The DuPont model incorporates profit margin and asset efficiency to find ROA. Profit margin is calculated from values on the income statement. Asset efficiency, as measured by total assets turnover, is calculated from values on the income statement and balance sheet.

$$\text{ROA} = \text{Profit margin} \times \text{Total assets turnover}$$
$$= (\text{Net income/Sales}) \times (\text{Sales/Total assets})$$
$$= \text{Net income/Total assets}$$

This can be taken a step further. If a company is only financed with common equity, then ROA equals ROE.

$$\text{ROA} = \text{Net income/Total assets}$$
$$= \text{Net income/Common equity}$$
$$= \text{ROE}$$

When a company is financed with debt, ROE is found by multiplying ROA by an equity multiplier (a company's financial leverage). As stated earlier, financial leverage is another term for debt and refers to the relative use of equity or debt to finance asset purchases. The equity multiplier will show if the company's use of borrowed money (debt) is driving ROE.

$$\text{Leverage} = \text{Average assets/Average shareholders' equity}$$

Or stated another way,

$$\text{Equity multiplier} = \text{Leverage} = \text{Total assets/Common equity}$$

And finally,

$$\text{ROE} = (\text{Net income/Total assets}) \times (\text{Total assets/Common equity})$$
$$\text{ROE} = \text{ROA} \times \text{Equity multiplier}$$

The next equation is an expanded DuPont equation that shows ROE is a function of three factors: (1) profitability, (2) efficiency, and (3) financial leverage.

$$\text{ROE} = \text{Profitability} \times \text{Efficiency} \times \text{Financial leverage}$$

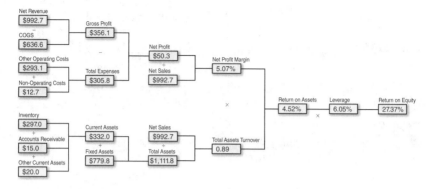

Figure 6.1 DuPont model.

Expanded to

$$\text{ROE} = (\text{Net income/Sales}) \times (\text{Sales/Total assets}) \times (\text{Total assets/Common equity})$$

The DuPont model (Figure 6.1) when created in a spreadsheet shows instantly how a change in any value affects ROA and ROE, among other financial and operational ratios. Inserting new values into the model provides immediate feedback about a company's operations, supply chain decisions, and policies.

To add more context to the ROE discussion, consider that the ultimate goal is to identify what is driving ROE. Is it driven by profitability, which measures management's ability to achieve high margins? Is it driven by management's ability to use their assets efficiently? Is it driven by management's assumption of additional debt? If ROE increases, this is generally positive. It is an indication that the return on shareholders' equity is rising. Increasing ROE could be because a company is satisfying customers, but without understanding the driver, one can only guess. If the company is increasing ROE through satisfied customers, it can hope that customers are willing to pay more for its offerings than they would pay for the same offerings at a competitor, thus allowing it to achieve higher margins. However, without a clear indication of the driver of increased ROE, one cannot assume this is the case.

Alternately, consider an investor's perspective. An investor might believe that a company with an increasing ROE is a worthwhile investment. However, if ROE increased only because the company took on additional debt, which increased its financial leverage, this bears reconsideration. Though ROE increased, the company may be a risky investment because it is taking on more debt. By breaking down ROE into components, the DuPont analysis provides great insight into how the company is operating and how leveraged it is.

Increasing ROE is generally good for an organization, while decreasing ROE is often viewed negatively. However, one should not so quickly jump to conclusions. ROE can decrease for many reasons, and if ROE is decreasing because debt is being paid off, this is positive for an organization. This is just one example of why scrutinizing ROE changes is important to have a true understanding.

The question must also be asked, what if ROE remains the same? As ROE is examined more closely, it may be that both profit margins and asset turnover have declined, thus reason ROE remained the same was because of an increase in the use of debt. Of course, this scenario would not be considered healthy for an organization.

Extended DuPont Model

The DuPont model is useful in many ways.

First, it allows users to isolate what is driving ROA and ROE. Are they driven by the company's ability to earn high profit margins (a measure of operating efficiency), or from its efficient use of assets (measured by total asset turnover), or from its use of debt financing (measured by financial leverage, equity multiplier)?

Second, the DuPont model can be used to conduct what if scenarios. Should capacity be increased and new workers hired for expected sales growth? Inserting expected wages and sales revenue into the DuPont model, immediately demonstrates how ROA and ROE change. In addition, if management states that its goal is to increase ROE by 10%, the DuPont model can help determine how should the goal be accomplished and what operational or supply chain activities will contribute.

Third, the DuPont model can be used as a risk-planning tool. What if a supplier goes out of business, so a new supplier is needed and shipments must be expedited. How will these changes impact ROE?

Finally, the DuPont model can be used as a sales instrument in business-to-business (B2B) commerce. Prospective customers can see how their ROE could improve if they buy one company's service or product instead of a competitor's.

The idea behind putting the DuPont model into practice is that as the business environment changes (or before it changes), one can understand the effects of these changes on a business. This is accomplished by inserting expected values in the DuPont model while observing changes in ROA and ROE along with other performance ratios.

Of course, many supply chain and operations processes and projects have an impact on ROA and ROE. Some examples of changes include (1) implementing new inventory and transportation IT systems, (2) consolidating or adding distribution centers, (3) implementing lean and quality management programs, and (4) changing suppliers. Each of these can affect ROA and ROE but to different degrees.

To illustrate this, consider the following example. You chose a supplier a few years ago and since then operations have been running smoothly. Upon further investigation, it appears your supplier is not as financially stable as it once was. An economic downturn or even slightly higher interest rates may seriously affect your supplier's ability to deliver the requested quantity of product. You can conduct scenario analysis using the DuPont model. Two scenarios seem reasonable: (1) a steady state position as seen in Figure 6.1 where the supplier continues to deliver as promised, or (2) the supplier is affected by higher interest rates and is unable to borrow additional funds, thus they are unable to produce in the quantities needed (Figure 6.2).

If scenario number two occurs, two outcomes are likely: (1) your revenue declines due to lost sales and (2) your costs increase from finding a new supplier, spending additional time working with your new supplier to coordinate processes and procedures, and from expediting shipments to meet current sales obligations. In this scenario

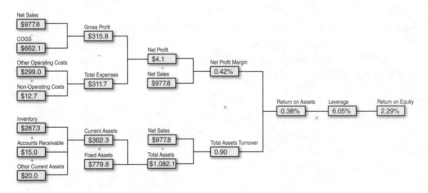

Figure 6.2 Revised DuPont model.

using the DuPont model, if you were to input reasonable estimates of the new values for revenue and cost, you will see the impact in ROE immediately.

Scenario number one, the current situation shows that ROA is 4.52% and ROE is 27.37%.

However, if scenario number two happens, it can be reasonably expected that

1. Revenue declines 1.5% due to lost sales
2. COGS increases 4% because of higher raw materials prices and expedited shipping
3. SG&A increases by 2% due to additional planning and coordination
4. Inventory decreases by 10%

Using new values in the DuPont model shows the resultant changes in performance are substantial. ROA is now 0.38% and ROE is 2.29%.

Adjusting accounts receivable and other current assets does not appreciably change the outcome. By doing this exercise, the gap between operations and supply chain performance and a company's financial performance is bridged. The output communicates how a change in suppliers can affect the company's financial performance.

Capital Budgeting

Capital budgeting is the process of identifying and selecting projects that the company should undertake and the allocation of money to start them. These projects are typically very expensive and long lasting, making it difficult to correct any initial poor acceptance decisions that have been made. Further, projects enable companies to remain competitive. These might be updating equipment, introducing new product lines, or implementing new information technology systems. Careful selection of projects is important if the company is to remain competitive and increase shareholder wealth.

Many quantitative methods are available to assist managers as they select projects that will add value to the company and to their shareholders. Although quantitative methods are helpful, it is important to note that qualitative factors such as corporate social responsibility and sustainability efforts compliment project selection decisions. In the following sections, net present value, internal rate of return, and payback are discussed.

Net Present Value

Companies implement projects to generate future cash flows, which in turn generate shareholder value; however, since companies have limited budgets, management has to decide which projects to undertake that will generate the highest returns. Net present value (NPV) is used to rank and select projects that return the greatest shareholder value. The higher the NPV, the higher the return on shareholder value, thus it would make sense to select the projects with the highest NPV. One caveat remains, while NPV is a quantitative method of deciding which projects to undertake, there may be qualitative factors with greater importance that affect decisions. It is possible that corporate governance, ethics, or environmental sustainability concerns make a project with a lower NPV more attractive to management and to company stakeholders.

NPV uses the concept of present value. Present value implies a dollar in your pocket today is worth more than receiving a dollar tomorrow. Three reasons explain this: (1) risk, (2) inflation, and (3) opportunity cost.

Risk: There is a risk that you will not see your cash again. Some projects have a higher probability of failing or not providing cash inflows than were expected.

Inflation: Inflation cuts into your purchasing power. Today, you can buy $1 worth of goods, but with a 3% yearly inflation rate, next year you can only buy $0.97 worth of goods with $1.

Opportunity cost: If you have cash in your pocket now, you can use it to generate more cash immediately. You might put the money in an interest bearing bank account and start earning interest income right away, or you might buy stock in another company and generate investment income right away. If you give your cash away or spend it somewhere else, you have lost the opportunity to earn income on that cash. For projects, you would expect to spend money upfront to get the project started, and then it is your hope that you would collect lots of cash at a later date once the project is implemented and then subsequently completed. You hope to collect cash in an amount that is at least equal to an amount as if you didn't undertake the project, but instead, put your money elsewhere.

For a new project, management typically spends money in the beginning stages; this is labeled as cash outflow or negative cash flow. Management does not increase shareholder wealth with cash outflows. The company hopes to reap rewards from the project and collect cash later. Generating cash from the project is labeled as cash inflow or positive cash flow. This is when the company generates value and wealth for itself and its shareholders.

Of course, projects have different amounts and timing of cash outflows, inflows, and different risk profiles. If given a choice, most people would rather spend less money upfront and generate higher cash inflows sooner, rather than spending more money now and waiting longer to receive cash inflows. Doing the former will generate higher shareholder value. To place projects on a level playing field, each project's risk profile is used to convert its cash outflows, inflows, and the timing of its cash flows to present values (PV). With this common language, management is able to compare each project and choose the project that provides the highest value to the company.

When using NPV for decision making, there is a need to provide an appropriate discount rate and an accurate estimate of future operating cash flows. The discount rate is a rate that is assigned based on the risk of the project and the cost of capital. The risk of a project is related to the possibility that future cash flows will be less than anticipated. If a risky project is undertaken, there must be a higher reward for taking it on. The discount rate will be higher for riskier projects. Further, if the cost of capital is 10%, the project needs to at least earn that amount to ensure all investors earn a return commensurate with their risk.

The discount rate enables a company to convert its expected future cash flows into today's value. Today's value is known as present value. For example, a company is going to embark on a 3-year project. In the third year, it expects to receive $1,500 (cash inflow) with a cost of capital of 10%. What is the present value of $1,500 the company will receive in 3 years from now? To determine this, use the formula:

$$PV = FV/(1 + r)^y$$

where PV is the present value, FV is the future value, r is the discount rate, and y is the time period when the cash flow is received from now.

$$PV = \$1,500/(1 + 0.10)^3$$
$$PV = \$1,500/1.331 = \$1,126.97$$

This indicates that the PV of $1,500 received in 3 years from now is $1,126.97. Stated another way, $1,126.97 in the company's bank account today is equivalent to receiving $1,500 in 3 years from now. The key point is that management is trying to make decisions based on future sums of cash receivable by transforming them into today's monetary terms.

To continue with this example, the company estimates that it will spend $2,500 this year to get the project running. It also estimates receiving $1,500 in each of the next 3 years from this project. Recall the discount rate is 10%. What is the NPV for this project? The formula to use:

$$NPV = -C_0 + \frac{C_1}{(1+r)^1} + \frac{C_2}{(1+r)^2} + \frac{C_3}{(1+r)^3}$$

where NPV is the net present value, C_i is the cash flow, r is the discount rate, and 0, 1, 2, and 3 are the time periods (years in our example). Notice the cash outflows are designated with a negative sign and cash inflows have a positive sign.

$$NPV = -2500 + \frac{\$1,500}{(1+0.10)^1} + \frac{\$1,500}{(1+0.10)^2} + \frac{\$1,500}{(1+0.10)^3}$$

$$NPV = -2,500 + \frac{\$1,500}{1.1} + \frac{\$1,500}{1.21} + \frac{\$1,500}{1.331}$$

$$NPV = -2,500 + 1,363.64 + 1,239.67 + 1,126.97$$

Adding up all of the present values, the net present value equals:

$$NPV = \$1,230.28$$

Should the company pursue this project? Yes, because NPV is positive. This means that the company is better off in present value terms by undertaking the project—their wealth as measured in today's terms has increased.

Decision rules for NPV are as follows:

1. If NPV is positive, accept the project. The project will add value to the company and shareholders.
2. If NPV is negative, do not accept the project. It will not add value to the company or shareholders.

3. If NPV = 0, the project's cash flows are exactly sufficient to repay the required rate of return to those who invested capital in the company.

4. If NPV is positive for more than one project and the budget is limited, select the projects that maximize total NPV across all positive NPV projects given the budget constraint.

What would happen to the NPV value if the discount rate was higher because the project appears to be more risky than originally thought? NPV would become lower. For example, with a 30% discount rate, NPV = $224, much lower than before. The more future cash flows are discounted because of higher risks or a higher cost of capital, the higher the discount rate will become, resulting in a lower NPV. Alternatively, if a project is less risky and the cost to borrow money is low, a discount rate lower than 10% can be assigned. In this scenario, NPV will increase. It is important to select a representative discount rate for a project. If the rate is inaccurate, a company might find that a project was undertaken when it should not have been, or a project was not undertaken when it should have been.

One of the most challenging aspects of conducting NPV analysis is forecasting future cash flows of a project. Many factors play into these forecasts making it difficult to obtain accurate estimates. Many departments within the organization share in the development of individual forecasts for revenue, costs, and demand.

Items needed for cash flow estimates are as follows:

1. *Revenue*: what price does a company expect to obtain for its products or services?

2. *Demand*: what is the demand forecast for products or services?

3. *Costs and cost savings*: what additional costs will be incurred and will there be a cost savings, if any, from the project?

4. *Taxes*: what is the tax rate and will it change?

5. *Depreciation*: what depreciation method is being used and will it change?

Making accurate cash flow forecasts even more challenging, analysts need to consider other factors such as:

Economic conditions: unemployment and interest rates

Company attributes: brand equity, product and service quality, reliability and responsiveness, and sales force effectiveness

Just as free cash flow is important to company valuation (Chapter 5), it is also important when evaluating projects. Relevant cash flows are used to evaluate projects. Relevant cash flows are the additional cash outflows and inflows that a company experiences if the project is undertaken.

As a reminder from Chapter 5 to calculate free cash flow, operating income (profit) is adjusted for taxes, depreciation, capital expenditures, and any change in working capital.

FCF = (Operating income × [1 – Tax rate] + Depreciation) – Capital expenditure – Change in net operating working capital

Similarly, free cash flow:

FCF = Income from operations + Depreciation – Taxes – Capital spending – Change in working capital

Change in working capital = Change in operating current assets – Change in operating current liabilities.

Operating current assets are those assets used to operate the business such as cash, inventory, and accounts receivable. Operating current liabilities are those liabilities that occur due to operations, such as accounts payable and accruals.

Estimating FCFs from a project is the culmination of estimating income from operations. This estimate is based on accurate estimates of revenue, costs, and expenses. Since depreciation is a noncash expense, it is added back into FCF. In addition, because cash is actually paid out in taxes, capital spending, and working capital, each reducing FCFs, these items are subtracted from the FCF.

When conducting NPV analysis, the terms nominal dollars and real dollars will be part of the conversation. Nominal dollars include the effects of inflation, whereas real dollars remove the effects of inflation. Nominal dollars are the actual amount of money making up cash flows; real dollars reflect the purchasing power of the cash flows. Real dollars are found by adjusting the nominal dollars for the rate of inflation. Inflation affects both projected cash flows and the discount rate. While either real or nominal values can be used in NPV calculations, nominal values are used more often. If projected cash flows are in real dollars, the discount rate used should be the real rate. If projected cash flows are in nominal dollars, the discount rate used should be the nominal rate.

Internal Rate of Return

Like NPV, internal rate of return (IRR) is a quantitative method used for project selection. IRR is popular among managers because it is easy to use. Unlike selecting a discount rate for NPV analysis, IRR is the discount rate that forces NPV to equal $0. If an analyst tries to find a discount rate using trial and error for an NPV calculation to make the present value of future cash flows $0 (NPV = $0), this discount rate would be the IRR.

$$\text{NPV} = -C_0 + \frac{C_1}{(1 + \text{IRR})^1} + \frac{C_2}{(1 + \text{IRR})^2} + \frac{C_3}{(1 + \text{IRR})^3} = \$0$$

Using the previous NPV example, IRR equals 36.31%. If a discount rate of 36.31% was assigned for the previous NPV example, NPV would equal $0.

Projects should be pursued if IRR is greater than the required rate of return, which encompasses the cost of capital and project risk. The required rate of return is also referred to as the hurdle rate. If IRR hurdles or is higher than the required rate of return, the project should be selected. Hurdling the required rate of return implies that there will be a surplus of funds after repaying the capital. The surplus of funds creates wealth for shareholders.

IRR does have drawbacks. One disadvantage of using IRR is that it assumes all cash flows will be reinvested at the project's IRR (discount rate). In reality these rates fluctuate, especially with longer term projects. IRR can be modified to mitigate this shortfall. Modified internal rate of return (MIRR) assumes that all cash flows are reinvested at the company's cost of capital, which is a more realistic view. IRR has another drawback: when cash flows turn positive and negative multiple times over the life of the project, as is the case for long-term projects, IRR does not provide an accurate picture.

So far examples have focused on independent projects. Independent projects are those whose cash flows do not affect one another. Mathematically, the NPV and IRR calculations will lead to the same accept or reject conclusions in these instances. Logically, one would choose the projects with positive NPVs or rank the projects first and select the projects with the highest NPVs. Likewise, projects with IRRs above the hurdle rate would be chosen or the projects would be ranked and the projects with the highest IRRs above the hurdle rate selected first.

Mutually exclusive projects, projects where one is chosen and another rejected, can lead to problems when ranking is based on IRR. The project size and the timing of cash flows affect NPV and IRR rankings. When comparing mutually exclusive projects, NPV should be used instead of IRR.

Payback Period

The payback period is the estimated time it will take to recoup the initial investment in a project. When comparing two projects based on payback periods, the project with a shorter payback period is more desirable than the project with a longer payback period.

As an example (Table 6.1), if the initial investment in a project is $2,500 and the expectation is to receive $1,500 for the next 3 years, how long will it take to recoup the $2,500 initial investment? At time zero ($t = 0$), the initial outlay is $2,500. At year 1, $1,500 is received. The cumulative cash flow through year 1 is the initial outlay of $2,500 plus $1,500 (−$2,500 + $1,500 = − $1,000). At year 2, the cumulative cash flow is the previous year's cumulative cash flow plus year 2 cash inflow of another $1,500 (− $1,000 + $1,500 = $500). By year 2, the initial $2,500 has been recouped, along with an additional $500. If in the second year, the cash flows were evenly distributed throughout the year, the payback period can be determined from the following formula:

Payback period = Year before full recovery + (Unrecovered cost at start of the year/Cash flow during the year)

Payback = 1 + ($1,000/$1,500) = 1.67 years

Some companies use another version of the payback period method. It is called the discounted payback period method, which considers the time value of money. The discount rate that is commonly used is the cost of capital for the company. Using the previous example from the NPV section, cash flows are discounted using a 10% discount rate (Table 6.2).

Payback = 1 + ($1,136/$1,240) = 1.92 years

Table 6.1 Payback Period

Project	Time 0	Year 1	Year 2	Year 3
Net cash flow ($)	−2,500	1,500	1,500	1,500
Cumulative cash flow ($)	−2,500	−1,000	500	2,000

Table 6.2 Discounted Payback Period

Project	Time 0	Year 1	Year 2	Year 3
Net cash flow ($)	–2,500	1,500	1,500	1,500
Discounted cash flow ($)	–2,500	1,364	1,240	1,127
Cumulative cash flow ($)	–2,500	–1,136	104	1,231

The payback period is longer when cash flows are discounted. When ranking projects based on these two variants of the payback period method, there can be conflicting rankings. The payback period method is the same as breaking even. The regular payback period method shows when cash flows equal cash outlay. Contrastingly, the discounted payback period method shows when cash flows equal cash outlay plus debt and equity costs.

Using the payback period method has several benefits. It uncovers the liquidity of the project, is easy to understand, and is intuitive. It also answers how long cash will be tied up in the project. One drawback for the regular payback period method: it does not take into consideration the time value of money. A drawback for both payback period methods is it ignores cash flows that occur after the payback. This can lead to rejecting positive NPV projects and/or accepting negative NPV projects.

Risk and Decision Making

Forecasts are often used in business decisions. Because forecasts are developed using assumptions, the uncertainty makes forecasts less accurate. To reduce the likelihood of making poor decisions, managers use decision trees and simulation tools to examine alternatives and a range of possibilities.

Decision Trees

Decision trees are useful when sequential decisions are made. They force decision makers to carefully consider the assumptions being made. In addition, decision trees incorporate any uncertainty that surrounds the assumptions in the decision-making process. Decision trees are used in many industries where multiple scenarios exist. Lawyers use them to determine whether or not to appeal verdicts; oil companies use them to determine whether or not to drill for oil;

and manufacturers use them to guide their new product development decisions.

To develop and use decision trees for decision making, three components are necessary: (1) more than one alternative (a choice of options), (2) probabilities of events occurring, and 3) payoffs (NPV, profit, and cost) for each alternative.

How are decision trees used in practice? The following example shows how to use a decision tree. Consider this situation: a management team must decide on the size of a new manufacturing facility to construct. They have two choices: (1) they will construct a small facility, or (2) they will construct a large facility. To make the best decision about the facility's size, the team recognizes that accurate demand forecasts are important. They also know that demand forecasts are never completely accurate. The management team has collected information regarding payoffs (cash flows, revenue projections, demand forecasts) and the probability of demand either being high or low. Management has constructed a decision tree to help determine what to choose to maximize company and shareholder value.

With this knowledge, it is time to construct the decision tree. Decision trees are built from left to right and solved from right to left. In Figure 6.3, box number one indicates that this is decision number one. Should a large or small facility be built? The circles in the decision tree indicate a chance of something occurring. There is a 70% chance that demand could be high and there is a 30% chance that demand could be low. Box number two indicates sequential decision number two is to be made. The second stage decision depends on the decision for stage one and if demand is high or low. For instance, if a small facility is built and demand is high, a decision needs to be made. Decision makers may do nothing, add extra shifts to meet the higher demand, or expand the small facility. Each decision has an expected payoff associated with it. In this example, NPVs indicate the payoff.

Solve the decision tree one branch at a time. Following the branches from right to left, there is a payoff and a probability of this payoff occurring.

> Branch 1: Small facility and low demand: $30,000 × 0.30 = $9,000
>
> Branch 2: Small facility and high demand: $45,000 × 0.70 = $31,500

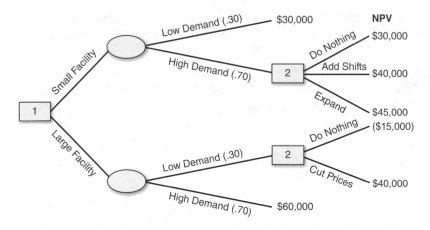

Figure 6.3 Decision tree.

Why choose the $45,000 option to expand the facility and not the $40,000 add extra shifts or the $30,000 do nothing options? When choosing among alternatives, select the alternative with the highest payoff.

> Branch 3: Large facility and low demand: $40,000 × 0.30 = $12,000

> Branch 4: Large facility and high demand: $60,000 × 0.70 = $42,000

A weighted average was computed for the two alternatives: (1) build small and (2) build large. The alternative with the highest expected value is chosen. The second alternative has the highest expected value with $54,000, thus the build a large facility is chosen.

> Alternative 1: Build a small facility (branches 1 and 2): $9,000 + $31,500 = $40,500

> Alternative 2: Build a large facility (branches 3 and 4): $12,000 + $42,000 = $54,000

Simulation Models

Simulation models are mathematical models that try to replicate realistic scenarios. Simulation can be applied to a variety of financial and operational settings. Continuing with the NPV example, NPV is only as good as the estimates of its inputs, such as revenue, costs, and demand patterns. These inputs are inherently uncertain. With this uncertainty present, each input is based on a best guess, resulting in a best guess NPV.

Simulation, on the contrary, incorporates uncertainty into the input variables. Simulation forces an understanding of the probability distributions that surround the variables. Simulation models are then performed thousands of times—called replications. The output provides a range of NPV possibilities. The range provides all possibilities from worst-case to best-case scenarios. In the NPV example, cash flows are estimated to be $1,500 for 3 years; however, cash flows could realistically be higher or lower than $1,500. What if cash flow estimates and resultant NPV were based on revenue projections using a price of $20 per unit, but the units could be sold between $10 and $30, considering competitive and market forces. Simulation will show a range of NPVs based on the distribution of prices.

Simulation models have several advantages. One advantage of simulation models is the full range of values provided, instead of just one value. A second advantage of simulation models is that managers can experiment with changing inputs without actually physically changing anything. For instance, airline managers do not have to physically change interiors of airplanes or configurations of ticket counters to understand how process changes and layouts might affect boarding or check-in times. Another advantage of simulation models is that managers can create relatively accurate depictions of what could happen in real life using less data. These advantages save companies large amounts of both time and money.

Break-Even Analysis

Think about new products that your company is considering launching or even a list of current products that it sells. Each has fixed and variable costs for production and a selling price. Variable costs are associated with producing additional units. As production levels rise and fall, so do total variable costs. Fixed costs are associated with producing products, too. However, total fixed costs generally do not change based on the volume of production. Fixed operating costs incurred during normal operation of the facility include rent, adding equipment, racking, automation, paying taxes, and paying salaries. These are fixed amounts and are paid whether or not 1 or 100 units are made.

Break-even analysis provides managers with information needed for introducing new products, offering sales promotions, and entering new markets. Managers would like to know how many units must be sold to break-even? The break-even number is simply the volume that must be sold to cover fixed and variable costs at a given price per unit. At break-even, the total cost of earning revenue equals revenue; the company is not earning a profit, but is not losing money either. It is crucial for managers to understand their fixed and variable costs; otherwise, disastrous competitive decisions could be made. If competitors are reducing their prices and a manager tries to chase them to the bottom, then the manager must know how low prices can go before profits turn to losses?

The general form of the break-even formula is:

Break-even point = Fixed costs/(Unit selling price – Variable costs)

Figure 6.4 shows the relationship between revenue and fixed and variable costs. Revenue and total costs increase as each unit is produced and sold, while fixed costs remain constant. Total costs combine variable and fixed costs. At some point total revenue equals total costs. This is the break-even point (break-even quantity).

As an example, a company is selling headphones for $150.00 per unit, with fixed costs at $10,000 per month, and variable costs at $16.50 per unit. How many headphones need to sell each month to break-even?

Break-even point = $10,000/($150 – $16.50) = 75 units

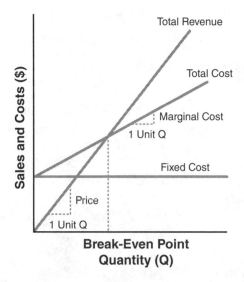

**Break-Even Point
Quantity (Q)**

Figure 6.4 Break-even analysis.

To break-even, 75 headphones must sell at $150 per month to break-even. If less than 75 units are sold at this price, then the company will incur a loss. However, if more than 75 units are sold at this price, a gross profit will be earned. The market will determine if it is possible to sell 75 headphones at $150 each month. Using the break-even formula and simulation allows management to experiment with cost and revenue changes. For instance, if the headphones could be sold for $160 per unit, then only 70 units per month need to sell to break-even. Another option is to drop prices because of competition. How many headphones need to sell to break-even if prices drop to $125 per unit? The answer is approximately 92 units per month. The next question to ask is related to capacity—is there capacity to produce and sell 92 units per month? Going a step further, management wants to know how reduced costs impact the break-even point?

Now, examine the denominator of the break-even formula:

Contribution margin per unit = Unit selling price – Variable costs

Contribution margin per unit is the remaining amount of revenue after all variable cost are deducted.

Contribution margin per unit = $150 – $16.50 = $133.50

A contribution margin of $133.50 implies that the company has $133.50 from each headphone sale to cover fixed costs and contribute to net income.

Contribution margin ratio is also a popular ratio among managers.

Contribution margin ratio = Contribution margin per unit ÷ Unit selling price

Contribution margin ratio = $133.50 ÷ $150 = 0.89 = 89%

An 89% contribution margin ratio implies that $0.89 of each dollar in revenue is available to cover fixed costs and contribute to net income.

Another useful detail that managers like to know is the revenue required to break-even. This is found by

Revenue break-even point = Units sold at break-even × Selling price

Revenue break-even point = 75 × $150 = $11,250

In many cases, management sets a target net income level. Then, management needs to determine how many units are needed in addition to how many units need to sell or the sales revenue to target.

How can management determine how many units need to sell or the amount of sales revenue needed meet the net income target? The contribution margin can be used to answer this question.

Required sales in units = (Fixed costs + Target net income)
÷ Contribution margin per unit
= ($10,000 + $15,000) ÷ $133.50 ≈ 187 units

Required sales in dollars = (Fixed costs + Target net income)
÷ Contribution margin ratio
= ($10,000 + $15,000)/0.89 ≈ $28,090

Break-Even and Make or Buy Decisions

Alternately, break-even analysis can be used as a make or buy and as a supplier comparison tool. Businesses need to determine whether or not to outsource manufacturing or other business processes based on production and facility capacity requirements. Break-even analysis can be useful in these decisions. In these types of scenarios, fixed and variable costs and expected production volumes are the focuses, not necessarily the price per unit. Break-even analysis is referred to as cost–volume analysis in such cases.

Cost–volume analysis becomes useful when fixed and variable costs can be identified and there is a need to review costs based on production levels. The better option, make or buy, becomes apparent over a range of production requirements when using cost–volume analysis.

The cost to produce items is a function of fixed and variable costs in addition to the number of units produced (Table 6.3).

Total cost to produce = Fixed cost + (Variable cost × Total units produced)

Next, the break-even point and total cost to make or buy are:

Total cost to make = $1,500,000 + ($125 × Total units produced)
Total cost to buy = $500,000 + ($275 × Total units produced)

Table 6.3 Estimated Costs and Annual Requirements

Costs	Make	Buy
Fixed ($)	1,500,000	500,000
Variable ($)	125	250
Annual requirements (unit)	10,000	

Break-even in units:

Total cost to make = Total cost to buy

$$\$1,500,000 + 125(x) = \$500,000 + \$250(x)$$

$$\$1,000,000 = \$125(x)$$

$$x = 8,000 \text{ units}$$

Total cost at break-even = $\$1,500,000 + (\$125 \times 8,000 \text{ units})$
= $\$2,500,000$

Or

Total cost at break-even = $\$500,000 + (\$250 \times 8,000 \text{ units})$
= $\$2,500,000$

If the monthly requirements are 10,000 units and our break-even is 8,000 units, should production be outsourced or should it continue in house (Figure 6.5)?

Total cost to make = $\$1,500,000 + \$125 \times 10,000 \text{ units}$
= $\$2,750,000$

Total cost to buy = $\$500,000 + \$275 \times 10,000 \text{ units} = \$3,250,000$

The difference in cost between the two options is $500,000 and favors keeping production in house.

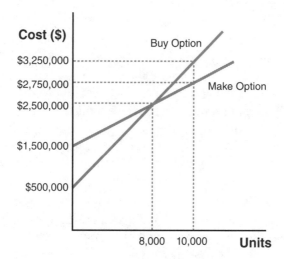

Figure 6.5 Cost–volume analysis and make or buy decision.

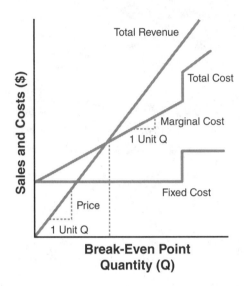

Figure 6.6 Cost–volume analysis and nonlinear costs.

One assumption often made is that costs are linear; however, that is not necessarily the case. It is possible for fixed costs to increase in steps as volume increases (Figure 6.6). Adding capacity as sales increase results in fixed costs increasing from activities such as adding shifts, labor, and equipment. In addition, small companies with low volume output may not be able to obtain quantity discounts for purchases, but as the company grows, they will able to do so. Large companies with increasing production levels might see wages increase substantially because of overtime pay.

As the production volume increases, total costs increase. However, as production increases, the total cost per unit tends to decline as fixed costs are spread out over a higher number of units produced. This phenomenon is called economy of scale. Economies of scale become apparent when the cost to produce a unit declines as the volume of production increases. If the cost per unit increases as volume increases, this is referred to as diseconomies of scale.

In practice, it can be difficult to compute an exact break-even point because of the varying demands of customers, differences in selling prices, fluctuating costs, and changing capacity levels. Nonetheless, break-even analysis is a useful exercise that provides many insights into a business.

Real Options

Many project investment decisions are the result of significant analysis of various projects. The decision is based on analyses and the assumption that the organization commits large sums of money upfront to a project, and if the project fails, the company has lost most if not all of the investment. This approach can be risky as the business environment changes. The viability of a project can be seriously questioned if the assumptions that led to a project being selected have changed. In the same way, a project that appeared unfeasible can become viable with changes in the business environment.

One way to minimize project risk and to increase the chance of project success is to use real options reasoning. Using this reasoning means investments in projects are less upfront and become greater as projects move forward. As the project moves forward, the assumptions made early on are updated with current information with which management can make further project related decisions. Using current information diminishes the uncertainty surrounding the project, which means less project risk. Management can therefore make more informed decisions about continued investment in the project, accelerating the project timeline, delaying further investment, or ending the project all together. By using real options, management is able to make sequential decisions based on current information, which reduces project uncertainty and risk.

Summary

Management decision making is broad and complex. This chapter introduced common tools management uses when making financial decisions. These tools help communicate the ways in which supply chain and operations projects affect the company financially. The DuPont model is useful in demonstrating how the company's financial performance changes relative to operational performance and risks potentially occurring. Then capital budgeting and project selection tools such as NPV and IRR were introduced. They identify if projects add value to the company and its shareholders. Payback period was then discussed. It reveals the liquidity of the project. Next, decision trees and simulation were discussed, showing how risk and probability distributions may be incorporated into managerial decision making. Finally, break-even analysis and real options conclude the chapter, showing how analysis informs decisions about project investment.

7

Project Management

Companies undertake projects for several reasons. Projects can improve the company's value, increase shareholder wealth, and help it remain competitive in the market place. Projects contribute to these goals by increasing cash inflows and minimizing cash outflows. Managing the projects is a critical part of the company's success. If a company routinely chooses unsuitable projects or sees projects fail often, the company's financial performance and reputation can be severely damaged. Therefore, successful project selection, implementation, and completion are of the utmost importance.

Projects vary greatly in scale, scope, and area of emphasis, even though all are designed to improve the company's operation in some way. Implementation of IT projects such as transportation planning, warehouse management, and contract management systems are found within companies. These types of projects are intended to improve organizational communication and efficiency throughout the supply chain. Other projects that are centered within the company may focus on:

1. Improving the customer experience
2. Improving the research and development process (faster new product launches)
3. Six-sigma improvements
4. Constructing or remolding facilities (new distribution strategies)

Some companies are project companies; their entire existence is based on projects. Construction companies are examples of this. They construct buildings, homes, bridges, and roads. Other companies construct roller coasters, while still others produce movies or music. The projects serve external customers and so the projects are actually completed outside the company, not for company improvement.

An important note in this regard is that projects are different from processes. Processes are the day-to-day, repetitive tasks that a company uses to function. Projects have more defined boundaries. Typical projects are as follows:

1. Are complex, one-time endeavors
2. Have limited and defined budgets
3. Have limited resources
4. Have limited time frames with defined start and end dates
5. Have clear goals

Managing Projects

The management of projects is critical. A project that appeared to be an excellent opportunity for the company can have negative consequences if the management is subpar. This happens all too frequently. As an example, look to the convenience store/gas station corporations, WAWA, Inc. and RaceTrac. The companies compete against each other and often build stores in close proximity. At one location in Southeast Florida, both started constructing stores at about the same time. One company finished their store months sooner than the other company. With project management strategies, one company executed their project more efficiently. A company that manages resources, time, and risk more effectively will come out on top. When a store is completed, revenues start flowing faster, loans can be paid off more quickly, and interest expenses can be reduced. Companies that outperform competitors through execution of projects create an advantage.

Understanding effective execution of projects is critical to project management. Consider the WAWA example. A subset of the WAWA construction project might look like this:

1. Obtain construction permits (36 days)
2. Hire subcontractors (36 days)
3. Excavate the land (21 days)
4. Pour the concrete foundation (7 days)

There are four tasks to be completed and a time estimate for the completion of each task. The question arises, how long will it take to complete all four tasks? The answer depends on how a project manager approaches the problem. One project manager would add the time

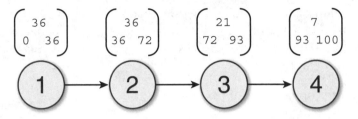

Figure 7.1 WAWA project. (36 days + 36 days + 21 days + 7 days) = 100 days.

estimates and indicate that it will take 100 days to complete all of the tasks. As each task is completed, the next one begins (Figure 7.1).

A second project manager, approaching the problem differently, might provide a different estimate. Obtaining permits and hiring sub-contractors at the same time can reduce the total days of the project (Figure 7.2). With this methodology, the project would only take 64 days.

A third project manager, perhaps one with more experience in project management, would anticipate times differently. Obtaining permits and hiring subcontractors can happen at the same time, as with the second manager; however, excavating the land will take 17 days instead of 21 days (Figure 7.3). The result is project completion in 60 days. Although the third network diagram does not change from the second network diagram, the activity times do.

Which of the three managers is correct? Each option is feasible; however, one option may be a more logical choice than the other two. The assertion is that companies that plan and execute projects more effectively generate benefits and value faster than their competitors.

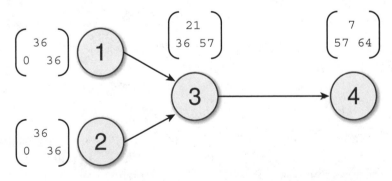

Figure 7.2 WAWA project revision one. (36 days + 21 days + 7 days) = 64 days.

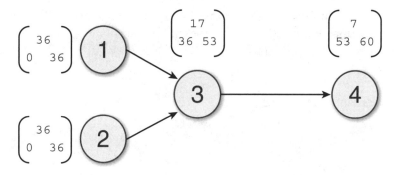

Figure 7.3 WAWA project revision two. (36 days + 17 days + 7 days) = 60 days

Reducing the number of days to complete projects benefits the company, shareholders, and customers. Effective project management minimizes costs and makes shareholders and customers happy. Knowing this, the 60-day estimate is the logical choice.

Wages, equipment rentals, and loan interest are typical areas where costs can be minimized. Minimizing cost, though, is not the only reason a company may want to finish a project early. A company may be awarded a bonus if they deliver a project early. Costly monetary penalties can be avoided by completing the project on time or early. With early project completion, cash inflows can begin and allow the company to break even in a shorter period of time.

Project Success and Failure

Successful completion is not easily achieved. A variety of challenges can derail a project. How is a project's success measured? A project can be considered successful when the stated goals and objectives are reached, it is delivered on time, it remains on budget, and it delivers on the specifications and value proposition promised.

The first step toward a successful project is selecting the right project. Then implementing it expertly, and finally, being open minded enough to learn from the process. Individual stakeholders determine success in different ways; many times these are conflict with each other. Consumers are concerned with product safety; suppliers are interested in open communication and predictability; government focuses on regulatory compliance; shareholders are interested in profitability; and management may be looking for ways to achieve bonuses.

A multitude of projects have been conducted and with some examination, common traits of successful projects emerge. Successful projects contain the following:

1. Communication flows free
2. Regular reporting
3. Stakeholder updates
4. Active risk management
5. Division of work into manageable parts

Similarly, looking closely at the projects reveals commonalities that often lead to failure. Active project management is critical to a project's success. Without proper active project management costs increase, delivery dates are missed, and customers and stakeholders quickly become dissatisfied. Common failure points include the following:

1. Frequent changes in project scope
2. Ineffective planning and scheduling
3. Ineffective cost estimation and control
4. Ineffective risk management
5. Unclear objectives
6. Poor leadership
7. Poor team commitment
8. Delays in problem solving
9. Delays in communication
10. Inaccurate and untimely information
11. Under funding projects

To recap, there are many advantages to successfully completing a project. Companies can maintain a positive image in their industry. They can also benefit from higher-than-expected cash inflows through cost savings and increased revenue. In addition, they reduce the chance for penalties or reduced shareholder value from lawsuits or from prolonged debt financing (interest payments).

Project Selection

In general, a company's finance department is responsible for capital budgeting. Smaller companies may be without dedicated finance department or project office. In these instances, the company will use a team of managers throughout the company to determine which projects to undertake. Project proposals come from all areas of the organization, thus there is great competition for a limited amount of dollars. Projects with the greatest chance of creating company and shareholder value from increased cash inflows are most likely to be undertaken. However, not all project proposals are created equally or ethically. To win acceptance of a proposal, bias can be built into the proposal by stating overly optimistic revenue and cost saving projections. Business projects are competitive as some managers see their chances for promotion hinging on project acceptance. Whether intentional or unintentional, such biases create a risk for the company. If the projected outcomes are unrealistic, the potential exists to hinder the company. Even with accurate projections, some companies are reluctant to undertake even the most promising high-value projects realizing that the initial investment will make their financial ratios decline. Such a view is shortsighted, but not uncommon in business.

Previous chapters have discussed extensively how companies choose projects. Financial analysis tools such as NPV, IRR, payback period, and ROI are commonly used when selecting projects. These tools allow company decision makers to identify projects that add value to the company and should be undertaken. In reality, a company has limited resources, such as cash, and cannot undertake all value-adding projects presented. There must be a way for management to determine which projects to take on. A company's objective should be to maximize NPV without exceeding its budget. Two tools, integer programming and profitability index (PI), can be used to rank and select projects based on budget constraints.

Table 7.1 displays five potential value-adding projects with positive NPVs and profitability indices. However, the cash needed to undertake all five projects is higher than the cash available.

Profitability index is related to NPV analysis. For simple projects that have an initial cash outlay followed by a series of cash inflows, profitability index is a good way to rank and choose projects when it is not possible to select all projects. Profitability index is the present value of the project's cash inflows divided by the project's initial cash outflow.

$$PI = \frac{\dfrac{C_1}{(1+r)^1} + \dfrac{C_2}{(1+r)^2} + \dfrac{C_3}{(1+r)^3} + \cdots + \dfrac{C_n}{(1+r)^n}}{CF_0}$$

Table 7.1 Selection of Projects Using Integer Programming and Profitability Index

Project Description	Project	Cash Required	NPV	Quantity	Total Cash Required	Total NPV	PI
Transportation management system	1	$4,500	$10,000	1	$4,500	$10,000	1.22
Updating recycling recovery system	2	$5,000	$10,500	0	$0	$0	1.10
Warehouse management system	3	$5,500	$12,000	0	$0	$0	1.18
Refit trucks w/natural gas	4	$6,500	$14,000	1	$6,500	$14,000	1.15
Network planning system	5	$6,500	$18,000	1	$6,500	$18,000	1.77
Budget		$17,500		3	$17,500	$42,000	

Using an example from an earlier chapter, estimate the expected cash inflows and then compute their present values. For example, the expected cash inflow for period one is $1,500. It is then converted to a present value using a 10% discount rate.

$$PI = \frac{\dfrac{\$1,500}{(1 + 0.10)^1} + \dfrac{\$1,500}{(1 + 0.10)^2} + \dfrac{\$1,500}{(1 + 0.10)^3}}{\$2,500}$$

The PV for period one cash inflows is $1,363.64. Sum each of the three years' present values and divide by the initial cash outflow (initial investment) of $2,500.

$$PI = \frac{\$1,363.64 + \$1,239.67 + \$1,126.97}{\$2,500}$$

The profitability index equals

$$PI = 1.49$$

A profitability index greater than 1 indicates the PV of cash flows is greater than the investment. This leads to a decision to accept the project. Notice, too, that if the profitability index is greater than 1, NPV will be greater than 0, thus PI and NPV lead to the same decision to accept or reject an individual project.

From the integer programming analysis (Table 7.1), projects 1, 4, and 5 should be selected. Given the budget of $17,500, this provides for a total NPV of $42,000. Any other combination reduces NPV or exceeds the budget. Profitability index analysis reveals that projects 5, then 1, and then 3 should be undertaken. Other projects should be declined. A company will take the highest profitability index projects until it reaches the allotted budget. By doing these three projects in this order, the company reaches a cash budget of $16,500 with $1,000 remaining. No other projects can be undertaken because projects 2 and 4 require more than $1,000 cash. The NPV total is $40,000.

Although financial analysis is important in project selection, other factors should also be considered. Successful project selection factors should include

1. Risks that hinder project success and completion
   a. Organizational
   b. Financial
   c. Development
2. Internal operating issues
   a. Ability to execute and implement the project
   b. Changes in operating and manufacturing facilities
   c. Workforce training and development
3. Ability to finance debt during project execution

Before selecting projects from the portfolio of projects in front of them, management should look at the project's strategic fit with the organization, the timing of cash flows, and the availability of company capabilities, skills, and expertise. For a company to implement projects, it needs resources, qualified project managers, and competent and available team members. Moreover, at the end of the project selection and evaluation process, managers and executives have to answer: (1) can we do it and (2) should we do it?

Project Implementation

Project implementation is an area where operations professionals shine and have a significant impact on the company's financial success (or failure). If a project is executed well, the likelihood of budget overruns is reduced, as are delayed cash inflows, and dissatisfied stakeholders. Operations professionals are tasked with:

1. Estimating activity times
2. Developing a project network
3. Reducing activity times
4. Reducing overall project duration
5. Managing risks

From the previous section of this chapter, the transportation management system (TMS) was selected as a project to undertake. One of the responsibilities of the project manager is to develop a project network, identifying the activities that need to be accomplished and how long each activity will take to complete. Table 7.2 shows a subset of a TMS implementation project for demonstration purposes. The table identifies the project's activities, expected activity times, and associated variances of the activity times.

Activity times are incredibly difficult to estimate. However, estimating accurate activity times is incredibly important. Accurate estimations can

1. Set reasonable expectations for the project's completion date
2. Estimate costs more accurately
3. Allocate resources appropriately
4. Predict break-even and cash flows with greater confidence

Accurate activity time estimation is a product of learning from past projects, though in many cases there is not a lot of history from

Table 7.2 Project Time Estimates in Days

Activity	Activity Number	Optimistic	Most Likely	Pessimistic	Expected Time	Variance
Migration	1	30	36	40	35.67	2.78
Deployment	2	28	30	35	30.50	1.36
Test	3	15	17	18	16.83	0.25
Customer handoff	4	6	7	11	7.50	0.69
Critical path					60.00	3.72

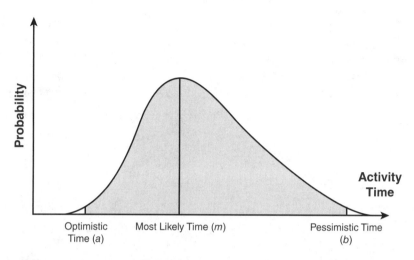

Figure 7.4 Distribution of three time estimates.(*Source: Heizer J and Render B, Operations Management: Sustainability in the Supply Chain*, 11th ed. Upper Saddle River, New Jersey: Prentice Hall; 2013.)

which to learn. Various techniques to estimate activity times exist, one of which will be discussed next. One technique used more often than other predictive methods is to have a team of experts estimate activity times. The team estimates activity times by first identifying three possible completion times for each activity. They will estimate a pessimistic completion time where difficulties with the activity are likely, thus delaying its completion. Next, they will estimate a most likely completion time. This is the most probable time to complete the activity. Finally, they will estimate an optimistic completion time where few to no difficulties will occur, and the activity may be completed early. Figure 7.4 provides an example of the three estimates. There is a higher probability of completing the activity in the most likely time frame, while there is a lower probability of completing activities much earlier. Likewise, in this situation, there is a lower probability of having to extend activity duration to complete it. Notice that the distribution is skewed. The most likely time can move between the optimistic and pessimistic times. It does not have to be centered between the two.

After the three estimates are determined, the following formula is used to calculate an overall expected activity completion time using the three time estimates:

$$t = \frac{a + 4m + b}{6}$$

Take, for example, activity 1, migration (Table 7.2). The experts have estimated three times in which this activity could be completed. They expect the migration activity to most likely be completed in 36 days, but it could take as long as 40 days if things do not go as planned or it could be completed in 30 days if things go well. Using the formula, the expected time to complete the migration activity is 35.67 days.

$$\frac{30 + 4(36) + 40}{6} = 35.67 \text{ days}$$

Management needs to recognize that the length of an activity will vary. This method of estimation helps examine risks that may cause delays in completing an activity or worse, the entire project. Included in the estimated activity times are risks associated with delays. Delays can be caused by weather and natural disasters, funding, the use of low cost labor, scope adjustment, and changes in the project.

Quantifying the variability provides insight into the range of possible completion times. Knowing this will help the company manage resources effectively and control costs and spending. Activities with the highest variance, which is a measure of risk, contain the greatest concern for project managers. These are the activities that run the risk of not being completed on time. Cost and time overruns are likely if these activities are not managed well.

The variance of each activity is found by using the following formula:

$$\sigma^2 = \frac{(b - a)^2}{36}$$

Continuing with the migration example, the variance for migration is

$$\frac{(40 - 30)^2}{36} = 2.78 \text{ days}$$

The migration activity has the highest variance of each of the four activities, thus the activity needs a higher level of attention by the project manager.

After computing each activity's expected completion time and variance, the next step is to create a project network diagram. Remember

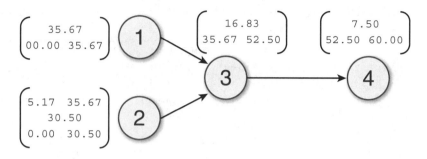

Figure 7.5 TMS project network diagram.

that the development of the project network is critically important. A poorly designed network can cost the company a large sum of money by extending a project unnecessarily.

Figure 7.5 shows the four activities for the TMS project implementation, including the expected activity times that were calculated.

As the project's network diagram shows, projects will have many paths. To complete a project, the activities in the project must be completed along some particular path. The paths are determined by which activities must be done before others can start. This particular project has two paths: path 1-3-4 and path 2-3-4. Notice that each activity contains the time the activity can start, how long it is estimated that it will take to complete, and when the activity is expected to be completed. Take activity 1, for example, which starts at time 0. The estimate is 35.67 days for completion, thus this activity should be completed 35.67 days from now. Activity 3 can start when activity 1 is completed (and activity 2, which will be completed 30.50 days from now). Since activity 1 ends in 35.67 days from now and activity 2 ends in 30.50 days from now, activity 3 can start in 35.67 days. Add 35.67 + 16.83 (the time expected for activity 3 to take) to find the estimate for finishing activity 3: 52.50 days after the project was started. Notice that activity 4 shows an end time of 60 days, which is how long the entire project is expected to last. By adding up the activity times for each path, one can see that path 1-3-4 is expected to take 60 days, whereas path 2-3-4 is expected to take 54.83 days.

Path 1-3-4 is the longest path and is considered the critical path. At least one path in every project network is considered the critical path. It is critical because it is the longest path and any delay in any one of the activities in this path will cause the entire project to be delayed. The critical path determines how long the project will take to complete.

It is important to identify the critical path because if activities on the critical path do not have high priority or are not managed well, there is a risk that the project will be delayed. However, if the activities on noncritical paths are not actively managed, this too could delay the project.

Look back to the TMS implementation example (Figure 7.5) and notice that activity 2 has two starting dates: time 0 and 5.17. Activity 2 can be started at the same time as activity 1 (time 0), or it can be started 5.17 days later. How can this be? Why 5.17 days later? Remember that for activity 3 to start, activities 1 and 2 must be completed. If both activities need to be completed by 35.67 days, and activity 2 takes only 30.50 days to complete, activity 2's starting date could be delayed (35.67 − 30.50 = 5.17 days) until 5.17 days after the project's start. The difference between when it is possible to start an activity and when it must be started called slack time. Activity 2 has 5.17 days of slack time in it. Also, notice that all activities on the critical path have zero slack time. If activity 2 is delayed beyond 5.17 days, then the entire project will be delayed.

Why does this matter? There are implications to identify which activities have slack time and those that do not. The real driver in these situations is when cash is being spent. Remember that when using NPV and IRR analysis for the financial feasibility of projects, the timing of cash inflows and outflows is an important consideration. For the sake of learning, consider delaying the start of activity 2. By delaying activity 2, some of the resources (e.g., people) that are no longer needed for activity 1 can be used for the second activity, thus reducing the number of people and wages necessary. If, on the contrary, there are no additional resources to borrow from activity 1, spending money on wages can wait until later. By managing the timing of cash outflows effectively, the risk of running out of cash before the project ends is reduced. Better yet, the cash can be used for other business needs.

To further illustrate why waiting may be beneficial, recall the WAWA example. Activity 3 is excavating land and activity 4 is pouring concrete. It is entirely possible to bring in the excavation equipment and the concrete trucks, along with workers and needed inventory early on in the construction process, but should that be done? By practicing just-in-time philosophy, there is potential to alleviate space, inventory, and cash flow concerns. There might not be enough space at the construction site to accommodate all of these pieces at once. Spending cash is also a consideration. Is the cash available to be spent, or should the company not hold the cash until it must be spent? Spending now requires the company to buy inventory and pay wages long before the materials and labor are needed.

Project Completion

Inevitably, the request to move up the completion date will come from someone involved. Reducing activity and project times is an important function of project and operations managers. Of course, there are good reasons to speed up the completion of projects; however, the benefits should outweigh the costs of doing so. Shortening projects can result in bonuses. It also allows the company to avoid late penalties, start cash inflows sooner, create company value more quickly, and free up resources, allowing the reallocation of resources to new or upcoming projects. Project duration can be reduced through careful network planning, eliminating unnecessary activities, running activities in parallel (consecutively), or by shortening activity times. Operations managers can play an important role in shortening activity times by transferring resources from noncritical path activities to critical path activities. Managers can also crash activities. Crashing means adding resources, not necessarily transferring resources, to shorten critical path activities.

When working with an executive who wants to complete the TMS project 5 days early, how can an operations manager confidently provide an answer? To offer an answer, the probability of achieving this can be calculated. The answer can be found by finding the Z value and its corresponding probability using the normal distribution table.

$$Z = \frac{\text{New duration} - \text{Expected duration}}{\sqrt{\sigma_p^2}}$$

The Z value is the number of standard deviations the new duration or target date lies from the mean or expected duration. To find the project's expected duration, add up the expected activity times for the activities on the critical path. Remember, the critical path consists of activities 1-3-4. The TMS project is expected to last 60 days. Remember there is a desire to reduce the project duration by 5 days to 55 days. Next, add up the variances for the critical path activities.

The total variance of these activities is 3.72 days. By taking the square root of the variance, the standard deviation of 1.93 days is found. Knowing this, then the Z value is –2.59.

$$Z = \frac{55 - 60}{\sqrt{3.72}}$$

$$= \frac{-5}{1.93} = -2.59$$

Next, find the corresponding probability from the normal distribution table. It turns out the probability of completing the TMS project 5 days earlier is only 0.48%, an extremely low probability. With such a low probability, the executives pushing for a shortened project completion time will not be satisfied. It is worth noting that this procedure may provide inaccurate project completion estimates. This is because it is based on just the current critical path when in practice other paths often become critical during execution. A more reliable way to estimate probabilities of completion is to use simulation. However, there is another strategy that operations managers can employ in an attempt to shorten a project.

To shorten the duration of the project, managers can crash it. Crashing a project means shortening the time to complete activities, thus finishing earlier than expected. When crashing a project, the main objective is to reduce the overall duration of the project. With this in mind, it is important to select the correct activities to crash first. Crashing inappropriate activities can be costly and provide no benefit to shortening the project.

Which activities should be crashed first? Consider these ideas when deciding which activities to select first to shorten the project:

1. Elimination of some activities
2. Shortening early activities
3. Shortening the longest activities
4. Shortening the easiest activities

Keep in mind that the overall goal is to shorten the entire project duration. Thus, when selecting activities to shorten (crash), focus on those activities on the critical path first. For instance, decreasing the time to complete activity 2 for the TMS project will not shorten the project duration; it will still take 60 days. Reducing either activity 1,

3, or 4 will change overall project duration; it will be reduced by the number of days, any one of these three activities is shortened.

Critical paths have zero slack time, whereas noncritical paths are identified by activities containing slack time. Crashing noncritical path activities where there is slack time would not have an impact on overall project duration and could be a waste of money. After all, the way to shorten the project is to increase the amount of resources, which costs additional money.

Activities 1, 3, and 4 are prime candidates for crashing, so which one should be crashed first? Compiling a table such as Table 7.3 helps answer this question.

Consider activity 4, Customer Handoff, as an example. It is estimated to take 7.5 days to complete this task. Adding resources to this activity can reduce the time by 3 days, thus completing the customer handoff in 4.5 days. However, it will cost $500 per day extra to reduce the activity time. Before crashing activity 4, $1,500 will be spent to complete this activity. If activity 4 is crashed by 1 day, it will cost $1,500 + $500 = $2,000. If this activity is crashed by all 3 days, it will cost $1,500 + $500 + $500 + $500 = $3,000. With this in mind, which activity should be crashed first if the project is to be reduced from 60 days to 59 days? For someone wanting to move quickly and not spend money, activity 2 for $100 looks like a good choice. After all, this is the lowest cost activity to crash. However, recall that activity 2 is not on the critical path and has slack time. Thus, reducing this activity time does not reduce the project to 59 days. The next choice should be activity 3 (test). This activity is on the critical path and it has the lowest cost per day out of activities 1, 3, and 4. Understanding which activities should be crashed and in what order is a vital skill to learn. Learning this skill will eliminate unnecessary costs from projects.

Table 7.3 Normal and Crashed Project Time and Cost Parameters

Activity	Activity Number	Expected Time	Total Allowable Crash Time	Normal Cost ($)	Crashed Cost ($)	Cost Per Day To Crash ($)
Migration	1	35.67	1	3,000	4,000	1,000
Deployment	2	30.50	1	200	300	100
Test	3	16.83	2	700	1,300	300
Customer handoff	4	7.50	3	1,500	3,000	500

A typical approach to crashing activities includes increasing resources or using overtime. Some companies use their own employees and others may contract out the duties; still others will use a mix of their own employees and contracted services. Although shortening projects is attainable, there are many practical implementation issues that interfere with this goal. One might expect that the actual work will progress at the same rate; however, studies have shown that the use of overtime time leads to a reduced rate of progress, leads to low morale, and creates an environment where burnout is common. It takes time to find additional resources and to have all employees produce at the same level. Further, quality may suffer because contractors may not have the same level of motivation to do a good job.

Projects and KPI Trees

To sum up why companies invest in projects, recall from Chapter 5 that ROIC and FCFs contribute to increasing company value (Figure 7.6). The goal is to drive ROIC and FCFs higher, and this can be done by driving operating profit (EBIT) higher. Operating profit is driven higher by investing in projects. By investing in projects companies are trying to drive operating profit higher by either increasing revenues or reducing costs (Figure 7.7). If projects are effectively managed, EBIT can be driven higher while minimizing the amount of capital investment needed. Managers are striving to increase the ratio of EBIT to invested capital. When projects are managed well, companies are managing the invested capital well.

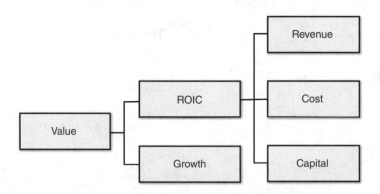

Figure 7.6 Drivers of company value.

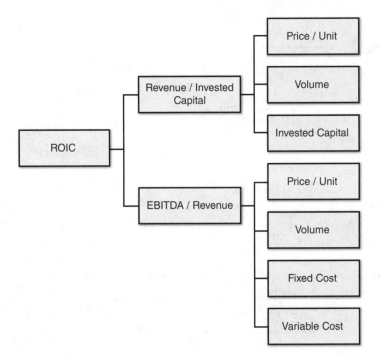

Figure 7.7 ROIC tree: price, volume, and costs.

Summary

Companies invest in projects for many reasons. Ultimately, they take on projects to increase company value. Projects are intended to increase ROIC and FCFs. They typically have long-term consequences; projects are expensive, and they are time and resource consuming. Thus, effective project management is critically important. Because there are many barriers to project success, it is important to recognize these ahead of time to mitigate their existence. Successful projects start with identifying the correct projects that add value to the firm. Next, projects need to be implemented smartly, including actively managing activity times, resources, and costs. Finally, companies are wise to learn from each project they undertake and transfer this knowledge to future project leaders and team members.

8

Supply Chain Network Design and Location Analysis

The design of supply chain networks is an important aspect for any organization. The design impacts costs and customer service levels. Companies have a choice of many different supply chain designs. Similar companies in the same industry often have different supply chain designs. However, companies with good designs have one element in common; they are in alignment with their customers' needs and with the company's business strategy. Yet, meeting customer needs and expectations is not that easy. The type of products and services offered, the location of acceptable materials and suppliers, and the transportation that connects all of these pieces together are quite a puzzle to assemble.

Business Strategy and Competition

Business executives realize companies use supply chains to gain a competitive edge. Efficient, well-designed supply chains result in higher profits, lowers costs, better operational performance, and higher consumer satisfaction. Of course, optimization models are available and used to design supply chains for the lowest cost, mileage, or time in transit. Design must consider more factors than strict quantitative measures. It can maximize different aspects, such as profits or service levels. Supply chain design requires an organization to make tradeoffs based on cost, service levels, and environmental impact to achieve the most optimal operation for that specific organization. A well-designed and managed supply chain brings many benefits to an organization, they are as follows:

1. Products and services delivered to customers in a timely manner, increasing customer goodwill

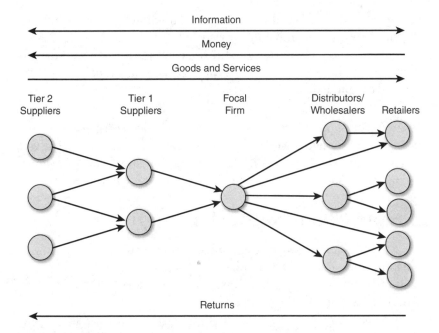

Figure 8.1 Generic supply chain network.

2. Total supply chain cost reduction
3. Financial and operational risks to the business can be minimized
4. Environmental impact reduction
5. Tax reduction

It is important to define supply chain network design. In essence, a supply chain network is a multipiece puzzle that when put together allows materials, information, and money to flow in a manner that aligns corporate and business strategies (Figure 8.1). There are many elements to consider in the design.

1. How many tiers in the supply chain are necessary?
2. What suppliers to use, how many of them are there?
3. Where facilities are located?
4. What channels of distribution are needed?

Before designing a new supply chain network or changing a current one, an organization must establish its mission, objectives, and goals, along with a business strategy. Each employee should understand the direction their leaders have set forth and how the business intends to compete in the market place. It is crucial to know if company intends to compete on cost, reliability, or responsiveness as these elements affect the supply chain design and financial performance. After all, supply chain management helps an organization attain its mission, objectives, and goals.

With a clear business strategy, supply chain professionals can begin to explore options to meet the organization's needs using the supply chain. A well-designed and well-managed supply chain network is vital to an organization. The connection among the supply chain strategy, the network, and the corporation's business strategy must be clear.

Supply Chain Network Design

Supply chain network design must consider several factors. Some obvious elements are the number and locations of suppliers, manufacturing and assembly plants, distribution centers, and warehouses. Yet, there is still more to consider.

Supply chain professionals need to consider the customer in the design. For example, it is important to know who the customers are and their buying behaviors. Ultimately, businesses are in business to satisfy the customers. It is imperative to find out what is important to them. In supply chain design, the answers to the following questions are crucial.

1. What products and services do customers want?
2. How long are customers willing to wait for products and services?
3. What service level are customers willing to accept?
4. What are customers willing to pay?

Of course, the cost to deliver a product or service is important. What cost is the organization willing to incur to deliver a product or service at the service level customers will accept? What are they willing to pay for the level of service they desire? If a network is designed to achieve high service levels, this could increase costs to a level where the revenue collected will not cover them.

The product or service is an important consideration in supply chain design. The product's physical attributes affect the ability of the supply chain to deliver. The lifecycle is an important aspect as well.

1. Is the product large or small, heavy or light?
2. Does the product have to be assembled near the customer location?

Heavy products, such as tractors, cost more to transport, thus assembling them closer to the customer will likely reduce transportation costs. Laptops and mobile devices, on the other hand, can be assembled in far-away places and still arrive in a timely manner and at a reasonable cost. Labor intensive industries such as apparel might locate operations or outsource production to Asia or Central America to take advantage of lower wages.

3. Does the product have stable demand and high volume?

For toothpaste, a stable demand and high volume product, it would be appropriate to design an efficient make-to-stock supply chain compared with a make-to-order supply chain that is less efficient but more flexible.

Knowing which lifecycle phase the product is in is important too (Figure 8.2). If the product is in the growth phase, the network is more likely to be designed, considering increasing facility and process capacities in the future. If the product is in the declining phase, capacities will be decreasing and fixed assets may need to be unloaded.

Where products and services are sourced from is always a consideration in supply chain design. The materials and services purchased may be found in limited geographical regions. Transportation costs coupled with our customers' location will dictate whether we

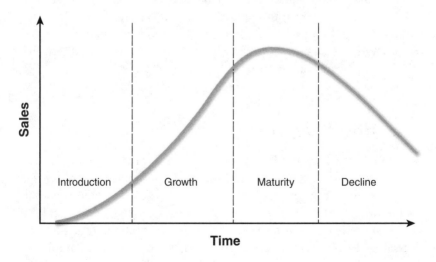

Figure 8.2 Product lifecycle.

ship materials to distant assembly plants or move the assembly plants closer to the point where the materials were acquired. An organization might also consider moving its suppliers closer to the assembly plants, much like how the automobile industry operates. Along with dispersed locations comes added risk.

Many business executives are concerned with mitigating supply chain risk. Businesses generally desire stability; they do not like surprises. Wall Street and shareholders do not like surprises either. Regional economic and political climates, and other associated risks can wreak havoc on the financial and operational performance of companies and entire industries. For instance, if governments impose tariffs arbitrarily, the supply chain is affected. If workers are allowed to strike often or currency valuations fluctuate greatly, these situations must be taken into account. Knowing the climate within which the supply chain operates informs the design; it is prudent and design supply chains according to its climate.

In addition to risk, executives are starting to realize that corporate social responsibility and sustainability issues are important factors to consider. Supply chains are being designed to minimize carbon emissions. Moreover, companies are reviewing supplier selection and oversight policies, making sure that workers are treated fairly and that they are provided with living wages and safe work places. Each of these areas has an impact on the supply chain design.

These are several essential factors that contribute to an effective supply chain design, but additional areas must be part of the conversation. Technology is required to operate the supply chain. Managing and operating a supply chain effectively requires access to communications and information systems. Ultimately, there is a need to transmit data and information accurately and in a timely manner.

Location Selection

Location analysis and selection is an important topic for all companies. Location decisions should not be taken lightly. Supply chains are global, even for the smallest of companies. Although global supply chains are part of the conversation, much of the discussion about location analysis is relevant to local and regional locations too. Location decisions affect cost, service, system and communication complexity, and the level of exposure to supply chain risk. Firms decide where to buy materials, where they want the goods produced, assembled, and stored, and subsequently sold. Before selecting a location for these activities, many factors are considered:

1. Trade agreements that reduce import duties and tariffs
2. Stable currency
3. Proximity to markets
4. Proximity to suppliers
5. Proximity to materials and material costs
6. Labor availability, skill, productivity, union rules, and wages
7. Government tax incentives
8. Land availability
9. Infrastructure to include transportation and utilities
10. Risk reduction to include financial, political, and natural disasters

Operating globally offers many advantages. One advantage is obtaining suppliers that can offer better pricing for higher quality materials. Access to talent and expertise with higher productivity levels is another opportunity provided by global operation. Companies might find that working around the clock, literally, taking advantage of time zones helps reduce the time to market. Higher productivity levels and reducing the time to market generate cash inflows faster, creating value for the organization.

At the same time, however, there are disadvantages of operating globally or over long distances. There are cultural differences and holidays that can interrupt the flow of goods and services. Some countries do not have regulations enforcing high labor or safety standards and are prone to currency exchange volatility. Although crossing time zones increases the time available to produce, this also increases the complexity of communicating with suppliers and customers.

Centralizing a network is often a topic of discussion among supply chain executives. Dialog surrounding these topics can be difficult, especially if closing a facility is part of the centralization process. There are general guidelines to follow once countries' characteristics are identified. Table 8.1 identifies country factors that favor reducing the number of facilities (centralize) or favor increasing the number of facilities (decentralize) in the network. For instance, a country that has stable exchange rates merits further investigation. Stable

Table 8.1 Centralize and Decentralize Country Factors

Country Factors	Centralize	Decentralize
Trade barriers, duties, taxes	Low	High
Exchange rates	Stable	Volatile
Government	Stable	Volatile
Fixed costs	High	Low
Value to weight ratio	High	Low
Product/service serves universal needs	Yes	No

exchange rates favor centralizing your supply chain to take advantage of the stability. On the contrary, if a country displays exchange rate volatility, decentralizing the network to mitigate the risk of unfavorable exchange rates in that country should be considered.

Cost Behavior

When the design of the supply chain network changes, so do certain costs. Transportation, inventory, and facility costs characteristically change as the number of facilities change in a distribution network (Figure 8.3). Take for instance, as the network is decentralized by increasing the number of distribution and warehouse facilities, total costs decline, then rise again. Inventory and facility costs increase, while transportation costs initially decrease, then increase again.

As the number of facilities increases, so do the costs to manage and operate them. To meet existing service levels, inventory costs rise due to additional safety stock requirements. The increase in safety stock is a result of the variation in consumer demand as the network is decentralized. Transportation costs tend to initially decrease as the outbound distance from distribution centers to their delivery points decrease. Lower costs remain as long as the inbound transportation to the facilities can maintain economies of scale. When inbound full-truck-loads (FTL) and/or full-container-loads (FCL) cannot be maintained any longer, transportation costs begin to increase. Transportation costs begin to grow when too many facilities are added. Outbound costs per unit tend to be higher since these are generally smaller lot sizes, whereas inbound lot sizes are generally larger.

Response time, the time it takes to serve a customer, is also affected by decentralization. It is a more difficult cost to measure.

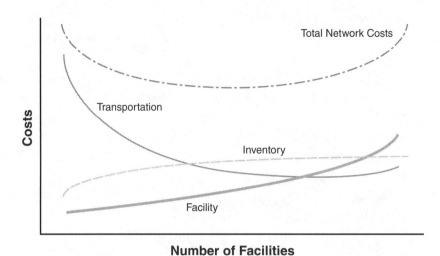

Figure 8.3 Relationship between number of facilities and costs.(Adapted from Chopra S, Meindl P. *Supply Chain Management: Strategy, Planning, and Operation.* 5th ed. Upper Saddle River, New Jersey: Pearson; 2013.)

Response time is critically important, though. Companies lose customers when response times are too slow. As the number of facilities increases, response time decreases.

Supply Chain Network Modeling

Companies often re-evaluate supply chain designs for a variety of reasons. Some reasons include acquisition of another company, cost savings, divesting certain fixed assets or product lines, or changes in consumer buying behavior that prompts a company to enter or leave a market. Moreover, executives are trying to make supply chains simpler by removing the complexity that has been built into the supply chain over time. Modeling the supply chain provides management with useful information for deciding if and how the design might change, and what the impacts to the organization might be if the change does occur.

Companies start by evaluating their current or base state. Analysts gather information surrounding:

1. Current and potential new locations of facilities, supply sources, and markets

2. Capacities of the facilities

3. Current and future consumer demand for their products and services

4. Current fixed and variable costs

5. Revenue generated from products and services for the various locations

6. Facility, labor, and material cost by location

7. Transportation costs between locations

8. Inventory costs by location

9. Taxes, tariffs, and duties

10. Response times

11. Risks

Next, companies consider a number of scenarios. By evaluating the current and possible new supply chain designs, management can answer questions such as:

1. How does the supply chain network total cost change if new facilities are added or current facilities are closed?

2. How does the cost change if facility locations change?

3. How many locations and facilities are needed to meet company goals, objectives, and consumer demand?

4. How does the network cost change if facility capacity increases or decreases?

5. How do costs change if service levels change?

Furthermore, management needs to evaluate if the suggested changes are realistic and make sense, given the current supplier network and customer base. If changes are made because of future consumer demand or to mitigate political, regulatory, or environmental risk, then will suppliers and customers adapt as well?

Case Example Mid-Atlantic Hospital System

Network and financial performance are connected, this much has been made clear. Consider the following example to better understand the concept. The fictitious Mid-Atlantic Hospital System will provide the opportunity to examine two supply chain network scenarios and perform financial analysis comparing them.

Mid-Atlantic Hospital System is a regional healthcare provider located in the Mid-Atlantic United States, covering Delaware, Maryland, and Virginia. Through a series of mergers and acquisitions, the hospital system has grown to six hospitals. Considering recent events such as rising healthcare costs, the implementation of the Affordable Care Act, and the hospital system's mission of *"providing quality care to anyone who needs it,"* Mid-Atlantic Hospital System is considering changing its distribution network in the hopes of greater cost savings. They recognize that *"the efficient management of the hospital system's assets is paramount to its long-term success and ability to provide patient care in line with the Affordable Care Act."*

Further, Mid-Atlantic Hospital System is a big supporter of the Institute for Healthcare Improvement's initiative, which states that health system performance designs must be developed to simultaneously pursue: (1) improving the patient experience of care, including quality and satisfaction, and (2) reducing per capita healthcare costs.

Mid-Atlantic Hospital System currently operates three distribution centers located throughout the hospital system's regional area that handles the distribution for medical-surgical supplies for the six hospitals. The VP of Supply Chain states, "There is nothing more important than to have resources available to our patients, nurses, and doctors when they need them." She goes on to say, "At the same time, though, it is no secret that healthcare costs are increasing for our patients so we need to take proactive measures to rein in costs, but we have to make sure our nurses and doctors have the right materials at the right time to serve our patients. We intend to rank high among our peers in both patient and employee satisfaction scores. We want to create a work environment where our associates feel like they have the tools they need to do a great job for their patients." The supply chain group is now evaluating different distribution designs that meet the hospital system's mission and objectives.

Network Design Analysis

The hospital's management team has made it clear that high service levels, high patient satisfaction, and low costs are important. Keeping these objectives in mind, analysts might consider adding an additional distribution facility. This would reduce response times,

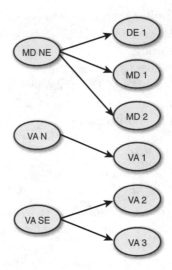

Figure 8.4 Current network design.

which should improve service levels and patient satisfaction by bringing supplies closer to the hospitals. In addition, total supply chain costs may be reduced.

The first task is to understand the current situation. The supply chain group collects data from various departments such as sourcing, logistics, finance, and accounting. From these data, the current system's design, costs, and materials routing information can be ascertained. The data collected should include current and future demand for its supplies, facility capacities, fixed and variable cost related to inbound and outbound transportation, the operation of the distribution centers, and inventory.

Figure 8.4 and Table 8.2 show the current network design. Three distribution centers that supply six hospitals are located in Northeast

Table 8.2 Current Network Design

	DE 1	MD 1	MD 2	VA 1	VA 2	VA 3	Shipped	Supply
MD NE	1,000	1,250	3,000	0	0	0	5,250	5,500
VA N	0	0	0	3,000	0	0	3,000	3,000
VA SE	0	0	0	0	2,000	1,500	3,500	4,000
Received	1,000	1,250	3,000	3,000	2,000	1,500		
Demand	1,000	1,250	3,000	3,000	2,000	1,500		

Table 8.3 Current Network Cost Per Unit

	DE 1	MD 1	MD 2	VA 1	VA 2	VA 3
MD NE	3.70	5.60	8.55	9.65	12.45	15.75
VA N	9.55	8.90	4.60	2.20	7.50	8.40
VA SE	16.90	18.20	11.05	7.25	5.80	2.50
Weekly total			$58,300			
Yearly total			$3,031,600			

Maryland, Northern Virginia, and Southeast Virginia. There is one hospital located in Delaware, two in Maryland, and three in Virginia. Table 8.2 provides the weekly demand rates, supply capacities, and number of units shipped between the distribution center and the hospital.

Based on the weekly capacity of the distribution centers and the demand rate for medical-surgical products by the hospitals, and the cost per unit to transport between any two points, the analysis shows, for example, that the Northeast Maryland distribution location has a weekly capacity of 5,500 units per week, of which 5,250 units are shipped to the Delaware and Maryland hospitals. The Delaware hospital received all 1,000 units that it demanded from the Northeast Maryland distribution location.

Table 8.3 provides the operating cost per unit to transport, handle, and store medical-surgical inventory between any two points in the network. For instance, it will cost $3.70 to ship one unit from Northeast Maryland to the Delaware hospital. The cost per unit includes relevant variable and fixed costs such as transportation costs, storage and handling, wages, and inventory holding cost. Relevant costs are those that will change when comparing two or more alternatives As an example, if analysis shows that one of the distribution centers may be disposed of, some fixed costs will disappear. The fixed costs that disappear are relevant and should be included in the analysis. If, on the contrary, fixed costs are not expected to appreciably change between the two scenarios, then fixed costs should not be included in the analysis. Based on the hospital's objectives, current demand pattern, and facility capacities, the hospital system does not anticipate fixed costs to disappear, thus only variable costs are included in the analysis.

Given the capacities, demands, and costs, Mid-Atlantic Hospital System has a weekly cost of $58,300 with an annual cost of $3,031,600 to operate the current distribution network. They also find that by

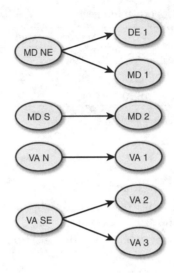

Figure 8.5 New network design.

shipping 11,750 units per week divided by total capacity of 12,500 units per week, they have a system utilization of 94%.

The second scenario includes the possibility of adding a fourth distribution center in Southern Maryland (Figure 8.5). The analysis was completed (Table 8.4) using estimated cost data for a fourth distribution center (Table 8.5).

Mid-Atlantic Hospital System finds that the estimated weekly cost for this network design is $46,150 with an annual cost of $2,399,800. They also find that they have a system utilization of 75.8% from shipping 11,750 units per week with a total capacity of 15,500 units per week. If Mid-Atlantic Hospital System were projecting future growth, the added capacity would be welcome. Even so, this system with lower

Table 8.4 New Network Design

	DE 1	MD 1	MD 2	VA 1	VA 2	VA 3	Shipped	Supply
MD NE	1,000	1,250	0	0	0	0	2,250	5,500
VA N	0	0	0	3,000	0	0	3,000	3,000
VA SE	0	0	0	0	2,000	1,500	3,500	4,000
MD S	0	0	3,000	0	0	0	3,000	3,000
Received	1,000	1,250	3,000	3,000	2,000	1,500		
Demand	1,000	1,250	3,000	3,000	2,000	1,500		

Table 8.5 New Network Cost Per Unit

	DE 1	MD 1	MD 2	VA 1	VA 2	VA 3
MD NE	3.70	5.60	8.55	9.65	12.45	15.75
VA N	9.55	8.90	4.60	2.20	7.50	8.40
VA SE	16.90	18.20	11.05	7.25	5.80	2.50
MD S	5.60	6.50	4.50	5.50	10.80	13.30
Weekly total	$46,150					
Yearly total	$2,399,800					

system utilization is less costly for the hospital system to operate. The yearly cost savings is $631,800.

Capital Budgeting

Next, the hospital system needs to determine if they should proceed and add a new distribution center in Southern Maryland. They will save an estimated $631,800 per year, but is the total savings sufficient and will the cash inflows come early enough to undertake the project? NPV, IRR, and payback period analyses are employed to answer these questions.

It is wise to begin with NPV and IRR analysis. The cost savings of $631,800 per year is the additional positive gross operating cash flow the company estimates it will realize. However, the NPV and IRR analysis requires net operating cash flow for a more precise and accurate analysis. Depreciation and tax expenses, salvage value, initial investment, and discount rate are needed for NPV and subsequent IRR analysis (Table 8.6).

Table 8.6 NPV Analysis Data

Depreciation	Straight Line
Useful life	10 years
Salvage value	$0
Tax rate	30%
Construction period	1 year
Initial investment	$3,000,0000
Discount rate	10%

As mentioned earlier, net operating cash flows must be obtained from gross cash flows. Net operating cash flow (Table 8.7) is found from the following simplified formula:

Net operating cash flow = EBIT + Depreciation – Taxes

Initial analysis looks at the cost savings from the new network design. Then, to find EBIT, one should subtract depreciation. EBIT is the amount from which the tax liability is computed. Once the tax burden is calculated, it is the time to calculate net cash flow. The noncash depreciation expense is added to EBIT, and then the tax liability is subtracted from this amount. The result is net operating cash flow, which will be used for the NPV and IRR calculations. NPV ends up being $270,507; a positive number that signifies the project will add value to the company and should be undertaken. IRR is 12%; a number that management decides is above their hurdle rate. Given that 10% was their discount rate, 12% IRR appears to clear the hurdle rate. Again, signifying that the project will add value to the company and the project should be undertaken.

Do not underestimate the significance of 12% IRR. Assume the supply chain redesign was on a global scale instead of a regional scale. In such a case, maybe a Central American or Eastern European location was needed. The discount rate in all likelihood would be higher to cover the additional risk. Increasing the discount rate would lower the NPV value making the investment less attractive. How much higher can the discount rate go before the project should not be undertaken? As you may recall, a 12% IRR signifies that if the discount rate were raised from 10% to 12%, NPV would become 0.

Payback period methods are quite useful to indicate the liquidity of a project, otherwise stated as, how long it will take to receive your initial investment. In these two examples, it will take payback period is found to be 5.64 years and the discounted payback period is 8.71 years, identified by the turn to positive cumulative cash flow (Table 8.8).

A summary (Table 8.9) comparing the two network designs shows that the redesign should be undertaken. There is a cost savings, NPV is positive, IRR clears the 10% hurdle rate, and utilization while at 76% allows for growth and supply chain flexibility.

Table 8.7 NPV Calculations

	Year 0	Year 1	Year 2	Years	Year 4	Year 5	Year 6	Year 7	Year 8	Year 9	Year 10
Gross Cash Flow	-3,000,000	631,800	631,800	631,800	631,800	631,800	631,800	631,800	631,800	631,800	631,800
Depreciation		300,000	300,000	300,000	300,000	300,000	300,000	300,000	300,000	300,000	300,000
EBIT		331,800	331,800	331,800	331,800	331,800	331,800	331,800	331,800	331,800	331,800
Tax		99,540	99,540	99,540	99,540	99,540	99,540	99,540	99,540	99,540	99,540
Operating Cash Flow = EBIT + DEP – TAX	-3,000,000	532,260	532,260	532,260	532,260	532,260	532,260	532,260	532,260	532,260	532,260

Table 8.8 Payback Period and Discounted Payback Period

Project	Time 0	Year 1	Year 2	Year 3	Year 4	Year 5	Year 6
Net Cash Flow	-3,000,000	532,260	532,260	532,260	532,260	532,260	532,260
Cumulative Cash Flow	-3,000,000	-2,467,740	-1,935,480	-1,403,220	-870,960	-338,700	193,560

Project	Time 0	Year 1	Year 2	Year 3	Year 4	Year 5	Year 6	Year 7	Year 8	Year 9
Net Cash Flow	-3,000,000	532,260	532,260	532,260	532,260	532,260	532,260	532,260	532,260	532,260
Discounted Cash Flow	-3,000,000	483,873	439,884	399,895	363,541	330,492	300,447	273,134	248,303	225,730
Cumulative Cash Flow	-3,000,000	-2,516,127	-2,076,243	-1,676,348	-1,312,807	-982,316	-681,869	-408,735	-160,432	65,298

Table 8.9 Summary of Results

	Current Network	New Network
Total yearly cost	$3,031,600	$2,399,800
Utilization	94%	76%
NPV		$270,507
IRR		12%
Payback period		5.64 years
Discounted payback period		8.71 years

DuPont Model

Supply chain network analysts must present a network design that management will find appealing. Using NPV, IRR, and payback period analysis, analysts can show how a distribution network redesign can reduce cost, adding value to the company and its shareholders. The next step is to show management how the network change affects a few of the important financial and operational performance measures. Here, the DuPont model can be used as a visual tool. Begin by showing the current state of the organization, which includes the current distribution network (Figure 8.6). Notice that the DuPont model is revised slightly from the one presented in Chapter 6. In many instances, financial reports vary by industry and by company, thus the reason for the revision. Many hospitals show operating and nonoperating expenses but not COGS or COS. The current state shows that ROA is 1.97% and ROE is 4.53%.

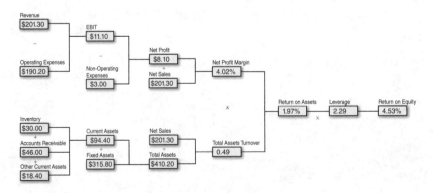

Figure 8.6 DuPont model current state.

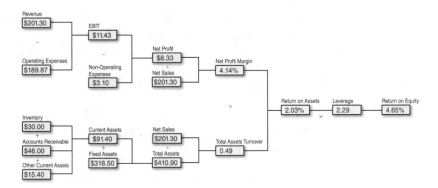

Figure 8.7 DuPont model revised state.

The DuPont model in Figure 8.7 shows how the revised network (adding a fourth distribution center) affects the hospital system's financial and operational performance from an accounting perspective. The revised network DuPont model represents your best estimate of how the hospital system's financial performance will change based on this network change.

Knowing that an investment is made before reaping any gains or cash inflows from the investment, the DuPont model should represent a benefit to the company.

Therefore, the results of analysis should reflect the end of the first year. This is the first period in which the organization will see cash inflows from their initial investment.

Even without the in-depth knowledge a company accountant has, supply chain analysts have enough knowledge to provide accurate estimates and assumptions when modifying the original DuPont model.

Before the network design change, the hospital system needs to invest an initial $3.00M. The initial investment covers fixed asset purchases and/or renovations, equipment, and installation costs. The finance department decides if the funds should come from their cash account in the bank, or if they should borrow the cash from a lender or sell shares to raise capital. In this example, you assume the cash came from Mid-Atlantic's bank account. Thus, other current assets have been reduced by the amount of the initial $3.00M cash investment.

$$\text{Other current assets} = \text{Current} - \text{Withdraw}$$
$$= \$18.40M - \$3.00M = \$15.40M$$

Next, consider operating expenses. Because the analysis found cost reductions in operating expenses, apply them here. Gross cash flow or cost savings is $631,800; therefore, operating expenses can be reduced by this amount. However, operating expenses need to be increased by $300,000 for the depreciation expense.

$$\text{Operating expenses} = \text{Current} - \text{Gross cash flow} + \text{Depreciation}$$
$$= \$190.20M - \$.6318M + \$.30M = \$189.87M$$

Income tax is a nonoperating expense, thus nonoperating expense should increase by the amount of tax, $99,540.

$$\text{Nonoperating expenses} = \text{Current} + \text{Taxes}$$
$$= \$3.00M + \$.0995M = \$3.0995M$$

Although it is possible that the balance sheet inventory account may stay the same or increase from carrying additional safety stock, inventory costs have been accounted for in the cash flow forecast. Recall that inventory costs flow from the balance sheet to the income statement after the inventory has been used. In this example, the average inventory balance does not change, but since inventory has been assumed to have been used, the cost is reflected in operating expenses.

$$\text{Inventory} = \$30.00M \pm \text{Change in inventory} = \$30.00M$$

Fixed assets have been adjusted to reflect the $3.00M investment, less the depreciation expense of $300,000.

$$\text{Fixed assets} = \text{Current} + \text{Purchased asset} - \text{Depreciation}$$
$$= \$315.80M + \$3.0M - \$.3M = \$318.50M$$

With the revised DuPont model, notice that ROA is 2.03% and ROE is 4.65%, both of which are improvements over the current distribution network. Furthermore, EBIT and net profit margin both improve (Table 8.10). While fixed asset turnover declined slightly, the overall improvements outweigh any slight decline in this ratio. Moreover, since earnings per share (EPS) is important to Wall Street and executives alike, seeing that EPS improves since net profit increased to $8.33M and provided the number of shares has not increased. However, if the company increased the number of shares to raise capital for this project instead of using their own cash, then EPS may decline.

Table 8.10 Summary of DuPont Models

	Current Network	**Redesigned Network**
ROA	1.97%	2.03%
ROE	4.53%	4.65%
Fixed asset turnover	0.637 times	0.632 times
Total asset turns	0.491 times	0.491 times
EBIT	$11.10M	$11.43M
Net profit margin	4.02%	4.14%
Net profit	$8.10M	$8.33M

Summary

Company value is created through increasing cash inflows and WACC. Cash inflows come from revenue growth and ROIC. ROIC is influenced by how well the company manages its operations. This includes how well it manages its operating costs. Several ways in which supply chain and distribution network analysis can increase company value were presented. One way was how companies can compete using supply chains. Part of this is identifying what factors managers and analysts should consider when designing supply chain networks. Who the customers are and what they are willing to pay for, the types of products and services we offer, and location and risk factors all are important to consider. Relevant costs and cost behaviors in network design must be part of the analysis. Finally, a case study demonstrated how an organization could model and analyze its distribution network, using this to make capital budgeting decisions that could increase value.

9

Inventory Management

Managing inventory is an essential function for any company. Too little inventory halts production and stifles sales. Having more inventory than necessary creates cash flow issues. Cash that is not tied up in inventory can be used for other business activities such as entering new markets, developing new products and services, and offering training, competitive pay, and benefit packages to employees. Knowing this, managers need to understand the financial and operational implications of effectively managing inventory. It is a balancing act between maximizing customer service levels and minimizing inventory costs. For these reasons, industry and financial analysts closely watch the method in which companies manage inventory. As an operations or supply chain professional, understanding and managing inventory is crucial to supporting your company's financial success.

Earlier chapters have discussed how and where inventory is represented in a company's financial statements along with the effect inventory levels have on several financial and operational performance ratios. This chapter will provide insight into how inventory management decisions affect inventory levels, thus changing the financial and operational performance ratios. Furthermore, because skilled inventory management decisions depend on accurate demand management, the chapter will show the connection between inventory management and demand forecasting. Inventory management and demand forecasting can inform one another. Demand forecasts help determine inventory requirements and at the same time, historical inventory demand is widely used for demand forecasting.

Many operations and supply chain professionals refer to inventory in units. However, to convey a company's financial performance, these units are converted to dollars. Recall that inventory noted on the balance sheet is stated at a cost, which is determined by one of the cost accounting methods. Once inventory is used and the product is sold, the cost of inventory is moved to the income statement as an expense labeled cost of goods sold (COGS). Further, the cash that is used to buy inventory is reflected on the balance sheet and cash flow statement. The cost of inventory includes other inputs besides the cost per unit of inventory; it includes all costs incurred to make the good available for sale. These costs may include transportation, duties, and taxes.

Inventory has many labels and uses. Inventory is generally classified as:

1. Raw materials—inventory that has not been worked on yet
2. Work in process—inventory that is being worked on but not yet ready for sale
3. Finished goods—inventory ready for sale
4. Inventory in transit—in the pipeline

Inventory is used to:

1. Satisfy demand
2. Satisfy backlog
3. Counter lead-time variability
4. Serve as a buffer to avoid a disruption in the flow of goods
5. Protect against stock-outs
6. Guard against price increases

The fundamental goal of inventory managers and planners is to minimize the amount of inventory while still meeting customer demand. To accomplish this, managers often ask two questions: (1) how much inventory should be purchased and (2) when should inventory be ordered? Answering these questions about quantity and timing may appear simple, but in reality, it can be difficult to answer them appropriately as many factors must be considered.

Before answering the two questions, there is a need to identify the characteristics of the inventory. Does the inventory have high volume, high cost, low number of SKUs, and stable demand or otherwise? In addition, a manager needs to identify what service levels the customers expect. It should become clear that inventory levels affect at least three comprehensive areas: organizational performance, costs, and customer service. Based on the characteristics that are uncovered, inventory can be categorized.

Continuing with the Mid-Atlantic Hospital System case from Chapter 8, the categorization and inventory management can be explained further. The hospital system has many different inventory items. Each item has a different cost, consumption rate, and has a different time period when it becomes obsolete. Knowing this, the supply chain group has segmented the inventory into the following categories: (1) food and other perishable items, (2) "hotel items," such as laundry, linen, soap, shampoo, and toothbrushes, (3) surgical tools, and (4) medical surgical items such as bandages, syringes, needles, and gauze. Now that the inventory is categorized, it becomes clearer how to manage the inventory.

How Much Inventory to Order

Several inventory models are available to determine the correct amount of inventory to purchase each time an order is placed and how often to place an order. Segmenting inventory helps identify the appropriate model to use. For instance, perishable items are not managed the same way as medical-surgical items. Thinking about it simply, ordering too much fresh fruit would result in some spoiled fruit; however, if bandages were over-ordered, they would not spoil. Thus, if a salesperson offered a quantity discount, a manager may not want to order larger amounts of fresh fruit to take advantage of the discount, but might order a larger quantity of bandages.

Often the inventory model chosen depends on the way inventory is tracked. Is inventory tracked perpetually (all the time), much like retailers and grocery stores do as the product's universal product code is scanned at checkout? Or is inventory counted at a fixed time interval (periodically), much like a small bar owner who counts the bottles of liquor in the storeroom each Thursday. A simple Economic Order Quantity (EOQ) model or a variation of this model, can be used if:

1. A continuous supply of an item is necessary.
2. The item's demand is fairly stable.
3. It is tracked continuously.

The simplest inventory model is the EOQ model. The basic idea in this model is that an optimal order quantity that minimizes cost exists. If the order quantity is above or below the optimum, costs increase. Costs can be placed into two categories: holding cost and order cost (also called setup cost). Knowing these two costs helps answer the first question managers ask, which is how much inventory to purchase each time an order is placed. Use the following equation to determine the optimal quantity:

$$Q = \sqrt{\frac{2 \times D \times S}{H}}$$

Where Q is the optimal order quantity, D is the annual demand for the product, S is the order cost, and H is the annual per unit holding cost.

Using the EOQ equation, if Mid-Atlantic Hospital System wishes to order bandages, how many should be ordered? The hospital system has forecasted that it needs 100,000 boxes of bandages this year. It has also calculated the order cost is $25.00 every time additional boxes are purchased and it costs them $1.50 to hold the boxes for a year. Demand and holding cost are for the same time period.

$$Q = \sqrt{\frac{2 \times 100,000 \times \$25}{\$1.50}} \approx 1,826, boxes$$

To minimize inventory costs, the inventory managers should order 1,826 boxes of bandages each time. The next section introduces the connection between order size and its effect on total inventory costs.

Total Inventory Costs

In Figure 9.1, notice the optimal order quantity is at the lowest point of the total cost curve. Moreover, this is the point where holding costs equal ordering costs. Notice too, at the lowest point of the total cost curve, it is fairly flat, which implies that even if the exact optimal quantity is not ordered, the total cost will not appreciably increase. In other words, a comfortable margin exists. The margin is important to understand because the exact quantity might force a manager to ask suppliers to break pallets or larger boxes up into smaller orders. A manager at the hospital will likely find that ordering more than the optimal quantity of bandages is less costly than asking the supplier to break up larger boxes in smaller orders and charging more for ordering an unusual quantity. However, it is possible that ordering higher quantities because a volume discount has been offered may actually reduce total costs. Volume discounts are discussed more in the next chapter.

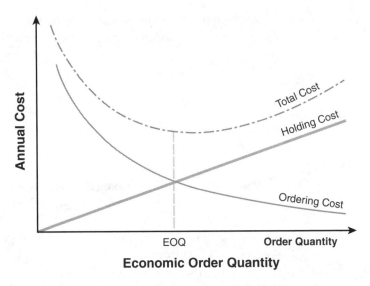

Figure 9.1 Total annual cost of holding and ordering inventory.

If the hospital system orders 1,826 boxes of bandages at a time throughout the year, how much will the yearly cost to hold and order bandages be? Using the total cost formula below, where TC is the total cost, Q is the order quantity in units, H is the holding cost, D is the annual demand in units, and S is the order cost, this question can be answered. The EOQ formula is used to find Q, while H, D, and S are the same values used in the EOQ formula.

$$TC = \frac{Q}{2} H + \frac{D}{Q} S$$

$$TC_{1,826} = \frac{1,826}{2} \times \$1.50 + \frac{100,000}{1,826} \times \$25.00$$

$$TC_{1,826} = \$1,369.50 + \$1,369.11 = \$2,738.61$$

Assuming that the inputs do not change during the year, it will cost the hospital system \$2,738.61 on average to hold and order bandages for the year. It may turn out that the number of orders per year may vary a small amount. If a quantity other than 1,826 is ordered each time, the total cost will increase. An in-depth understanding of holding cost and order cost is necessary for managers to make informed decisions that will affect total cost. Next, these two concepts will be explained.

Holding cost is typically stated as a percentage of the average inventory dollar amount for the year. The percentage is used because it is difficult to exactly determine the dollar amount for holding every item of inventory. For example, if Mid-Atlantic Hospital System reports that the average inventory is $30M per year and the holding cost rate is 15%, then the annual cost of holding inventory is $30M × 0.15 = $4.5M.

The rate at which the inventory holding cost is predicated on is difficult to determine. To complicate the situation, the costs that make up an organization's total holding cost are spread throughout the organization. Total holding cost is made up of individual costs related to:

1. Facilities
2. Utilities
3. Insurance
4. Damage
5. Obsolescence
6. Theft
7. Taxes
8. Administration and wages
9. Cost of capital

Allocating these costs to holding inventory is neither simple nor precise. However, by striving for precision, inventory decisions become more accurate. One thing experienced managers know is that money will be spent if inventory sits on a shelf. This is the basis for the preoccupation with measuring inventory turns and days of inventory. The faster the inventory turns over, then the lower the number of days of inventory, and the lower the cost to hold inventory.

A number of methods can be used for calculating inventory holding cost. In general, each includes the costs associated with noncapital (costs 1–8 from above) and capital cost (cost 9 from above). For example, the hospital system would add up all of its costs stated above and divided by the average annual inventory. To calculate this, the hospital system adds up the costs (1–9 from above), which totals $4.5M. With an average annual inventory of $30M, then the holding cost rate would be 15% ($4.5M/$30M = 0.15 × 100 = 15%). This means that for every dollar of inventory that the hospital system has, it spends $0.15 to hold the inventory. Managing holding costs is important, just as is managing order cost.

Each time a company orders inventory it incurs additional costs. These are called order costs, sometimes referred to as setup costs. Order costs include:

1. Wages
2. Transportation and delivery
3. Taxes, duties, and fees

For manufacturing companies, there are also costs associated with:

1. Equipment and assembly line change-overs

Purchase and buying processes play a large role in the costs that the company incurs. The more often a company orders inventory, the higher the order costs. Currently, Mid-Atlantic Hospital System orders bandages approximately 55 times per year. This is calculated by:

$$\frac{100,000 \text{ boxes annual demand}}{1,826 \text{ units order quantity}} = 54.76 \approx 55 \text{ times per year.}$$

At $25.00 per order, they spend ≈ $1,369.11 in order costs annually.

After a company has a handle on the amount spent on holding and ordering costs, it can calculate an optimal order quantity that minimizes these costs. In addition, it can calculate how often to order the optimal quantity. These ideas feed into reorder points. To what point can inventory decline before an order must be placed to minimize stock-outs and risk losing sales?

When to Reorder Inventory

The statistical reorder point (ROP) tells managers when to place an order to replenish inventory. When the quantity of an item drops to a particular number, the item is reordered. The ROP is the lowest inventory level at which a new order must be placed to avoid a stock-out. To determine the ROP, it is necessary to understand:

1. The rate of consumer demand or usage rates
2. The lead time
3. Demand and lead-time variability
4. Desired service level

Since demand and lead time are never certain, there is a need for safety stock. Safety stock reduces the likelihood of a stock-out. Safety stock is the amount of stock that is held in excess of expected demand and expected lead time due to variable demand and variable lead time. Lead time is time between submitting a purchase order and receiving the purchased items. Lead time, of course, can and does fluctuate. Lead-time variability is the byproduct of:

1. Unreliable suppliers
2. Material quality issues
3. Poor supplier inventory management
4. Transportation delays and port closings
5. Government inspection delays

Desired service levels stipulate the degree of stock-out risk acceptable to management.

The following formula is used to determine the statistical ROP.

$$\text{ROP} = \overline{d} \times \overline{L} + Z \sqrt{\sigma_d^2 \times \overline{L} + \sigma_L^2 \times \overline{d^2}}$$

Where $\overline{d}$ is the average daily demand, $\overline{L}$ is the average lead time in days (demand and lead time need to be in the same unit of time), Z is the z-score corresponding to the service level, σ_d^2 is the variance of demand, and σ_L^2 is the variance of lead time. An important note is that everything to the right of the plus sign is used to calculate safety stock. If the variability in demand or lead time was not present, only ROP= $\overline{d} \times \overline{L}$ would be needed to calculate the ROP.

The ROP formula can be used for the Mid-Atlantic Hospital System to identify when to order bandages and how much safety stock is required. From past performance, the hospital system has found:

$$\text{Average demand} = \frac{100,000}{365 \text{ days}} \approx 274 \text{ boxes per day}$$

$$\text{Average lead time} = 4 \text{ days}$$
$$\text{Variance of demand} = 50 \text{ boxes}$$
$$\text{Variance of lead time} = 1 \text{ day}$$
$$\text{Service level} = 95\%$$

Note: The Z value for a 95% service level is 1.645. A normal distribution table was used to find the Z value. If the service level is increased, the Z value increases. If the service level value is decreased, the Z value decreases.

$$ROP = 274 \times 4 + 1.645 \sqrt{50 \times 4 + 1 \times 75{,}067}$$
$$= 1{,}096 + 1.645 \sqrt{200 + 75{,}067}$$
$$\approx 1{,}096 + 452$$
$$\approx 1{,}548$$

The ROP formula indicates that Mid-Atlantic Hospital System should order bandages when the inventory declines to 1,548 boxes. Of the 1,548 boxes, 452 boxes are safety stock.

Although this example may seem simplistic since only one item is being considered, the idea is to understand that the same factors used to order one item apply to multi-item orders. For all orders, managers must consider demand rates, lead-times, variability, and service levels. Just as there are many different models to help determine how much inventory to buy, there are many models available to help determine when to buy. The challenge is to find the appropriate models for the situation. Knowing that inventory levels significantly affect the business, inventory managers will eventually look for ways to reduce inventory levels and at the same time try to maintain high customer service levels.

Inventory Reduction

Company managers are interested in reducing inventory for a number of reasons. Reducing inventory levels exposes problem areas in the business that needs to be addressed. Excess inventory masks problem areas such as poor supplier performance, unreliable delivery, and poor quality. Moreover, reducing inventory improves operational performance measures such as inventory turns, days of inventory, and asset utilization, leading to an increase in available cash. Fewer units of inventory on the property at a time require less storage capacity, which translates to less property, or fewer and smaller facilities. Remember, too, reducing inventory levels does not mean consumer demand will be unmet. Reducing inventory does not reduce the ability to meet consumer demand. The company becomes more effective with spending cash and inventory management, all the while still meeting consumer demand.

Safety stock and Just-in-Time philosophy are two areas that deserve more attention. If managers want to reduce inventory levels, these two areas are a good place to start.

Safety Stock

Through reducing safety stock, total average inventory is reduced. Using the ROP formula can help reduce safety stock. Remember the factors for calculating safety stock include:

1. Demand and demand variability
2. Lead time and lead-time variability
3. Desired service level

Process improvements targeted at minimizing demand variability, lead-time variability, and average lead time would reduce the need for additional safety stock. Centralizing inventory can reduce demand variability. Centralization diminishes information complexity, so demand patterns can be more clearly identified. It is important for managers to be aware, though, the centralization will require some tradeoffs. Centralizing inventory increases delivery time, thus increasing the time to respond to customers. Managers should be cautious in thinking that reducing demand variability through centralization is the only answer to minimize safety stock. Reducing lead time and lead-time variability can be achieved and assist in reducing safety stock. Some means are effective communication, coordination and collaboration with manufacturing, materials, and transportation suppliers.

Another way to reduce safety stock is to review desired service levels. Reducing service levels reduces the need for extra safety stock. However, reducing service levels increases the possibility of experiencing more stock-outs. Although, if service levels are unnecessarily high in the first place, reducing them will reduce safety stock and improve the company's cash position. Because there are trade-offs, it is necessary to answer the question, "Does the cost of safety stock outweigh the cost of losing a sale?" If the cost of losing a sale is higher, then it is necessary to carry additional safety stock. By carrying extra stock, decreases in performance measures such as inventory turns, days of inventory, and asset utilization are likely. However, these declines could be acceptable if they are offset by customer retention.

The amount of safety stock is also affected by how inventory is tracked and counted. The ROP example from earlier assumes that the inventory count is always known. This is called a perpetual inventory system where the use of automated systems, such as RFID, POS, and UPC, is to track and count inventory. The perpetual system updates the inventory counts instantaneously. This type of system requires less safety stock.

If a periodic system is used, where inventory is tracked and counted at certain time intervals, additional safety stock is needed. Why? Because demand variability makes it difficult to know what the inventory position is until it is counted again. If consumer demand rose during the week and more items were sold than expected, managers would not know this immediately. Thus, more safety stock is required to mitigate this uncertainty.

Further, timely and accurate information among supply chain participants replaces the need for extra safety stock. Communication about actual sales demand and updating lead times and delivery schedules can remove uncertainty, thus reducing the need for safety stock or excess inventory. Open communication and coordination in the supply chain can reduce inventory levels, thus improving the firm's financial performance.

Just-in-Time

The basis for the just-in-time (JIT) philosophy stems from reducing waste. Excess inventory is considered waste. To reduce excess inventory levels and to more closely match supply with demand, inventory managers are ordering fewer units at a time, but are ordering more often. In essence, JIT means getting the right amount of inventory, at the right time, and at the right place. JIT works best where demand is fairly stable and in efficient supply chains, rather than flexible supply chains.

Recall from the earlier example, where Mid-Atlantic Hospital System should order 1,826 boxes of bandages for each order to minimize inventory costs. Currently, it is ordering approximately 55 times per year (100,000 annual demand in units/1,826 units per order = 54.76 orders per year). If the order size was reduced to 1,000 units per order, the hospital system would order 100 times per year. By doing so, it would nearly double the order cost. Thus, the total cost to hold and order inventory would be:

$$TC_{1,000} = \frac{1,000}{2} \times \$1.50 + \frac{100,000}{1,000} \times \$25.00$$

$$TC_{1,000} = \$750 + \$2,500 = \$3,250$$

There is an increase in total inventory costs of $3,250 – $2,738.61 = $511.39, an increase of 18.67%, just from ordering fewer units more often. Many in the industry believe that implementing JIT will result in a reduction in inventory costs. In this case, there was a reduction in holding costs but not order costs. Even though average inventory was reduced—resulting in holding costs being reduced from $1,369.50 to $750, a savings of $619.50, this was not nearly enough to offset the increase in the order costs. Simply, if per order cost is not reduced first, the total inventory costs will increase. Knowing that a reduction in average inventory is desirable and that order costs need to be reduced first, then determining the target order cost is also desirable.

What should the per order cost need to be if 1,000 units are ordered each time? Using the following formula will help determine this:

$$S = \frac{H \times Q^2}{2D}$$

where

H = Holding cost per unit per year

Q = Desired order quantity

D = Annual demand

$$= \frac{\$1.50 \times 1,000^2}{2 \times 100,000}$$

$$= \frac{\$1,500,000}{200,000} = \$7.50$$

For orders of 1,000 boxes instead of 1,826 boxes, it is necessary to reduce order costs to $7.50 from $25.00.

How can the order cost be reduced?

The automotive industry provides a good example. They focused on reducing transportation costs and shortening the lead times by moving suppliers and assembly plants closer to one another. In addition, automation and making order processes simpler and less complex reduces transaction times, human involvement, and wages.

Inventory Tracking

Tracking inventory is a critical component of determining safety stock levels. It is the role of the inventory manager to consider what methods are necessary for inventory tracking. Inaccurate tracking of inventory is risky for a business and can affect many aspects of the operation.

Without accurate inventory tracking there is a risk of:

1. Lost sales (even if the item is in the store, personnel may not be able to find it)
2. Greater forecast errors due to inaccurate data
3. Expending substantial extra effort managing inventory
4. Having products at incorrect stores and facilities
5. Having a need for greater end of season markdowns

Inventory managers must decide whether or not implementing inventory management technology is worthwhile because of the cost associated with it. The cost of technology must be weighed against the cost of holding safety stock. Managers use technology to assist in inventory management for several reasons. Accurately tracking and counting inventory allows for better inventory decisions regarding quantity and timing of orders.

Using technology to effectively track inventory can produce the following results:

1. Reducing out of stocks
2. Increasing sales
3. Increasing store and supply chain productivity
4. Lowering cost of inventory
5. Improvement in the speed to market
6. Reducing labor costs
7. Generating data for better decision making
8. Preserving brand integrity and consumer satisfaction
9. Reducing shrink

Source: CSCMP's Supply Chain Quarterly, 4/2013.

While numerous reasons to acquire technology driven inventory tracking and counting systems exist, it is necessary to first identify the desired goals and objectives of a system. Using a system that does not match a company's needs can be a source of stress and frustration. With a system that fulfills the company's needs for accurate inventory tracking and counting processes, then demand forecasts become more accurate and reliable. Technology is a useful tool for managing inventory with greater precision, though implementing it does have a cost; however, more accurate demand forecasts benefit the company.

Demand Forecasts

Accurate demand forecasts help companies make inventory, capacity, and other operational decisions with greater confidence. Inaccurate forecasts lead to a mismatch between the supply and demand for capacity and inventory. This mismatch produces unhappy customers, idle resources, and a drain on the company's cash. Of course, forecasts are not perfect, but a lack of understanding of all the factors leaves greater room for error.

Forecasts are inaccurate for many reasons. Knowing the factors that make forecasts less accurate can help make them more accurate. Some factors include:

1. Bias on behalf of those providing information
2. Lack of communication
3. Using an incorrect forecast technique
4. Using inaccurate information
5. Using ineffective performance metrics or sales incentives
6. The forecast horizon moves further into the future

Inaccurate forecasts are detrimental to the business, so it is vital that they are as accurate as possible.

Although entire books have been written about demand planning and forecasting, this chapter will narrow the focus to a few ways operations and supply chain managers can improve forecasts. One way is to reduce lead times. Forecasts are more accurate when the time horizon is reduced. To relate this to a common experience, consider weather forecasts. The 1-day forecast is more accurate than the 7-day forecast. Therefore, in the case of demand forecasts, the same principle applies. For demand forecasts, the forecast time horizon has to be only as long as the lead time. If it takes 45 days to order and receive inventory, then the forecast would have to be a 45-day forecast. Shortening lead times result in more accurate demand forecasts.

Another way to improve forecast accuracy is through standardization. Standardization removes variability. Whenever materials and products can be standardized, thus reducing SKUs, forecasts become more accurate. With this method, there is no need to create forecasts for multiple items. Forecasting demand for multiple SKUs increases the variance of the forecasts, which makes the forecasts less accurate.

Table 9.1 Lindt Truffle Sales Aggregated

Week	Truffle Sales Caramel	Dark	Milk	Total
1	34	23	56	113
2	23	25	58	106
3	45	32	54	131
4	56	31	48	135
5	43	26	47	116
6	45	40	59	144
7	37	35	60	132
Total				877.00
Average				41.76
Variance				155.69

However, customers want variability. They do not always want or need the same items. In the case of variability, demand planners can provide an aggregate demand forecast. For example, consider the Lindt Chocolate Company that wants to forecast the number of 75 piece truffle bags needed to meet demand. The demand forecasts tend to be more accurate when forecasting the total number of 75 piece truffle bags (Table 9.1) rather than trying to forecast the number of bags of each flavor: milk chocolate, dark chocolate, and caramel (Table 9.2).

Table 9.2 Lindt Truffle Sales Disaggregated

Week	Truffle Sales Caramel	Dark	Milk	
1	34	23	56	
2	23	25	58	
3	45	32	54	
4	56	31	48	
5	43	26	47	
6	45	40	59	
7	37	35	60	
Average	40.43	30.29	54.57	41.76
Variance	107.95	36.57	27.29	171.81

Forecasting in the aggregate (Table 9.1) tends to be more accurate than forecasting in disaggregate (Table 9.2). Over a 7-week period, the average number of bags sold in the aggregate is 41.76 bags per week with a variance of 155.69. The averages in disaggregate are 40.43, 30.29, and 54.57 and an overall average of 41.76 bags and a total variance of 171.81. The higher variance indicates more uncertainty about the accuracy of the forecast, even though the average is the same.

Knowing this, operations managers forecast for capacity and plan for execution. Instead of solely relying on a forecast for each SKU (different truffle flavors), operations managers plan their process to accommodate the fluctuation in demand at the SKU level. Capacity will be sufficient to produce approximately 42 bags of truffles regardless of the flavor. If extra dark chocolate falls out of favor for a time, Lindt will have planned flexibility into their systems and processes to make other flavors as real-time demand is known. Further, Lindt understands that if ingredients can be standardized and used in each truffle flavor, they are able to handle the fluctuations in consumer demand for each flavor of truffle more readily.

As shown in the Lindt example, historical data are often used for forecasting and capacity planning. If historical demand data are to be used, an accurate depiction of what occurred in the past is needed. Accurate information is incredibly important but can be difficult to obtain.

Coordination and open lines of communication in the supply chain can provide more accurate information; however, information does not always flow freely. When communication is lacking, companies upstream in the supply chain typically use past orders instead of actual demand to produce forecasts. Unfortunately, past orders may not translate into shipments or actual demand. Orders, production, shipments, and actual demand each can be significantly different. Quantity discounts and large lots, pricing policies and promotions, purchase incentives, and company safety stock policies all can skew actual demand.

Because actual demand for products is difficult to know upstream in supply chains, suppliers often carry high levels of inventory unnecessarily. Higher inventory levels are a direct result of closed lines of communication and lack of coordination causing upstream suppliers to use inaccurate and unsuitable data for planning. Even with open lines of communication and coordination, the information transmitted has to be accurate and portray what is occurring correctly.

Information can easily be distorted, even if data are being collected in real time. For example, consider a supermarket that provides bonuses to its employees based on customer wait times and queue lengths at the checkout counters. In such a scenario, obtaining inaccurate demand information is common. To demonstrate, a cat owner comes into the supermarket and buys 12 small cans of wet cat food in 4 flavors. Knowing that the supermarket values short wait times and minimal lines, the cashier scans one can 12 times. The store got what it wanted: a quick customer checkout; however, it was at the expense of accurate data. To a data analyst, the data show that one particular flavor is popular, when in fact four flavors were purchased. Although technology such as point of sale (POS) systems assist in collecting accurate and timely data, managers should understand how performance and bonus incentives might not be in alignment with the objectives of the company.

Technology advances have companies rethinking the value in forecasting. Companies are relying less on historical information and traditional forecasting; instead they are trying to predict behavior in real time and developing supply chains with built in flexibility to accommodate changing demand patterns. Throughout the chapter, managing inventory to meet expected demand, at a desired service level while minimizing cost has been the focus so that companies can effectively operate.

Financial Performance

Many times it is difficult to connect operational changes to changes in financial performance. The DuPont model is a useful tool to demonstrate this, especially during meetings with executives. What follows is the use of the DuPont model to demonstrate how inventory levels affect relevant financial and operational performance measures.

The DuPont model for Mid-Atlantic Hospital System (Figure 9.2 and Table 9.3) identifies the current financial and operational performance of important performance measures. The current DuPont model provides a starting point from which to measure the effect of changing inventory levels. Currently, the inventory account is $30M. Observe the effects of reducing the inventory balance from $30M to $20M (Figure 9.3 and Table 9.3).

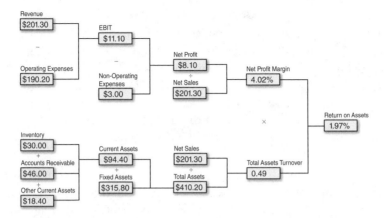

Figure 9.2 Current inventory condition.

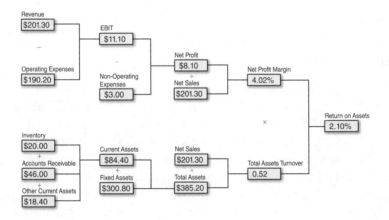

Figure 9.3 Improved inventory condition.

Table 9.3 Comparison between Inventory Levels

Performance Measure	$30M (Before)	$20M (After)	Unit
Inventory turnover	6.71	10.07	Times
Days inventory	54.40	36.26	Days
Fixed asset turnover	0.64	0.67	Times
Total assets turnover	0.49	0.52	Times
Return on assets	1.97%	2.10%	
Basic earnings power ratio	2.71%	2.88%	

Compare the two DuPont models: the inventory account is reduced, as are the fixed assets. It is reasonable to expect that if inventory is reduced, the need for capacity is also reduced. This leads to reducing fixed assets (PP&E). Although operating expenses (and COGS in other scenarios) remain the same in this example, it is not unreasonable to see this particular account decrease when inventory moves from the balance sheet to the income statement as inventory is sold. If operating expenses and COGS accounts decrease, profit margins increase.

Notice that each of the inventory and asset performance measures improves (Table 9.3). Inventory and asset management are becoming more efficient. Inventory is turning over faster; it is spending fewer days sitting in the hospital's facilities. Moreover, assets are being used more efficiently. The supply and demand for fixed asset capacity is better matched.

Summary

Effective inventory management is critical to a company's operational and financial success. In trying to find success, inventory managers often have to make tradeoffs. On one hand, they have to make customers happy by minimizing stock-outs. On the other hand, they have to minimize cost, and maximize inventory turns and return on assets. Timely and accurate information play a critical role in the inventory manager's success when confronted with these tradeoffs. With the right information, forecasting and capacity planning improve, thus making better inventory order amount and timing decisions. Furthermore, showing the expected financial results using the DuPont model can validate inventory decisions.

10

Sourcing and Supply Management

All organizations purchase goods and services; however, this task is not as simple as it appears. The importance of sourcing cannot be overstated. Sourcing and supply management are vitally important for organizational success and competiveness. Sourcing decisions are both strategic and operational. Each has financial, environmental, and social consequences. Further, sourcing decisions directly impact company revenues and costs, in addition to exposing it to risk factors.

Sourcing and supply strategies, policies, and processes should be extended and be in alignment with the corporation's mission, objectives, and competitive advantage (Figure 10.1).

Since companies compete and are driven by different factors, there is no one right sourcing strategy or set of purchasing processes. Some companies are motivated by responsiveness, while others are driven by cost or by social or environmental concerns. Each reason entails different sourcing strategies, policies, and processes. These differences affect the organization's financial and operational performance, thus tradeoffs are common. Although the sourcing function

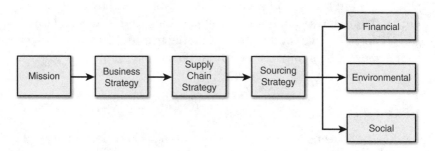

Figure 10.1 Sourcing strategy alignment.

has traditionally been a cost centered function, it is transforming into a cross-functional strategic center for many organizations.

Terminology surrounding sourcing and supply management can be unclear, so it is important to address this before delving into the chapter. The use of different expressions such as procurement, sourcing, and supply management can be somewhat unclear. Some use procurement to describe transactional buying, whereas sourcing and supply management take this further to include global purchasing, relationship building, information sharing, and collaborative strategy development. In this chapter, each term will be used interchangeably, leaving the debate for another forum.

Why Is Sourcing and Supply Management Important

Sourcing and supply management use other parties and companies to obtain goods and services that are critically important for organizational success and competiveness. These transactions, partnerships, and relationships have consequences if not managed properly. Sourcing goes beyond typical cost and quality control factors. Although cost control is important, each strategic and operational sourcing decision has a greater financial, environmental, and social consequence. Consequences are the result of the types of materials companies purchase or the suppliers used and relationships they develop. Responsible sourcing, sourcing decisions based on environmental and social factors, is becoming more prevalent because it considers all stakeholders, not just stockholders. Companies and their executives are being held accountable for damage they cause to the environment and communities in which they do business. The way the company sources and operates is reflective of the company decision makers, which impacts their brand image and ultimately impacting their financial performance.

Financial

The purchasing and sourcing functions have long been focused on reducing the organization's materials and services costs. Recall from earlier chapters that inventory purchases are captured in the inventory account on the balance sheet. Inventory purchases include the amount paid to suppliers to acquire inventory, freight costs incurred for the delivery of products, import costs, and taxes. Once this inventory is used, the cost is expensed and captured in the COGS account on the income statement. If the inventory and subsequent COGS balances are reduced, a direct and quantifiable result is observed. Lowering sourcing costs results in lower COGS on the income statement.

However, purchasing is not just a matter of lowering costs and inventory levels any longer. The purchasing function has transformed itself, becoming a collaborative nucleus of communication and information sharing for the purpose of driving the organization's competitiveness. To increase financial performance, it is necessary to coordinate activities and collaborate with other departments to achieve a competitive advantage. Success requires coordination in several areas: finance and accounting, production and manufacturing, and sales and marketing.

Collaboration and coordination with other departments and with suppliers can increase revenues and profit margins through higher service levels and customer satisfaction. A teamwork approach leads to an increase in the quality of goods and services, and a reduction in rework, waste, and warranty work. In a lean manufacturing environment, collaboration and coordination is important. The delivery of smaller orders more often requires reliable transportation and miniscule damage rates. Further, in this type of environment, a focus on reducing setup and ordering costs is imperative; otherwise, these costs will increase dramatically as an increase in the number of orders is placed.

The profit leverage effect (PLE) is widely used to show how a reduction in COGS leads to improved profits faster than a corresponding increase in sales. A question often contemplated is, should the company increase sales or decrease costs to improve profitability quicker? Using a simplified profit and loss statement (Table 10.1), PLE is demonstrated. As viewed in the table a base state is provided, and then increasing sales by 10% and reducing costs by 10% are compared.

Suppose that Green Design and Build has an operating profit of $250,000 and total sales of $1 million in a given fiscal year, the base case in Table 10.1. It has an operating profit margin of 25%. This means that for every dollar of sales, they generate $0.25 in operating profit. Further, if Green Design and Build has $3.5 million in total assets, its return on assets is ($250,000/$3,500,000) or 7.14%. What strategic initiatives can help improve these figures?

As observed in the table, a 10% decrease in spending (COGS) is more advantageous than an equivalent percentage increase in sales. A decrease in cost results in an 18% change in profit, where an increase

Table 10.1 Profit Leverage Effect

	Base Case	Decrease Cost (10%)	Increase Sales (10%)	Increase Sales (18%)
Gross sales	1,000,000	1,000,000	1,100,000	1,180,000
–Cost of goods sold (45%)	450,000	405,000	495,000	531,000
= Gross profit	550,000	595,000	605,000	649,000
–Sales, general and administration (30%)	300,000	300,000	330,000	354,000
= Operating profit	250,000	295,000	275,000	295,000
Change in profit		18%	10%	18%

Notes: COGS and SG&A are calculated as a percent of sales. In the decrease cost scenario, COGS is reduced 10% from the COGS in the base case scenario.

in sales results in a 10% increase in profit. The PLE example reveals that to earn revenue, SG&A expenses that hold back operating profit are always incurred.

The next question that a sales manager might want answered is, "How much of an increase in sales would it take to see an 18% change in profit, equivalent to decreasing cost 10%?" The last column in Table 10.1 demonstrates this scenario. Consider the fact that every dollar saved in purchased materials increases operating profit by $1. Therefore, Green Design and Build would have to generate $18 in sales to get the same improvement in operating profit as cutting $1 from its COGS. This profit-leverage effect is particularly important for low-margin businesses. In addition to affecting profits, reducing the cost of materials also would reduce the amount of money invested in inventory, consequently, generating a higher ROA. Table 10.2 shows operating profit margins and ROA for each scenario that was presented in Table 10.1.

Environmental

Sourcing practices impact the environment in which people work and live. Pressure by stakeholders is making environmental issues less likely to be ignored by executives. Environmental issues are increasingly visible to company leaders. Sourcing decisions are more likely to consider the impacts to the environment today than in the past. Decisions about how to reduce global warming and carbon dioxide emissions, how to dispose of hazardous materials, and how to harvest and replenish raw materials are quite common.

Table 10.2 Operating Profit Margins and ROA

	Operating Profit Margin[a] (%)	ROA[b] (%)
Base case	25.0	7.14
Decrease cost (10%)	29.5	8.43
Increase sales (10%)	25.0	7.86
Increase sales (18%)	25.0	8.43

[a]Operating profit margin = Operating profit/gross sales.

[b]ROA = Gross sales/$3.5 million (assume total assets are $3.5 million).

Not doing what society perceives to be the "right thing" can harm a company's brand image, reduce future revenue, and increase costs through litigation and fines. Customers, environmental advocates, and other stakeholders can be extremely vocal if companies' actions are deemed inappropriate. Many companies have found that using suppliers who are destroying natural resources, wasting raw materials, or polluting ground water often result in unwanted press coverage.

Many companies are involving the sourcing department and their suppliers in the implementation of agriculture and forestry resource conservation programs aimed at reducing energy use, greenhouse gasses, and water usage. Others are in the midst of changing energy sources from oil-based fuels to alternatives such as biofuels. Although environmental decision making is front and center, there can be a monetary gain from environmental programs. Packaging materials and transport suppliers find that a focus on reducing environmental impact has decreased the amount of packaging materials needed and uncovered improved routings that lessen environmental impacts and operating costs.

Social

Beyond financial and environmental sourcing decisions, companies have a significant impact on the fair and equitable treatment of employees. Companies continue to use low-cost suppliers taking advantage of low wages. However, low wages brings issues related to labor practices, human rights, and employees' health and safety. There are a number of examples of companies using suppliers whose employees work in deplorable conditions, in unsafe environments, and work long hours without breaks, food, or water. Such working conditions have caused injury and death.

Stakeholders and customers are demanding the fair and equitable treatment of employees, providing them with living wages, safe working conditions, and environments free of discrimination and harassment. Just as in the case of environmental issues, not doing the "right thing" in a social context can harm a company's brand image and reduce future revenues. As stated earlier, customers, social advocates, and stakeholders can be extremely vocal if companies act in ways that others find inappropriate. Stakeholders want companies to be ethical as well as follow the laws that govern the industry.

There are environmental and social compliance elements to which companies must adhere when sourcing certain materials. If left to their own devices, companies may not act in the best interest of the communities they work in or the people they work with, so laws have been enacted to protect people and environments. For example, two European Union regulations outline requirements for data collection, labeling, and disposal procedures that must be undertaken if certain materials are sourced and used in production. REACH (Registration, Evaluation, Authorization and Restriction of Chemicals) aims to improve the protection of the environment and human health from the risks imposed by chemicals. What REACH does for chemicals is just like what RoHS does for electronics. The Restriction of the Use of Certain Hazardous Substances in Electrical and Electronic Equipment protects the environment and society from the harmful disposal of electronic equipment or e-waste.

In the United States, the Dodd–Frank Act requires certain companies using conflict minerals in their products to disclose the source of these minerals. Conflict minerals are minerals mined in conditions of armed conflict and human rights abuses, mostly in the eastern provinces of the Democratic Republic of the Congo. After mining, these minerals are then passed to a variety of intermediaries before being purchased mostly by multinational electronics companies. The profits from the sale of these minerals finance continued fighting and human rights abuses.

Organizational Purchasing Structure

The sourcing department supports the organization's competitive position and its organizational structure has implications to meeting this position. The organizational structure affects the speed and accuracy of information exchange and can affect service levels, inventory

Table 10.3 Comparison of Purchasing Structures

	Advantages	Disadvantages
Centralized structure	Greater buying specialization	Lack of business unit focus
	Greater buying leverage-clout	Distance from users
	Common suppliers	Tendency to minimize legitimate differences in requirements
	Proximity to corporate decision makers	Sharing of information is limited to one way
Decentralized structure	Speed of response	Difficult to communicate between business units
	Effective use of local sources	Operational vs. strategic focus
	Easier coordination with business unit	Tendency to focus too much on local sources
	Use of appropriate political, cultural, social, and currency environment	Lack of purchasing leverage-clout

continuity, and sourcing costs. Companies that are simple and lack the complexity of multiple business units initially tend to fall into a centralized purchasing structure. As companies grow and become more complex, their organizational structures gravitate over time to a decentralized purchasing structure. Many of these corporations are finding that a hybrid structure may be more beneficial, thus returning to a more centralized structure but maintaining some decentralized functions where appropriate.

There are advantages and disadvantages to each structure (Table 10.3). A centralized system has the advantage of using fewer suppliers, which drives purchase price reductions using its larger size for leverage. However, the centralized structure also lacks the clarity and emphasis of each business units' needs. The decentralized structure tends to be quicker and has local knowledge, though it loses the ability to leverage its size and reduce purchase prices.

Hybrid structures might centralize certain functions, such as implementing the corporation's strategic direction, policies and procedures, recruitment and training, and auditing supply performance and suppliers. Hybrid structures also decentralize the execution of actually sourcing materials and services. Typically, each business unit is responsible for its own profits and losses, thus business units want control over their own spending.

No matter which organizational sourcing structure is in place, common decisions have to be worked through, such as

1. Recruitment and training
2. Supplier relationships and collaboration
3. Information sharing
4. Leveraging organizational buying power
5. Auditing supplier performance

Business decisions such as these require careful forethought in the way sourcing processes, procedures, and systems are designed and implemented.

Sourcing and Supply Management Objectives

Realizing the importance of supply management in terms of financial, environmental, and social goals leads to the sourcing department's core objectives. To improve the company's competitive position, the sourcing department operates with the following objectives in mind:

1. Develop purchasing strategies that support the business strategy and organizational goals
2. Maintain supply continuity
3. Obtain and develop suppliers
4. Manage sourcing processes efficiently and effectively

Purchasing Strategies that Support Organizational Goals and Objectives

The sourcing department is responsible for developing strategies that support organizational goals and the business strategy. Before appropriate strategies can be determined, objectives to reach established goals should be stated. Goals often include

1. Cash flow preservation
2. Cost reductions
3. Improve social responsibility
4. Improve margins

5. Minimize inventory investment

6. Reduce environmental impact

To achieve the company's objectives and goals, the sourcing department has many decisions to make, such as

1. Which suppliers to use and where they are located

2. Which materials to use

3. When and how much inventory to purchase

4. Who holds the inventory and when the title transfers ownership

Using local compared with global sources of supply reduces complexity and generally allows for quicker information flows between buyers and suppliers, shorter lead-times, and fewer delivery delays. Though, global sourcing has benefits, too. It is possible that the only place to find materials and technical expertise is abroad; it is also possible that the total cost of ownership may be less through the use of regional trade agreements. Whether or not local or global sources are being used, the management of inventory and choices in transportation and materials will impact financial performance and the environment.

Of course, the sourcing department will eventually decide from whom and from where to purchase materials. Then, they will have to formulate a purchasing strategy. The strategy typically will consider when the money will change hands. This approach contemplates the timing of cash inflow and outflow. Typical purchasing strategies are

1. Spot purchasing

2. Volume and quantity discount

3. Just in time

4. Forward and hedging

5. Product lifecycle

Spot Purchasing

Spot purchasing is a purchasing strategy that is used to meet the current needs of the company. This type of purchase is often unplanned, but used when materials are needed immediately to complete or project or continue operation. Spot purchasing is also used when the company is experiencing low cash inflow and their remaining cash must be preserved. Further, spot purchasing is used when the price of materials is anticipated to decline, thus buying only for current needs and waiting until prices decline to buy for future needs.

Volume and Quantity Discount Purchasing

Suppliers will often offer volume or quantity discounts to buyers. These discounts provide cost reductions to the buyer but are a way to reduce cost for the supplier as well. Suppliers' cost reductions are seen in the form of reduced production cost (fewer setups and longer production runs) and in distribution where full truckloads can be used instead of multiple less-than-full truckloads. The buyer, of course, should decide whether or not to take the volume discount. Does the buyer need the additional units and will the quantity discount reduce or increase cost over the long term? Using the following example, answers to these questions can be determined.

For example, use a café franchise that purchases coffee beans from a South American distributor. The coffee shop plans to buy 250,000 pounds of coffee beans this year, the holding cost is $5.45 per pound per year and the order cost is $150 per order. Recall from an earlier chapter that the following formula can be used to determine the optimal order quantity, where Q is the optimal order quantity, D is the annual demand for the product, S is the setup/order cost, and H is the annual per unit holding cost.

$$Q = \sqrt{\frac{2 \times D \times S}{H}}$$

Using the formula, if the café wishes to order coffee beans, how many pounds of beans should they order each time?

$$Q = \sqrt{\frac{2 \times 250,000 \times \$150}{\$5.45}} \approx 3,710 \text{ pounds}$$

To minimize inventory costs, the inventory managers should order 3,710 pounds of coffee beans in each order. But, what if the coffee bean distributor offers a quantity discount as shown in Table 10.4?

Using the total cost of inventory formula below, where TC is the total cost, Q is the order quantity in units, H is the holding cost, D is the annual demand in units, S is the order cost, and P is the unit cost, the café can determine whether or not they should take the quantity discount.

Table 10.4 Coffee Bean Discount/Volume Purchase Prices

Pounds of Beans	Price per pound ($)
1–5,000	3.25
5,001–10,000	3.00
10,001 and more	2.75

Total cost of inventory = Holding cost + Ordering cost + Purchase cost

$$TC = \frac{Q}{2} H + \frac{D}{Q} S + PD$$

If the café orders 3,710 pounds each time an order is placed at a cost of $3.25 per pound, the total annual cost to the café franchise will be $832,717.57.

$$TC_{3,710} = \frac{3,710}{2} \times \$5.45 + \frac{250,000}{3,710} \times \$150.00 + \$3.25 \times 250,000$$

$$TC_{3,710} = \$10,109.75 + \$10,107.82 + \$812,500 = \$832,717.57$$

If the café orders 10,001 pounds each time they order—just enough to take advantage of the quantity discount of $2.75 per pound, the total annual inventory cost to the café franchise will be $718,502.36.

$$TC_{10,001} = \frac{10,001}{2} \times \$5.45 + \frac{250,000}{10,001} \times \$150.00 + \$2.75 \times 250,000$$

$$TC_{10,001} = \$27,252.73 + \$3,749.63 + \$687,500 = \$718,502.36$$

From this example, it would behoove the café to take the volume discount and order additional pounds of coffee beans each time since the total cost is less when applying the volume discount. Although holding cost increases, this is offset by the lower order cost and price per unit.

Just-in-Time Purchasing

Just-in-time (JIT) purchasing allows an organization to receive the items just as they are needed. It is commonly used to reduce inventory, improving inventory and asset performance ratios. Purchasing in this manner is planned and is ongoing. It works best for products with stable and continuous demand. Because JIT purchasing is rooted in lean principles, it induces a higher number of orders and with fewer amounts in each order. The result is that buffer inventory is reduced. Because of this, highly reliable deliveries and high-quality materials are needed. Major problems occur if transportation infrastructure and suppliers are not reliable.

Making the switch to JIT purchasing is not simply focused on ordering less to reduce inventory levels. Ordering less means that more purchase orders are required to fulfill demand, which requires reducing order costs first. To illustrate, if the café from the previous example is not offered a quantity discount, but instead has opted for JIT purchasing, how would cost be affected as coffee beans are purchased more often but in smaller quantities?

It was shown earlier that the café should order 3,710 pounds of coffee beans to minimize yearly inventory cost.

$$TC_{3,710} = \frac{3,710}{2} \times \$5.45 + \frac{250,000}{3,710} \times \$150.00 = \$20,217.57$$

What would happen to the cost of inventory if the café ordered 2,000 pounds of beans instead without reducing the order cost first? Total cost would increase not decrease as hoped for.

$$TC_{2,000} = \frac{2,000}{2} \times \$5.45 + \frac{250,000}{2,000} \times \$150.00 = \$24,200.00$$

Depending on the situation, reducing order cost might entail reducing transportation or wage costs associated with performing purchasing functions. Increasing efficiencies through process improvements and automation may be useful in these situations.

Forward and Hedging Purchasing

Forward and hedging are similar purchasing strategies, but differ in the way their contracts are composed and administered. Both look into the future and try to determine if prices for materials will increase. Forward purchasing is a commitment to purchase in anticipation of future requirements. It is most often used when item shortages are anticipated due to instances such as employee strikes or droughts, or when material prices are expected to increase. Hedging is a purchasing strategy using commodity exchanges, in which a premium is paid now to cover price changes or losses later, similar to an insurance policy.

Forward and hedging are used to offset price and exchange rate risk but neither is a guarantee. Over the years, some airlines used hedging strategies to offset future fuel price increases. Airlines thought the price of fuel was going to increase, so they bought fuel on the futures market at prices less than what they thought fuel was going to be in the future. However, fuel prices did not increase, they actually declined and the airlines that hedged fuel prices were forced to pay higher prices than the spot market price (e.g., buying at the pump). Hedging takes some skill and experience, so this strategy is not best suited for everyone or every industry.

Product Life Cycle Purchasing

The stage of the life cycle that a product is in directly affects how that item and related items should be purchased. In the introduction stage, the focus is placed on purchasing low quantities but reliable materials. The new product has to work when it is first introduced. During the growth phase, sourcing focuses strategies that work well with greater quantities of materials and more capacity. During the mature stage, efficiencies and steady cost controls are employed. As the declining stage is entered, the focus is on reducing quantities and further reducing cost, maintaining ample supplies for remaining sales and warranty work.

Supply Continuity to Support Operations

Maintaining an uninterrupted flow of materials and services is necessary to meet the requirements of a business's operations. It is crucial that materials meet necessary specifications, be the right price, and be delivered at the appropriate time at the needed location. As simple as this appears on the surface, it can be difficult to accomplish. Without a continuous flow of the correct materials and services, production stops and sales revenue declines. To make matters worse, cash inflow slows down, but cash outflow continues because fixed costs still need to be paid. Further, if products are not available for customers, they become unhappy. This can also affect investment or stock prices.

To maintain supply continuity successfully, sourcing professionals work to open lines of communication between their company's internal functional departments and with external suppliers. Communication reduces the risk of supply chain disruptions. Many areas in a supply chain can cause an interruption in the flow of goods: operational, financial, relational, and informational. For instance, inaccurate or untimely information about sales promotions that result in increased demand, which affects the company's ability to fulfill orders. Conversely, actions that lead to a disruption could be port closures, labor strikes, terrorism, natural disasters, supplier failure, quality, and political uncertainty.

There are a number of reasons for the increased risk of disruption. One reason is that supply chains are more global; increasing the length and complexity of supply chains increases the opportunity for problem areas. Another reason is that companies are focusing on lean and efficient supply chains, rather than effective ones. As a result, the supplier base is reduced and more "focused" type manufacturing facilities are being used, leading to centralization. This leaves little room for error.

Not all risks are alike. Some risks do more harm than others, some are dependent on specific company and industry characteristics, and all risks change over time. Ideally, a supply chain manager should have a true understanding of the supply chain before taking any specific steps to manage supply chain risk. A simple risk management program starts with the following four steps:

1. Map and understand the supply chain
2. Identify the critical paths and infrastructure
3. Manage the critical paths and infrastructure
4. Improve supply chain visibility

Once a comprehensive picture is drawn, it is time to categorize risks from devastating to inconsequential. This will help identify where efforts should be focused when implementing and managing supply chain risk. It is valuable to complete the following four-step process while using this simple formula. The higher the value at risk, the more attention should be given to this risk element.

Supply chain value at risk = value lost if event occurred
× probability of the occurrence happening

1. Identify all of the risk elements
2. Assess the dollar impact or value lost if the event occurred
3. Determine the probability of the occurrence happening
4. Prioritize the risks for monitoring and prevention

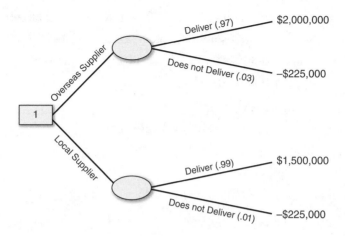

Figure 10.2 Decision tree for selecting suppliers.

A common supply chain risk that sourcing departments grapple with is the inability of their suppliers to deliver products and services when promised. This is especially prominent when choosing between global or domestic suppliers. Global suppliers generally have a higher risk of failure to deliver on time.

Using decision trees can assist in making supplier selection decisions in the face of risk and uncertainty (Figure 10.2). As an example, suppose an airplane wiring company has just secured a winning bid to provide wiring harnesses to an aircraft manufacturer. The airplane wiring company is now deciding between an overseas supplier and a local supplier for one of its wiring harness products. The overseas supplier can supply the product at a cost of $50 per unit, whereas the local supplier can supply the product at a cost of $55 per unit. The airplane wiring company expects to sell 100,000 harnesses at a price of $70 to the aircraft manufacturer. If the airplane wiring company fails to deliver the harnesses by the delivery date, they estimate that they will incur a loss of goodwill, future revenue, and penalties of $225,000.

After considering the possibility of the suppliers failing to deliver products on time, the aircraft wiring company has determined that there is a 97% chance that the overseas supplier will deliver on time and a 3% chance that they will not. There is a 99% chance that the local supplier will deliver on time and a 1% chance that they will not. With the information provided thus far, payoffs for each branch of the decision tree are calculated as follows:

Overseas supplier delivers: $(70 - 50) \times 100,000 = \$2,000,000$

Overseas supplier does not deliver: $-\$225,000$

Local supplier delivers: $(70 - 55) \times 100,000 = \$1,500,000$

Local supplier does not deliver: $-\$225,000$

The next step is to use the payoff values and the probabilities to calculate the expected values for each alternative.

Alternative 1 Use overseas supplier: Overseas supplier delivers and does not deliver:

$$(\$2,000,000 \times 0.97) = \$1,940,000$$
$$(-\$225,000 \times 0.03) = -\$6,750$$
$$\$1,940,000 + (-\$6,750) = \$1,933,250$$

Alternative 2 Use local supplier: Local supplier delivers and does not deliver:

$$(\$1,500,000 \times 0.99) = \$1,485,000$$
$$(-\$225,000 \times 0.01) = -\$2,250$$
$$\$1,485,000 + (-\$2,250) = \$1,482,750$$

In the end, this computes a weighted average for the two alternatives. The alternative with the highest expected value is the better choice, thus the overseas supplier is selected.

In addition, decision trees are useful when selecting suppliers in the same markets. Take, for example, two auto parts suppliers in the same city. Both suppliers are reliable, they provide high-quality parts and their prices are comparable. However, what affect would sudden turn in the market or a significant disruption in their business have on each? Could this leave them vulnerable or bankrupt and unable to deliver? Thorough audits and reviews, along with placing appropriate mitigation techniques in place before this occurs are wise.

Obtain and Develop Suppliers

Supply chains are about more than managing goods, services, money, and information. They are becoming relationship chains. Outsourcing is common as corporations and their supply chains become less vertically integrated. A weak supplier or a weak network of suppliers can seriously damage a company's brand image, along with its financial and operational performance. Continuity, quality, and cost cannot be achieved without a well-functioning, interconnected supply chain supplier network.

Important decisions about suppliers include:

1. Selecting and evaluating suppliers
2. How many suppliers to use
3. Supplier involvement and development

To manage the supplier network effectively, it is important to learn how to select and evaluate suppliers, determine and use an appropriate number of suitable suppliers, and manage the relationships that come from using various suppliers.

Reasons to Outsource

In the previous section, decisions surrounding suppliers were introduced. Before examining this in detail, it is important to understand why companies need suppliers. Typically, it is because the supplier can provide a service or there is a competitive position the organization wants to maintain. Examples of outsourcing to suppliers include sourcing raw materials, outsourcing the manufacturing of components, and outsourcing services. Sourcing and outsourcing decisions are influenced by the availability of resources, skills and expertise, and cost. Reasons to outsource can be viewed in three general categories:

1. Financial
2. Improvement
3. Organizational

Financial: Companies outsource with the intention of reducing costs. They want to reduce fixed costs and replace them with variable costs. By doing so, return on assets improves by selling unnecessary assets and from reducing inventory levels.

Improvement: Companies outsource with the intention of improving the quality of their products and services. This is accomplished by obtaining expertise, skills, and technologies that are otherwise unavailable in-house. Further, companies can improve productivity and shorten cycle times for introducing new products to market.

Organizational: Companies will outsource to improve their effectiveness by focusing on what they do best. In addition, companies can increase their product and service value by moving closer to customers and improving response times to better match customer requirements. Companies that have products and services with volatile and uncertain demand can increase flexibility by using outsourced companies.

Just as risk evolves and changes over time, so do outsourcing decisions. If outsourcing was favored in the past, there is nothing wrong with reversing this decision at a later date. Economic, social, and competitive reasons could favor insourcing. Airlines and computer companies outsourced call center support only to find that this move reduced customer satisfaction to the point that these companies reversed their earlier decisions.

Selecting and Evaluating Suppliers

Several characteristics exist with which one can evaluate and select potential suppliers. Traditionally, cost, quality, and service were the three main criteria for supplier selection. Today, there are many more to consider:

1. Certification—ISO
2. Environmental and social sustainability
3. Financial condition
4. Innovation, process, and design capabilities
5. Long-term relationship compliance
6. Management competence
7. Regulation compliance and transparency
8. Responsiveness
9. Risk profile

To help narrow the selection and evaluation criteria and the list of potential supplier candidates, it helps understand the degree of interfirm collaboration that is required. The level of interfirm collaboration dictates the type of suppler relationship needed. Where firms reside on the relationship continuum depends on who the end customer is, what they expect, and the type of product or service being provided.

Interfirm collaboration can run from an arm's length transaction all the way to vertical integration. Interfirm collaboration can also include several points in between these two extremes including partnerships, strategic alliances, and joint ventures. The need for information technology integration, openness, communication, and trust each become more important the closer the relationship requirements gravitate toward vertical integration.

Airlines are a good example of the relationship continuum. There is independence as well as interdependence among them. Airlines may "code-share," coordinate baggage handling and transfers, and integrate information technology. They may even take an equity stake in another airline. Even though they have done well in building relationships, they do fall short in some areas. Passenger complaint resolution and customer service are not always seamless between airlines due to differing policies or lack of coordination.

No matter what the relationship or the selection and evaluation criteria, the overarching goal is to select suppliers and partners who will help the firm compete, retain customers, and generate sales.

How Many Suppliers to Use

A decision the sourcing department must consider carefully is how many suppliers to use. One thought is that if more suppliers are used, then the competition between them will drive down prices. In some instances, this may not be an option. For highly technical and specific items, only one supplier may available. On the contrary, if fewer suppliers or single-sourcing strategies are used, the relationship between the supplier and buyer will be enhanced. However, if more suppliers are available and used, a multisourcing strategy can be used to reduce risk of item shortages.

As a general rule, if commodity items, such as stationary and letterhead, are being sourced, using more suppliers to promote competition to lower prices is appropriate. The disadvantage is that it does not promote long-term relationships and collaboration. For more technical components, such as jet engines, fewer suppliers is often the most viable option. Also, for products that are more valuable to the company, the general thought is that using fewer suppliers makes sense. Although maintaining reasonable costs is necessary, technical support, technical expertise, and service are more important, so the relationship aspect becomes an essential factor.

For most companies, the numbers of suppliers rise over time. After a while, the number of suppliers gets to an unmanageable number. If this happens, it becomes necessary to optimize (reduce) the supply base. Reducing the supply base frees time resulting in improved

Figure 10.3 Number of suppliers per category.

communications and relationships with critical suppliers. Pareto charts are useful tools to help determine where to focus attention and efforts for this reduction. Figure 10.3 displays the number of suppliers in each category from high to low, thus identifying where the bloat is occurring. In this example, print suppliers would be reduced first.

The number of suppliers is not the only factor to consider. Knowing the amount of money spent in each category is also imperative. If cost reductions are to be made, they should be made where there is the greatest effect. A 10% reduction in logistics spending is much more lucrative than a 10% reduction in training and development spending (Figure 10.4).

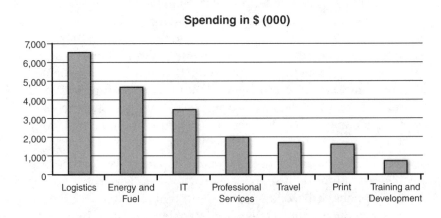

Figure 10.4 Dollar amount of spending per category.

Supplier Involvement and Development

Another aspect firms contend with is deciding how involved suppliers should be and to what extent firms should develop their suppliers. Should suppliers be involved in product development and other critical decisions? Larger companies with complex material and component requirements are beginning to take a proactive approach with their suppliers. They are finding that buyer and supplier relationships can mitigate new product development costs and risks. Early supplier involvement can produce better designs, decrease production costs, and yield faster idea-design-production-sale timelines.

Furthermore, a joint buyer–supplier quality program can reduce the amount of defective product and service instances. The cost of rejecting materials and shipments for noncompliance increases costs related to transportation and testing, among others. Working with suppliers can reduce the amount of defective and nonconforming products and services.

Firms may also seek to help their suppliers develop into high-functioning organizations. The goal is to increase supplier and firm performance by focusing on alignment of critical processes such as new product development, material replenishment, and cash-to-cash cycle time. By helping suppliers reduce lead times, increase their research and development capabilities, providing expertise, and providing capital to their suppliers, suppliers can therefore be a competitive asset to the firm and the supply chain.

Moreover, working with suppliers to improve productivity results in better positive cash flow for the buying firm. Recall from an earlier chapter that break-even analysis was used to assist in the make or buy decision. If the time to reach break-even is reduced, working capital and the time to achieve positive cash flow is also reduced. Many companies are finding it beneficial to help their suppliers improve using lean and quality approaches. Buyers find that the suppliers can pass along cost savings to the buying firm while the supplier still maintains their profit margin.

Managing the Sourcing Process Effectively and Efficiently

A major objective for the sourcing organization is to operate effectively. This may range from being highly efficient to being extremely flexible, or somewhere in between. Depending on what is

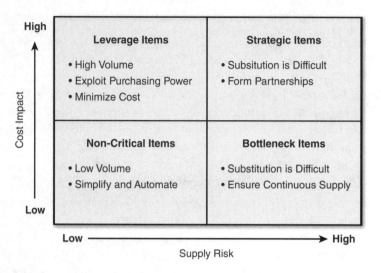

Figure 10.5 Purchase portfolio matrix.(Adapted from Kraljic P. *Purchasing Must Become Supply Management.* Harvard Business Review, 1983.)

being purchased and from whom, appropriate purchasing strategies, processes, and policies can be implemented. A mismatch between purchasing and its related processes can result in excessive purchasing costs, a lack of material continuity, and lower service levels. Sourcing requires a range of relationship structures and knowing the type of relationship that is required allows for the implementation of suitable purchasing strategies, processes, and policies to operate effectively and efficiently as necessary.

The purchase portfolio matrix can assist in the selection of the most appropriate purchasing strategies and processes (Figure 10.5). It helps identify where close well-developed relationships are needed and where automation is more suitable. The 2 × 2 matrix considers risk as measured by the number of suppliers available and the cost impact to the company. A high-supply risk indicates few available suppliers, whereas a low-supply risk indicates that many suppliers are available. A high-cost impact indicates that the cost of purchases is high, whereas a low-cost impact indicates that the cost of purchases is low. For example, an aircraft jet engine has few available suppliers (high risk) and the cost to purchase a jet engine is high (high-cost impact). On the contrary, there are an enormous number of suppliers for stationary and letterhead (low risk), while stationary and letterhead are inexpensive (low-cost impact).

How can the purchase portfolio matrix be used? First, segment purchased goods and services into one of the four quadrants. Once the purchases are segmented, develop the appropriate purchasing strategies, policies, processes, and relationships.

Strategic and bottleneck items: Unique products and service designs, few suppliers.

Strategic items: Develop supplier relationships and partnerships, switching suppliers is difficult, increase role of selected supplier, strive for effectiveness, supply continuity, and technical expertise is more important than price, prepare contingency plans, and requires a great deal of negotiation.

Bottleneck items: Ensure supply continuity, continuity is more important than price, design alternate materials or parts, reduce dependence on these items through diversification, seek substitute parts, strive for effectiveness, and strive to move to noncritical or leverage quadrants.

Noncritical and leverage items: Common products and service designs, many suppliers, highly redundant, automate and simplify acquisition processes, use electronic procurement systems, and standardize procurement processes.

Noncritical items: Consider supply base rationalization, use standardized parts, implement competitive bidding, minimize administration costs, use electronic support systems, strive for efficiency and effectiveness, and strive to move from noncritical to leverage quadrant to reduce costs.

Leverage items: Large number of suppliers, buyer has high spending power, push for lower prices and preferential treatment, and strive for efficiency and effectiveness.

Supplier Location and Total Cost of Ownership

As mentioned earlier, potential suppliers are located all over the world. The location of suppliers should not be taken lightly. Lower wages is a major contributor for choosing suppliers in the Asia-Pacific region. However, wages are increasing in some of these historically low-wage regions. Thus, companies are starting to choose suppliers closer to customers. They realize that wages are not the only concern for choosing a supplier. To illustrate, as inventory is reduced through lean practices, focus is shifted to reducing setup and order costs. Lean implementation has a better chance of success if these costs are reduced first. Moving suppliers and assemblers closer together reduces transportation costs, a large part of order costs.

When suppliers are further away from customers and assembly plants, other costs increase too. Because lead-time increases, so do safety and buffer stock levels. As inventory needs increase, cash flow is reduced, requiring the need for additional working capital. Given that there are additional costs beyond unit price, the total cost of ownership needs to be considered before choosing a supplier and making a purchase.

When sourcing globally, it should be recognized that hidden costs are prevalent. These costs include:

1. Additional buffer inventory and safety stock
2. Commissions paid to customs brokers
3. Customs documentation and translation costs
4. Finance fees related to letters of credit
5. Foreign exchange rates diminishing sales and cost savings
6. Foreign taxes and import duties
7. Insurance, warranty, and legal issues

Purchase at Lowest Total Cost of Ownership

Supply managers incur various costs when purchasing goods and services and they should take every opportunity to reduce or avoid these costs whenever possible. In the past, purchasers were only interested in the price per unit when making purchasing decisions. Often overlooked were other costs incurred but not considered. Total cost of ownership (TCO) considers these other costs that are beyond the cost per unit of an item being purchased. These costs are often significant and if left unchecked can cause unnecessary additional costs to the company.

Total cost of ownership is especially important when deciding to use low-cost wage countries. In addition to the hidden costs that were discussed in the previous section, other costs can be prevalent when sourcing globally that reduces the advantages of low wages. When considering a supplier, figure the following costs into your total cost calculations. It can be costly if these elements are not considered.

1. Acquire the product (wages, productivity)
2. Disposal (end of product life)
3. Installation and maintenance (technical support)
4. Landed cost (unit price, transportation, custom duties)
5. Reliability (service)
6. Rework (quality)
7. Service the product (technical support)
8. Storage and inventory costs
9. Timeliness (service, productivity)
10. Training (service)

After all relevant costs are accounted for, it is entirely possible that a supplier who was considered a frontrunner is no longer in that position. Since total cost of ownership can change over time, it is necessary to extend TCO analysis into the future. Table 10.5 reveals an example of TCO analysis for purchasing 500 laptop computers.

Although the example is simplistic, it does represent how TCO is calculated. It identifies and includes all of the relevant costs from the present day's initial cash outflow, and since IT equipment typically has a useful life of about 3 years, the analysis extends into the future. This exercise would be repeated for each supplier under consideration. The supplier with the lowest TCO is the most logical choice if cost were the only decision criteria. Of course, other criteria should be included in the decision-making process, which have been introduced throughout this chapter.

Supply Management and the Financial Connection

DuPont Model

As discussed earlier, the sourcing department has an incredible opportunity to improve corporate financial and operational performance. They have the ability to lower COGS, increase profit margins, reduce inventory, and improve inventory and asset performance ratios. The DuPont model is once again used to demonstrate these effects. Using the income statement and balance sheet, the DuPont model is created for a company's current position or base case (Figure 10.6).

Table 10.5 Total Cost of Ownership

Cost Elements	Cost Measures	Present	Year 1	Year 2	Year 3
Purchase price per laptop					
Equipment	$700 per laptop	$350,000			
Software	$200 per laptop	$100,000			
Acquisition price					
Sourcing	1 FTE @ $65K for 2 months	$10,833			
Administration	1 PO @ $150, 12 invoices @ $25 each	$150	$300	$300	$300
Usage costs					
Equipment support	$60 per month per laptop		$360,000	$360,000	$360,000
Network support	$70 per month per laptop		$420,000	$420,000	$420,000
Warranty	$90 per laptop for a 3-year warranty	$45,000			
Opportunity cost-lost productivity	Downtime 10 hours per laptop per year @ $55 per hour		$275,000	$275,000	$275,000
End of life					
Salvage value	$50 per laptop				($25,000)
Total		$505,983	$1,055,300	$1,055,300	$1,030,300
					$3,646,883

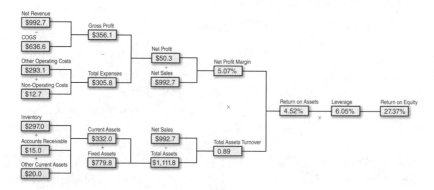

Figure 10.6 DuPont model base case.

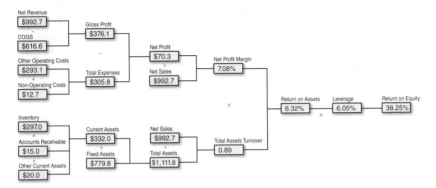

Figure 10.7 DuPont model COGS change.

Suppose upper management has implemented certain profitability goals for the company, thus an effort begins within the sourcing department to reduce COGS. The improvement is shown in the DuPont model (Figure 10.7). COGS sold were reduced 3.14% from $636.6 million to $616.6 million, resulting in an improvement in profit margin, ROA, and ROE.

The leaders of the sourcing department believed more improvement could be made. Thus, another effort is undertaken to reduce inventory levels. Along with the COGS reduction, inventory was reduced 6.73% from $297 million to $277 million. The results are seen in Figure 10.8.

Table 10.6 summarizes the results for each of the three scenarios. The three DuPont models and the following table provide a good

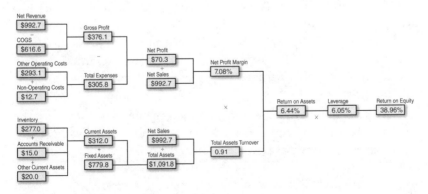

Figure 10.8 DuPont model COGS and inventory change.

Table 10.6 DuPont Model Comparison

	Base Case	COGS Change	COGS and Inventory Change
Gross profit margin	35.87%	37.89%	37.89%
ROA	4.52%	6.32%	6.44%
ROE	27.37%	38.25%	38.96%
Inventory turnover	2.14 times	2.08 times	2.23 times
Days of inventory	170.29	175.81	163.97

visual representation of how certain performance measures change and their interactions. Reducing COGS improves profit margins, ROA, and ROE, but decreases inventory turnover and increases days of inventory. Reducing inventory further improves ROA, ROE, inventory turnover, and days of inventory.

Accounts Payable Turnover

Companies negotiate and employ policies that prescribe when they pay their suppliers. Conventional wisdom would suggest that the longer you wait to pay your suppliers, the better. Keeping cash in your own bank account longer allows the company to earn interest income and reduces the need for additional sources of working capital to operate the business. However, this does leave your suppliers in a bit of a quandary. They may need to be paid without delay to operate their own business. If they are not paid in a reasonable amount of time, one cannot expect a high level of service. To gauge how quickly suppliers are paid, the accounts payable turnover ratio, which is an accounting liquidity metric, is used. The ratio measures the number of times in a given period a company pays its accounts payables. Accounts payables turnover can help a company assess its cash situation. Just as accounts receivable ratio is used to assess a company's incoming cash from buyers, accounts payable turnover assesses how a business handles its outgoing payments to suppliers.

The accounts payable turnover ratio is computed by taking the total purchases from suppliers made on credit and then dividing them by the average accounts payable during the same period. This number shows how many times per period the company pays its average payables amount. For example, if a company has $45,500 in credit purchases from suppliers in a year and has an average accounts payable of \$4,575 in the same year; the accounts payable turnover ratio is approximately 9.95 times (\$45,500/\$4,575).

$$\text{Accounts payable turnover} = \frac{\text{Total inventory purchases}}{\text{Average accounts payabley}}$$

$$= \frac{\$45,500}{\$4,575} \approx 9.95 \text{ times}$$

Since there is no single place to find credit purchases within financial statements, it is necessary to use the following formula to calculate purchases made:

Purchases = Cost of goods sold + Ending inventory − Starting inventory

$$= \$46,172 + \$4,409 - \$5,081 = \$45,500$$

If the account payable turnover ratio is trending down from one period to another, this indicates that the company is taking longer to pay its suppliers than it was before. It may also indicate the financial condition of the company is worsening. If the ratio is trending up, the company is paying its suppliers at a faster rate.

As with the accounts receivable turnover ratio, accounts payable turnover can be stated in the number of days it takes to pay suppliers as follows:

Average payment period = Days payable outstanding (DPO)

$$= \frac{365}{\text{Accounts payable turnover ratios}}$$

$$= \frac{365}{9.95 \text{ times}} = 36.68 \text{ days}$$

There is a balance between paying earlier or later. Although it may seem beneficial to delay payment as long as possible, this tactic could put suppliers in a precarious financial position. The untimely cash inflows create a need for them to borrow more money for working capital, and it reduces their ability to increase their capabilities for research and development. Further, gaining a reputation as a company that delays payment, reputable and high-quality suppliers may be less willing to do business. If they are willing to supply this type of company, they likely will not extend favorable credit terms.

Summary

The act of sourcing goods and services plays a crucial role in any organization. There are financial, environment, and social concerns that continually need to be addressed. The strategies employed to source goods and services directly affect cash flow, profitability, and asset utilization. Further, sourcing strategies affect the environment and social climates of the communities the firm occupies thus having a direct impact on company's brand equity. Success of the sourcing department depends on their ability to select and work with appropriate suppliers. Enhancing coordination and collaboration among purchasers and suppliers through open lines of communication is essential to establishing high-functioning supply chains. By implementing appropriate strategies, processes, and policies, the sourcing department can transform itself from a cost saving centered organizational function to a truly competitive asset.

11

Supply and Value Chain Metrics

Supply chain and operations departments have the distinct capability of impacting a corporation's financial performance from several vantage points. Moreover, they are in a position to carry out the corporation's mission and business strategies, enabling the company to compete in the marketplace. It has also been demonstrated that revenue streams, material cost, use of assets, and resultant cash flows are greatly affected by supply chain and operations activities. This chapter summarizes and connects many of the ideas presented in this book and where supply chain and operations managers can make substantive improvements within their companies.

Competition in the marketplace is necessary, so it is important to have a holistic view of it. Generally speaking, companies compete in four areas. They compete on quality, service, time, and cost. Companies that lead in their peer groups provided some combination of increasing quality and service and/or reducing time and cost. If a company is focused on competing through quality, then quality is a focus throughout the entire company. The focus on quality will be evident in supply chain and operations, service departments, call centers, human resources, and all aspects of the business. Likewise, if a company wants to compete using service, then service is a central theme throughout the entire organization. However, it is not enough to focus on one or two functional areas. All areas need to work in concert with each other for the company to be competitive.

Once the company determines how it is going to compete, metrics are applied to gauge performance in these areas. Of course, the metric by itself is of limited value. Interpreting the metrics to identify what is going on behind the scenes that are driving them it crucial. For instance, contemplate measuring the percentage of accurate invoices as an example of quality. First, determine if knowing this information would be useful. If it is, next think about the necessity of knowing how accurate the invoicing system is, or is there other information that can be gleaned from the accuracy of invoices? A high percentage of inaccurate invoicing can impact other areas of the business. One problem that occurs downstream is that the company will see accounts receivables increase as customers delay payments while waiting for accurate invoices. A second problem is that the additional time to correct inaccurate invoices results in additional wages from the time spent redoing the work. Impact to customers should also be given thought—inaccurate invoices waste their time and likely frustrated them.

In this chapter, certain supply chain metrics are presented; remember that this is not an exhaustive list and that there are many metrics that are suitable for different operations. However, no matter the metrics used, thought and intentionality must be used in making the choice. The metric should uncover details about the operation that go beyond the metric itself.

Supply Chain and Competition

How can supply chain and operations assist the corporation in competition? Quality is a key area. There is little debate that quality products and services improve customer satisfaction, leading to increasing revenues. What specifically can the supply chain do to improve customer satisfaction? A number of ways to improve quality and improve customer satisfaction exist. For example, reducing product defects, adhering to delivery schedules and executing perfect order fulfillment are ways to accomplish customer satisfaction. Other areas that can be measured (among many others) to ensure quality include:

1. Accurate invoicing
2. Complete orders
3. Damage-free deliveries
4. Forecast accuracy
5. On-time deliveries

These metrics identify wasteful practices. In addition, these metrics identify any defects and to what extent the defects are affecting the organization.

Service is another major category in which companies compete. Service is a catchall category and contains aspects that do not fit into the other three competition categories. There is a misconception about customer service (actions) and service experience (design of the interactions) being the same thing. Although customer service is important, this is a limited view. The customer experience should be the focal point. This is the journey from the customer's first interaction until their last one. Though, the goal is to keep the interactions in perpetuity. After all, companies want to keep customers.

Customers, especially business-to-business (B2B) customers, like to praise and refer companies that provide great service. Although, it is not uncommon to hear customers criticize companies for their lack of service. Service can come in many forms, a few areas are:

1. Availability of information
2. Minimum order quantity
3. Change order timing

Service is affected by many factors. Companies that implement effective and efficient communication processes, resulting in timely and accurate information, pay attention to details, and are perceived to operate more effectively. They eliminate runarounds and do not ask customers to repeat themselves. In addition, they do not leave customers wondering or searching for the status of orders or delivery times. It is not uncommon for customers to ask suppliers for a reduction in the required minimum order or ask for changes in the timing of the orders. After all, their demand patterns do not necessarily match the suppliers' preset orders. How capable or willing are suppliers to accommodate these requests? Being accommodating reveals a great deal about the company's willingness and ability to serve customers. Supply chain coordination is a key component of ensuring high service levels.

Many operations professionals will tout the idea that time is money, and they can demonstrate how this is true. In this instance, it is not simply being on time but also reducing time to complete tasks and processes. Customers from every tier in the supply chain value timeliness. Timeliness improves customer satisfaction and reduces supply chain risk. Further, timeliness improves a company's cash position, reducing working capital needs and providing higher returns to shareholders. Common metrics that measure timeliness include:

1. Cash-to-cash cycle time
2. Delivery cycle time

3. Forecast/planning cycle time

4. Order and fulfillment cycle time

5. Project completion time

These metrics uncover how fast (or slow) processes and projects take. Speed is important because it has a direct effect on cash inflows. Companies are valued by their expected future cash flows as has been noted throughout the book. A company that can design, produce, sell, and collect payment quickly earns a higher company value.

One area that deserves more attention and demonstrates that time is money is the cash-to-cash cycle or cash conversion cycle (CCC) time. The CCC is an area gaining more attention from supply chain leaders and executives, and for good reason. It shows how effectively a company manages cash outflows to vendors and cash inflows from customers. The CCC is the time period between when a company pays cash to its suppliers and receives cash from its customers.

The CCC directly affects cash flow, which affects working capital requirements and corporate value. CCC is used to determine the amount of cash (working capital) needed to fund ongoing operations. Cash that is unavailable because it is tied up in inventory or because customers still owe to the company cannot be used for ongoing operations. A company that is not operating efficiently will see an increase in working capital.

The formula to calculate CCC is composed of three individual measures and is calculated as follows:

$$\text{Cash conversion cycle} = DIO + DSO - DPO$$

$$CCC = 25 + 45 - 30 = 40 \text{ days}$$

Days inventory outstanding (DIO) reveals how many days it takes a company to sell its entire inventory; a smaller number is desired.

$$DIO = \text{Average inventory/COGS per day}$$

Days sales outstanding (DSO) measures the average number of days that a company takes to collect revenue from a buyer after a sale has been made; a smaller number is more desirable.

$$DSO = \text{Average accounts receivable/Revenue per day}$$

Days payable outstanding (DPO) measures the average number of days that it takes a company to pay its suppliers; a higher number is generally better, keeping in mind that buyer–supplier relationships play a major role in the timing of payment.

DPO = Average accounts payable/COGS per day

The CCC in the example above reveals that the business must support its ongoing operations for a period of 40 days. Cash to support the operation must come from somewhere. It can come from the company's cash bank account if it has the cash or it can be borrowed from creditors if the company is credit worthy.

Like all ratios, the CCC is useless unless it is used over multiple time periods or compared to competitors. In general, the lower the number of days is best. A CCC that is decreasing or steady is good, while rising ones should encourage an examination of each of the components of the calculation. A thorough examination can lead to more efficient processes and policies, such as tightening credit to customers, requiring payment in advance, or negotiating longer payments terms with suppliers. Interestingly, the CCC can be negative. This means that a company doesn't pay its suppliers for the goods that it purchases until after it receives payment for selling those goods.

Finally, and it should be no surprise, some companies compete on cost. This is different than reducing and controlling costs, which is crucial for all companies. Companies that compete on cost must be the lowest cost and, thus, there can only be one with the lowest cost. Because of this, companies that choose to compete on cost face a difficult field of competitors and a constant struggle. In many cases, as low cost is emphasized, quality, service, and timeliness are neglected. This is not to say that companies cannot compete on cost, but they cannot allow it to be an excuse for the other areas of the business to suffer. Common metrics used to ensure cost is in line with expectations are:

1. Cost to serve
2. Total delivered cost
   a. COGS
   b. Inventory holding costs
   c. Material handling costs
   d. Transportation costs
3. Cost of excess and shortfall capacity

Throughout the book, the DuPont model has been used to show how an operational performance change can affect a company's

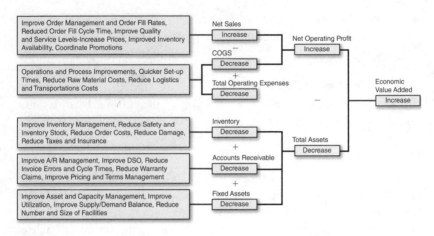

Figure 11.1 Supply chain and operations improvements.

financial performance. A section of the DuPont model is provided in Figure 11.1 displaying where several operations and supply chain processes and policies discussed throughout the book can be applied to improve a company's financial performance.

It has been established throughout the book that managing cash inflows and outflows is a crucial element to running a successful and ongoing business. Going forward, let us examine the DuPont categories again showing how supply chain and operations can affect cash flow.

Revenue: A focus on supply chain effectiveness drives up reliability and responsiveness, both of which can increase a company's level of quality and service. Company characteristics such as these increase revenue in two ways: increased sales volume and better yet, increased revenue per unit sold. Two specific ways to improve revenue are

1. Increasing reliability through perfect order rates
2. Increasing responsiveness by driving down order fulfillment cycle times

Just as there are ways to increase revenue, there are ways that it can be reduced. Gaining insight into how revenue can be impacted provides opportunities to lessen the effect. It is common to see the three following expenses reduce revenue:

Discounts: Discounts of 1% to 2% if invoices are paid early or providing discounts to buyers so that they buy in the present quarter instead of next. These are generally not good business practices. Buyers have a tendency not to pay early but still expect the discounts, and enticing orders through discounts further reduces revenue, and provides erroneous demand information and leads to a production whipsaw (bullwhip) effect, where there is a constant flux of over/under capacity.

Promotional allowance: Getting a retailer or distributor to push a product, even at lower prices or discounts to sell near beginning, ending or holiday season.

Volume discounts: Large customers demand volume discounts. Volume discounts can be applied successfully if long production runs are made or if you are capable of reducing setup time and costs.

A focus on supply chain efficiency is a key component of driving down costs.

COGS: An increase in gross margins can be achieved by reducing COGS, such as material costs. There are many ways to achieve this, including buy in volume, using an alternate supplier and using different materials. Of course, these alternatives are not as simple as they sound. Buying in volume may actually cost more in the long run; a company may not want a new supplier because their technical expertise is highly valued; and using different materials may substantially affect the performance and functionality of merchandise.

Material costs can be further improved by making sure the bill of materials (BOM) is accurate. Obtaining assistance from the production staff that puts products together and from the purchasing staff that buys the materials that are put together can improve BOM accuracy. Further, modifying outsourcing policies, lowering logistics and transportation costs, and improving production processes reduce COGS.

Operating expenses: COGS and SG&A make up operating expenses. Certain SG&A expenses when left unchecked can cause operating profits to decline unexpectedly. Support for suppliers, invoice accuracy, and employee wages from production and operations decisions affect SG&A, thus impacting operating profits.

Advertising support: Advertising expenses could include payments to distributors for carrying a product. These are expenses that may not be directly taken out of revenue or COGS.

Bad debt expense: For uncollected invoices. Increasing quality, conducting credit risk and financial audits, and open lines of communication can reduce the amount of bad debt expense.

Employee wages: Increase unexpectedly for a variety of reasons.

1. *Overtime increases* due to poor production scheduling, lack of communication from marketing and sales, unplanned promotions, and discounts.
2. *Poor production processes* increase employee hours from poor quality management and high setup times.
3. *Hiring unqualified personnel* at lower pay rates expecting that training would get them qualified, only to find out that the time and effort is not worth it. Unqualified personnel reduce productivity and break-even takes longer.
4. *Production managers* are not balancing the production line and not distributing the work evenly.

Asset deployment and utilization: Are essential functions for any organization. Matching capacity with demand is difficult, and if not done well, cash, inventory, accounts receivable, and fixed assets each will move in the wrong direction causing financial stress for the company. Managing assets well liberates working capital and provides the right amount of capacity to deliver high levels of service to customers. Improving forecast accuracy is a good start to aligning capacity with future demand.

Inventory: Requires constant focus. Reducing stock-out rates improves service levels and buyer satisfaction. Without inventory, the company cannot earn revenue. Too much inventory (as seen by slower inventory turns) reduces the company's cash position, thus reducing company value.

Causes of over purchasing and excessive inventory include:

Raw materials: A specific buyer in the team is not an effective buyer and may need additional training; a finished good has been eliminated from the product mix, but the raw materials are still being purchased needlessly; poor inventory tracking; too much safety stock is needed because of poor processes and a lack of accurate and timely information.

Work-in-progress (WIP): Unsuitable production scheduling causing overproduction and inefficient downstream production.

Finished goods: Incorrect demand forecasting and obsolescence.

Accounts receivable: Reduces cash inflows. To improve cash inflows and reduce the accounts receivables, a focus on shortening the time it takes to collect what's owed is necessary (DSO).

Ways to do this include:

1. Reduce invoice errors and cycle times
2. Improve product and service quality
3. Reduce warranty claims
4. Improve pricing and terms management
5. Reduce order cycle time (order to cash)
6. Improve order completion rate
7. Improve on-time delivery
8. Improve credit risk analysis of buyers

Fixed assets (PP&E): Are expensive, they are not liquid, and can burden a company's cash flow if they are out of sync with actual consumer demand. Many companies are looking for ways to make their fixed assets "less fixed" and more flexible instead. Volatility in demand and quick changing consumer preferences may require leasing (with flexible leasing terms) over buying PP&E. Good inventory management may also allow for divesting unused assets improving return on assets, utilization, and reducing capital expenditures. To improve asset utilization or to gauge how well assets are currently being utilized consider measuring:

1. Return on working capital (higher is better)
2. Return on supply chain fixed assets (higher is better)
3. Cash-to-cash cycle time (lower is better)

A Case of Outsourcing Production

It can be challenging to connect and apply the concepts introduced throughout this book. The following case introduces a practical application that summarizes and applies many of the concepts discussed.

Mr. Chuck Akin is employed at an electronics firm that produces video graphics cards. He is leading a collaborative team that needs to provide a recommendation to the VP of supply chain and logistics, Mrs. Alicia Turner, about where production should occur for a new video graphics card. The team recognizes that executives are interested in using financial information when making operational decisions. With this in mind, the team has decided that their recommendation should include financial measures that compare alternatives. Since they know that cash flows are important to every company and that cash flows are used to make capital expenditure decisions, the team members have decided that they should calculate NPV, and since ROI is a common financial measure that their executives use, they decide to include this, too. To get to an NPV calculation, the team will have to estimate cash inflows and outflows first. After a few brainstorming meetings, the team has decided upon requisite revenue and cost categories. These categories are outlined in Table 11.1, return on investment across countries.

The team provides an explanation into their thought process.

Sales: An accurate and timely demand forecast helps determine future capacity needs and an estimate of future sales revenue (cash inflows). The sales and marketing departments can provide insight into pricing and promotions.

Labor: Labor cost per hour is a major outsourcing and location criterion. Although knowing wages per hour is somewhat useful, combining this with productivity is better. The speed of production is an important consideration because it determines the time to the break-even point, the point at which cash inflows equal cash outflows.

Material: Material costs directly affect COGS and profitability. For these reasons, material costs are a major cost component that requires great attention.

PP&E: As an accurate forecast was determined, improved make-buy, outsourcing, and other capacity decisions can be made. In addition, other PP&E-related costs could be estimated more accurately. Since the depreciation schedule is needed to calculate an accurate NPV, the accounting department was consulted.

Custom duties and transportation: Realizing that the total cost of ownership is a superior framework than only cost per unit to gauge overall cost, customs duties and transportation costs are added into the mix to determine total purchasing costs.

Inventory: Inventory and safety stock levels and resultant inventory costs are affected by expected demand, lead-time, their variability, and service levels. Distance and crossing country borders affect inventory-ordering policies and directly affect inventory costs.

Sales and distribution expenses: Costs are incurred when selling products. The sales, marketing, and logistics departments may be brought in for their expertise in these areas.

Table 11.1 Comparison of NPV and Return on Investment Across Countries

	Parameter	USA	Poland	Vietnam
Sales				
Annual demand (Unit)	500,000	500,000	500,000	500,000
Selling price in U.S. market ($)	$ 120.00	120	120	120
Annual sales in U.S. market		60,000,000	60,000,000	60,000,000
Labor				
Labor hours needed per unit of product (labor productivity)		2	3	5
Total labor hours		1,000,000	1,500,000	2,500,000
Labor cost per hour		35	15	5
Total labor costs		35,000,000	22,500,000	12,500,000
Labor costs per product unit		70	45	25
Materials				
Material costs per unit (assuming sourcing locally)		18	14	8
Total material costs		9,000,000	7,000,000	4,000,000

(*Continued*)

Table 11.1 (Continued)

	Parameter	USA	Poland	Vietnam
PP&E				
Initial plant investment (depreciated over 5 years w/o salvage value)		8,500,000	3,575,000	2,500,000
Annual depreciation cost		1,700,000	715,000	500,000
Allocated depreciation cost per unit		3.40	1.43	1.00
Customs				
Customs value per unit (summing labor, materials, PPE costs)		91.40	60.43	34.00
Customs cost per unit	7%	—	4.23	2.38
Transportation				
Estimated transportation cost per unit		4	12	16
Total transportation costs		2,000,000	6,000,000	8,000,000
Purchasing (labor + materials + depreciation + customs + transport costs)				
Total purchasing costs per unit		95.40	76.66	52.38
Inventory				
Unit demand per day during lead time (assuming constant demand)	365 days per year	5,479.45	20,547.95	41,095.89
Average lead time (days)		4	15	30
Standard deviation of lead time		1.5	6.0	8.0

Table 11.1 (*Continued*)

	Parameter	USA	Poland	Vietnam
Customer service level 95% (z)	1.645	0.95	0.95	0.95
Safety stock requirement (unit)		13,521	202,808	540,822
Value of safety stock		1,289,860	15,547,298	28,328,252
Total costs of safety stock (obsolescence, damage, etc.)	25%	322,465	3,886,825	7,082,063
Cashflows				
U.S. domestic selling expenses		2,500,000	2,500,000	2,500,000
Annual net cashflows		8,187,675	(264,173)	(4,100,315)
Risk adjusted discount rate		20%	30%	25%
PV of cashflows over 5 years		24,486,159	(643,412)	(11,026,895)
NPV		15,986,159	(4,218,412)	(13,526,895)
ROI (return on initial plant investment)		1.88	(1.18)	(5.41)

Adapted from: X-SCM: The New Science of X-treme Supply Chain Management, University of Maryland, Supply Chain Management Center

Results: Now that cash inflows and outflows have been calculated from each category, net annual cash flows can be determined. Next, appropriate discount rates are assigned to each location. NPV calculations for each region can be computed and analyzed now. The result is that the U.S. manufacturing option has a higher NPV, making the U.S. option the logical choice. ROI is calculated by initial plant investment/NPV. The U.S. option again is higher and the better financial choice. The team recommends that video graphics card production should occur in the United States.

Mr. Akin believes his team has carefully thought through the issues, gathering the relevant information and providing a financial perspective. The analysis provided the information Mrs. Turner was looking for so that she could make an informed decision.

Summary

Companies compete on many fronts, quality, service, time, and cost. As the business narrows its focus and decides on the mission and business unit strategy, the supply chain and operations divisions can get to work. Since the supply chain plays a central role in the operation of the organization, there are many moving pieces at any one time that must be coordinated. Much of the work entails collaboration and communication with internal and external constituents. As these relationships begin to evolve, the supply chain strategy can be implemented. Effective supply chain networks can be developed, relevant suppliers can be selected, applicable resources can be allocated, and appropriate processes and performance measures can be implemented. All of these important activities working in tandem, like a well-choreographed performance, pave the way to impeccable financial performance, and delighted customers and other stakeholders.

Index